D95 .C35 1959
Casson, Lionel,
    The ancient mariners

Seafarers and Sea Fighters
of the Mediterranean in Ancient Times

Spring Valley Library
Colorado Mountain College
3000 County Road 114
Glenwood Springs, CO 81601

Seafarers and Sea Fighters of the

The Ancient Mariners

Mediterranean in Ancient Times

Lionel Casson

MINERVA PRESS

© LIONEL CASSON 1959

LIBRARY OF CONGRESS CATALOG CARD NUMBER: 58-12437

PUBLISHED BY ARRANGEMENT WITH
THE MACMILLAN COMPANY

PRINTED IN THE UNITED STATES OF AMERICA

2   3   4   5   6   7   8   9   10

FUNK & WAGNALLS PUBLISHING COMPANY, INC.

To

My

Girls

Foreword

THE STORY OF WHAT the ancients accomplished on the sea has never been put between the covers of one book. A few episodes have been dealt with so often, in handbooks and histories, that they are as familiar as Caesar's assassination. But once off these well-trodden paths, the searcher for information is forced to make his way through a miscellany of scholarly publications, more often than not articles in obscure journals, in a variety of languages; and he will find that there are some topics that have never been treated at all.

The present book is an attempt to fill this lack. I have tried to sketch, in a continuous narrative, the impressive record of the ancient mariner: how he perfected his trading vessels until from little more than rowboats they grew into huge freighters whose size was not to be matched until the eighteenth century of our era; how he perfected his fighting ships until from little more than oared transports they grew into mighty and complex rowing machines capable of carrying over a hundred marines, even of mounting artillery; how his maritime commerce progressed from timid coastal voyaging to an integrated network that stretched from Spain to Malay; how much that is popularly believed of him to his detriment—that he manned his galley with slaves, that he could not sail against the wind, and so on—is utterly wrong.

Probably this story could not have been properly told until now. Up to a half-century or so ago we had only the writings of ancient authors to supply information. Today we can draw on the findings of hundreds of archaeological excavations; these have laid bare maritime civilizations hitherto unknown, yielded an infinite variety of objects of trade, and even turned up priceless written documents, from the official records of the Athens Naval Base on imperishable stone to a tattered fragment of a maritime contract between some obscure businessmen on fragile papyrus. Moreover, in the last decade, the new science of underwater archaeology has enabled us to explore the actual remains of ancient wrecks. There are still gaps in our knowledge, but far fewer than there were fifty years ago.

The Ancient Mariners is addressed first and foremost to the general reader. Yet, since there is no other book in any language that covers the field, I have tried to straddle the fence and make it useful for scholars as well. I have given the sources of all illustrative material and citations. Though there are no footnotes, I have included two appendices that I hope will to some extent replace them. One is a selected bibliography: the books listed not only supply the source of most of the information in the text, but enable whoever is interested to pursue any phase in greater detail. The other is an index of Greek and Latin nautical terms cross-referenced to the text; a reader can, by looking up these words in the large lexicons, find many of the passages in ancient authors which have supplied significant information. I hope, too, that the index will prove useful to those who still take pleasure in reading the literature of Greece or Rome in the original; nautical terms can be a stumbling block to even an accomplished classicist, for the standard lexicons all too frequently define them in ways that are either meaninglessly vague or downright wrong.

Many people helped me in many ways with this book; I have space to acknowledge only my most important debts. A fellowship from the John Simon Guggenheim Memorial Foundation, by providing a precious opportunity to travel abroad for over a year, enabled me to investigate the sites of scores of ancient Mediterranean harbors, to search obscure corners of museums and come upon evidence that I would otherwise never have known of, and to use the unique facilities of half a dozen European libraries. I took particular pains to secure apt and clear illustrations; a number of institutions and individuals were of great assistance and their help is acknowledged at appropriate points in the list of plates. I must mention in particular Mr. Ernest Nash of the Fototeca Unione in Rome; I owe much to his eager and fruitful cooperation and to the splendid resources of the archive he heads. A number of the chapters have benefited from the remarks of my good friends, Professor Saul Weinberg and Professor Naphtali Lewis. Chapter 13 owes much to the generous cooperation of Fernand Benoit, Director of the Museum of Archaeology at Marseilles. But far and away my greatest debt is the one I owe my father. He passed a careful and critical eye over the language and phrasing of every sentence in the manuscript; as a result, there is hardly a page in the book that has not profited from his comments and suggestions.

Contents

	Foreword	vii
1	Down to the Sea in Ships	1
2	International Trade Begins	4
3	War on the Sea	27
4	Raiders and Traders	43
5	The Dawn of Maritime Exploration	58
6	Westward Ho!	66
7	The Wooden Walls	89
8	The Merchants of Athens	108
9	Beyond the Pillars of Hercules	128
10	The Age of Titans	141
11	Landlubbers to Sea Lords	157
12	East Meets West	173
13	Sea Digging	189
14	The Pirates of Cilicia	198

15	Rome Rules the Waves	206
16	All Routes Lead to Rome	223
17	An End and a Beginning	240
	Table of Dates	247
	Selected Bibliography	251
	Glossary of Greek and Latin Nautical Terms	263
	Index	271

Figures

		Page
1	Hatshepsut's fleet at Punt.	12
	From A. Mariette, *Deir-el-Bahari* (Leipzig, 1877), pl. 6. See pp. 13-14, 16.	
2	Arrival of a fleet of Phoenician vessels in an Egyptian port.	19
	From *Journal of Egyptian Archaeology*, 33 (1947), pl. vii. See pp. 17-18, 22, 25.	
3	Ramses III's fleet defeats the Northerners of the Isles.	40
	From *Medinet Habu*, vol. 1 (Publications of the Oriental Institute, University of Chicago, no. 8, 1930), pl. 37. See pp. 33, 41.	
4	Reconstruction of the *corvus*.	161
	From H. Wallinga, *The Boarding-Bridge of the Romans* (Groningen, 1956), fig. 11. See pp. 161, 162, 164, 166.	
5	Anchor with removable stock from one of Caligula's barges. Made of iron sheathed in wood.	196
	From G. Ucelli, *Le navi di Nemi* (Rome, second edition, 1950), fig. 270. See p. 197.	
6	Reconstruction of the sailing maneuvers pictured in Plate 13a. See p. 221.	221

Maps

2 The Eastern Mediterranean — 6–7
3 Africa and Western Europe — 130

Plates

(Plates 1 through 8 follow page 90.)

1 Early Boats

    a. Clay model of a sailing (?) skiff found at Eridu in southern Mesopotamia. Ca. 3500 or 3400 B.C.
Photograph by Frank Scherschel, reproduced by courtesy of *Life* Magazine; copyright 1956 Time Inc. See p. 2.

    b. Drawing of a sailboat on pottery from southern Egypt. Ca. 2900 B.C.
From H. Frankfort, *Studies in Early Pottery of the Near East* (London, 1924), pl. xiii-1. See p. 2.

    c. Merchantman on a Minoan seal. Ca. 2000 B.C. The high end is the prow.
From A. Evans, *The Palace of Minos at Knossos,* vol. 1 (London, 1921), p. 118, fig. 87–7. See pp. 25, 216.

    d. Sailor fighting a sea monster. On a Minoan seal, ca. 1600 B.C.
From Evans, *Palace of Minos,* vol. 1, p. 698, fig. 520. See p. 23.

    e. Galley on a Minoan seal. Ca. 1600 B.C.
From Evans, *Palace of Minos,* vol. 2, part 1 (London, 1928), p. 243, fig. 139. See pp. 25, 216.

2 Egyptian Seagoing Ships

    a. Ship of Pharaoh Sahure, ca. 2550 B.C. Model in the collection of the Department of Classics of New York University. See pp. 15, 27.
    b. Model of Ship of Queen Hatshepsut, ca. 1500 B.C. Made by Mr. V. O. Lawson and now in the Art Gallery and Museum, Glasgow. Photograph courtesy of the museum. See p. 16.

3 Aegean Warships, 2000–800 B.C.

    a. Warships drawn on the backs of mirrors found on Syros in the Cyclades. Ca. 2000 B.C.
    From Evans, *Palace of Minos*, vol. 2, part 1 (London, 1928), p. 241, fig. 138. See p. 41.
    b. Galley, probably 50-oared, on a cylindrical clay box found at Pylos. Ca. 1200–1100 B.C.
    From *Archaiologike Ephemeris* (1914), pp. 108–109, figs. 14–15. See p. 41.
    c. Galley on a vase found at Asine. Ca. 1200–1100 B.C.
    From O. Frödin and A. Persson, *Asine. Results of the Swedish Excavations 1922–1930* (Stockholm, 1938), fig. 207-2. See pp. 41, 84.
    d. Galley on a cup found at Eleusis (Eleusis Museum 741; on the original the ship faces left). Ca. 850–800 B.C.
    From A. Köster, *Das antike Seewesen* (Berlin, 1923), pl. 30. See pp. 83, 86.

4 Greek Warships, 800–700 B.C.

    a. Galley, probably 20-oared, cruising.
    From an Athenian vase now in the Louvre (Louvre A517). Reproduced from Köster, pl. 18. See pp. 83, 84.
    b. Galley, probably 50-oared, preparing to shove off. From a bowl found at Thebes and now in the British Museum. The vessel has only one bank of oars: the artist, wanting to include both port and starboard rowers but not able

to handle the perspective involved, naïvely portrayed the one above the other.
From Köster, pl. 19. See pp. 83, 84.

c. Forward part of a galley showing the key-like tholepins.
From an Athenian vase now in the Louvre (Louvre A527). Reproduced from Köster, pl. 21. See pp. 83, 84, 85.

d. After portion of a galley in action.
From an Athenian vase now in the Louvre (Louvre A531). Reproduced from Köster, pl. 24. See pp. 83, 84.

5 Greek Warships, 600–500 B.C.

a. Galley, probably 20-oared, cruising.
From an Athenian bowl in the Metropolitan Museum of Art (Metro. Mus. 07.286.76, Rogers Fund 1907). Photograph courtesy of the museum. See p. 85.

b. Galley, probably 50-oared, cruising.
From an Athenian pitcher in the Louvre (Louvre F61). Photo Giraudon. See p. 85.

c. Galleys cruising under sail; note the ports in the gunwales for the oars.
From an Athenian cup in the Louvre (Louvre F123). Photo Giraudon. See p. 85.

6 Merchantman and Two-Banked Warships, 700–500 B.C.

a. Merchantman on a vase from Cyprus, ca. 700–600 B.C. In the Metropolitan Museum of Art (Metro. Mus., Cesnola Collection 761, purchased by subscription 1874–74); photograph courtesy of the museum. See p. 87.

b. Two-banked galley, probably 50-oared, in action.
From an Etruscan pitcher of the sixth century B.C. in the British Museum (Brit. Mus. B60); reproduced from H. B. Walters, *Catalogue of the Greek and Etruscan Vases in the British Museum. Vol. II, Black-Figured Vases* (London, 1893), pl. 1. See p. 86.

c. Relief from Sennacherib's palace in Nineveh showing a two-banked Phoenician galley. Ca. 705–686 B.C. Now in the British Museum; photograph courtesy of the museum. See p. 86.

Plates xvii

7 Merchantman and Pirate Craft, Ca. 540–500 B.C.

   a. Hemiolia, 50-oared, overtaking a merchantman traveling under shortened sail.
From an Athenian cup, ca. 540-500 B.C., in the British Museum (Brit. Mus. B436); photograph courtesy of the museum. See pp. 86, 87.

   b. From the same cup as *b*. The hemiolia has now secured the upper bank of oars abaft the mast and is preparing to lower the mast—it already leans slightly aft—as a preliminary to boarding. The merchantman now has all its canvas drawing in the effort to escape. See pp. 86, 87.

8 The Greek Trireme

   a. Reconstructed cross-section of a fifth century Athenian trireme showing the arrangement of the rowers; flat platform at right represents the waterline.
From a model made by J. S. Morrison of Trinity College, Cambridge, and now in the National Maritime Museum, Greenwich. Photograph courtesy of Mr. Morrison. See pp. 92, 93.

   b. A fifth century Athenian trireme cruising. Sketch by Mr. I. S. Michelman of New York City. See p. 92.

(Plates 9 through 16 follow page 218.)

9 The Standard Ancient Shipping Container: the Clay Jar

   a. Amphorae from a wreck, dating around the end of the first century B.C. or the beginning of the first A.D., on the sea floor near the Île du Levant off Hyères on the French Riviera.
Photograph by Y. de Rolland of the Club Alpin Sous-Marin in Cannes, supplied through the courtesy of F. Benoit, Director of the Musée Borély, Marseilles. See pp. 192, 194.

   b. A Roman merchantman traveling under sails and oars with a full deck-load of amphorae. Mosaic of the second or third century A.D. from Tebessa in Algeria. See pp. 193, 214, 215, 216.

10 Roman Warships

   a. One of the heavy ships that fought in the Battle of **Actium in** 31 B.C. (symbolized by the crocodile); relief found at Palestrina near Rome and now in the Vatican Museum. The vessel has two banks of oars, each oar probably manned by multiple rowers. It is cataphract, that is, fenced in on top (by a deck) and sides. Forward is the mast for the artemon and, behind it, a turret. The flat relief of the head of Medusa perhaps represents the vessel's name; the niche behind has a female bust, possibly of a goddess.
   Photo Alinari. See pp. 92, 99, 145, 148, 213, 214.
   b. A portion of the relief decorating the column of **Trajan** (A.D. 98–117) in Rome. Two-banked Liburnians under oars, and a trireme under oars and the artemon, arrive at a port. See pp. 92, 94, 146, 213.

11 Roman Warships and Merchantmen

   a. Two-banked galley on the Nile, most likely a Liburnian attached to the fleet stationed at Alexandria. From a mosaic of the late first century B.C. or the first A.D. found at Palestrina and now in the Palazzo Barberini there. The stern ornament is virtually the same as that found on Greek warships of the sixth century B.C. (pl. 5). See pp. 92, 210, 213.
   b. Mosaic on the floor outside the office maintained at Ostia by the Shippers of Sullecthum ([*Navic*]*ulari Syllecti*[*ni*]), a town on the Tunisian coast very near Mahdia; second to third century A.D. Two merchantmen, one entering and one leaving, a harbor; in the background a lighthouse. The vessel on the left has three masts and the bow profile with projecting forefoot. See pp. 146, 214, 216, 218, 226.

Plates xix

12 Merchantmen in the Harbor at Portus. Relief found at Portus and now in the Torlonia Collection, Rome; ca. A.D. 200. Behind the dock at the right a triumphal arch, with a chariot drawn by elephants on top, is visible. In the upper right-hand corner is Liber, god of wine, after whom the vessels are named; note his picture carved on their prows. See pp. 174, 195, 214, 216, 217, 218, 220, 225, 235.

13 Merchantmen and Warships of the Roman Empire

    a. Three merchantmen at the entrance to the harbor of Portus. Relief from a sarcophagus of the third century A.D. probably found at Ostia and now in the Ny-Carlsberg Glyptothek, Copenhagen.
Photo Alinari. See pp. 214, 216, 217, 219, 220, 225.
    b. Detail of the above showing the sprit.
    c. Roman warships, probably Liburnians, racing across the waters of a harbor. Fresco from the Temple of Isis in Pompeii and now in the Naples Museum. First century A.D.
Photograph Fototeca Unione, Rome. See pp. 92, 213.

14 Merchantmen of the Roman Empire

    a. Model of a large merchantman.
In the collection of the Department of Classics of New York University. See pp. 214, 216, 217, 218.
    b. Small freighter, probably the type used to carry grain from Portus or Ostia to the docks on the Tiber; fresco, of the second or third century A.D., found at Ostia and now in the Vatican Museum. Since the mast is stepped rather far forward, the vessel probably had some form of fore-and-aft rig, perhaps a sprit. It is named the *Isis Giminiana.* Farnaces, the skipper (*magister*), stands by at the steering oars. Stevedores carry sacks of grain aboard which are emptied into an official measure under the eyes of the vessel's owner, Abascantus, and of a government inspector (holding an olive branch). A steve-

dore who has already emptied his sack rests in the bows. The fresco probably adorned Abascantus' tomb.
Photo Alinari. See pp. 214, 216, 219, 225.

15 Small Craft of the Roman Empire

  a. A shipwright at work; relief on a tombstone in the museum at Ravenna. The inscription means, "Longidienus pushes ahead on his work." See pp. 214, 216.
  b. Skiff in the act of warping a vessel into harbor; relief on a tomb, presumably that of the owner, a "tugboatman," in the Isola Sacra, the cemetery for Portus. The towing line runs from the stern upward and off to the left. The steering oar is oversize to provide enough leverage to direct the clumsy tow. With the mast set so far up in the bows, the boat must have carried some form of fore-and-aft rig, probably a sprit.
  Photograph Fototeca Unione, Rome. See pp. 214, 219, 225.
  c. Boat rigged with a short-luffed lug. Relief on a tombstone found in the Piraeus and now in the National Museum, Athens.
  Reproduced from A. Conze, *Die attischen Grabreliefs* (Berlin 1893–1922), vol. 4, no. 2064, pl. 451. See pp. 214, 219.
  d. Vessel traveling "wing and wing" under two spritsails. Relief on a tombstone in the Archaeological Museum, Istanbul. Photograph courtesy of the museum. See p. 219.

16 The Byzantine Age

  a. Model of a dromon of the tenth century A.D. Made by R. H. Dolley of the British Museum. Photograph courtesy of Mr. Dolley. See p. 243.
  b. Ship of the fleet of Emperor Michael II (A.D. 820–829) destroying an enemy with "Greek fire."
  From an illustration in a fourteenth century manuscript of Ioannes Scylitzes in the Biblioteca Nacional, Madrid. Photograph courtesy of the Biblioteca. See p. 243.

The

Ancient

Mariners

*Seafarers and Sea Fighters
of the Mediterranean in Ancient Times*

1 Down to the Sea in Ships

IN THE VERY BEGINNING men went down, not to the sea but to quiet waters, and not in ships but in anything that would float: logs that could be straddled, rafts of wood or of bundles of reeds, perhaps even inflated skins.

But these were floats, not boats. The first true boat—something that would carry a man upon water and at the same time keep him dry—was very likely the dugout, although experiments with bound reeds or with skins stretched over light frames must have been made quite early too. And, when the desire or need arose for something bigger than what could be hollowed out of the largest logs available, the boat made of planks came into being. This was one of prehistoric man's most outstanding achievements; the credit for it probably goes to the Egyptians of the fourth millennium B.C.

As long as they stayed in shallow waters, men could propel their boats with punting poles. Farther out they used their hands—and this led them to devise the paddle, a wooden hand as it were, and soon afterward the oar. Then they hit upon something that revolutionized travel: they learned how to use the wind. For the first time they harnessed a force other than their own muscles, their servants', their animals' or their wives'. It was a discovery whose effects reached down the ages: from this moment on, the easiest and cheapest way of transporting bulky loads over distances of any appreciable length was by water. This is the point at which the story of the ancient mariners really starts; the scene again is Egypt, or perhaps Mesopotamia.

In southern Egypt archaeologists have found hundreds of pictures of boats which, shortly before 2900 B.C., were drawn helter-skelter on rock outcrops or which were included as part of the decoration on pottery (Pl. 1b). Among them are some which show, stepped amidships or forward of amidships, a mast with a broad squaresail hung upon it.

No representations of sails discovered elsewhere come near to being as old as these. However, in Mesopotamia, a land whose civilization is as old as Egypt's, something has been unearthed that perhaps pushes this epoch-making invention as much as a half-millennium further back. Not long ago, while digging at Eridu, in the level that dates around 3500 or 3400 B.C., excavators came upon a little clay model of a boat (Pl. 1a). The town is now well inland; but the coast line in its vicinity has changed and in those days it sat upon the shores of the Persian Gulf. The model is of a small skiff, no doubt the sort used for fishing or short trips along the coast. In the center of the floor, somewhat forward of amidships, it has a sturdy round socket and, on either side, a hole has been pierced in the gunwale. The socket may have held a figure or a standard of some kind, but it looks very much as if it was there to receive a mast, and the holes a pair of stays.

Who first realized the far-reaching potentialities of the sailing ship and dared to use it to strike out beyond their own shores? For the age that predates recorded history there is nothing to go on beyond what the archaeologists dig up, and this is ambiguous: you can never be sure whether a prehistoric object of one country that turns up in another got there by sea or land. Yet, in the light of what follows (pp. 4-10), it seems most likely that the first true sea voyages were made by Egyptians who worked northward along the coasts of Palestine and Syria or southward down the Red Sea, and by Mesopotamians who sailed down the Persian Gulf and perhaps into the Indian Ocean.

Egypt and Mesopotamia, then, had a head start over the rest of the world in the art of sailing, as in so much else. But, as time passed, all along the coasts of the Mediterranean men started to go down to the sea. In the prehistoric age and long thereafter these shores did not have the bare aspect they show today but in many places were mantled by forests which provided logs for the earliest dugouts and timber for the keels, ribs, and planks of their more complicated progeny.

How far did these primitive Mediterranean mariners sail? Did they by and large stick to their own shores or did they venture on long voyages? That their ships were probably quite frail need not have stopped them; Polynesian sailors covered impressive distances in boats that were very likely no sturdier. There are tantalizing archaeological clues which seem to imply trade links between the older civilizations of the eastern Mediterranean and western Europe of prehistoric times: beads of Egyptian faience have turned up in Britain, and there are carvings on Stonehenge that look for all the world like the symbol of the double-ax which the Cretans favored (p. 20); in Brittany necklaces have been found of a mineral, a rare green phosphate, that seems to be native to the Near East; Spanish pots and figurines bear an odd resemblance to types found in Asia Minor. Were such objects carried by ships along trade routes that had been carved out in remote prehistory? Perhaps. But it seems simpler to conclude that they arrived at their distant destinations after long overland journeys, passing from hand to hand in village after village.

2 International Trade Begins

"BRINGING OF FORTY SHIPS filled with cedar logs." So wrote an ancient scribe in listing the accomplishments of Pharaoh Snefru, ruler of Egypt about 2650 B.C. This handful of words brings one across the threshold into the period of history proper. The dim tracks of potsherds and other like objects are still important—giving them up is a luxury that the student of the history of shipping cannot afford at any stage in the ancient period—but now there exists, for the first time, the strong light of written words to serve as a guide.

As in the case of so many phases of civilization, the record begins in Egypt. Very little wood grows in the valley of the Nile. Cedar most certainly does not, and to get it Snefru had to look overseas. So he sent to Phoenicia where a famous stand grew on the mountain slopes of Lebanon. Snefru was blazing no trail, for Egypt had been in touch with this area even before his time. Archaeologists have found in the tombs of pharaohs and nobles of earlier dynasties jars and flasks and pitchers which were made in Palestine and Syria, and they have dug up in the latter countries objects that unquestionably came out of Egyptian workshops. Were these carried overland or by boat? Before the time of Snefru there is no way of telling. But his words remove all doubt: some three thousand years before the birth of Christ a fleet of forty vessels slipped their moorings, sailed out of a Phoenician harbor, and shaped a course for Egypt to bring there a shipment of Lebanese cedar. It is the world's first articulate record of large-scale overseas commerce.

On the coast, not far north of where Beirut stands today, was the port of Byblus whose beginnings go back beyond recorded memory. It was here that, among other things, the timber of Lebanon in Snefru's day and for centuries thereafter was brought to be loaded for shipment, and copper from the rich deposits in Cyprus was ferried in for transshipment. So constant was the trade between this city and Egypt that from earliest times seagoing merchantmen were called "Byblus-ships" whether they actually plied between there and Egypt or not, just as in the last century "China clippers" and "East Indiamen" were used on runs other than those they were named for. Hundreds of years later, when Egypt lost much of her power and could no longer maintain her overseas contacts, she felt the loss of this commerce keenly. "No one really sails north to Byblus," wailed one sage some four or five hundred years after Snefru's time. "What shall we do for cedar for our mummies, those trees with whose produce our priests were buried and with whose oil nobles were embalmed?" It wasn't only the Egyptian shipwrights and carpenters who needed Lebanese timber; the undertakers depended on it too.

There was another important region which figured early in overseas trade. East of the Mediterranean, and separated from it by mountains, lay Mesopotamia, the land watered by the two mighty rivers, the Tigris and Euphrates. Here the ancient and highly developed civilization of the Sumerians and the Babylonians arose. Cut off as they were, their Mediterranean contacts had to be through middlemen, probably the merchants of the coast, including, no doubt, those of Byblus. But, to the south, the twin rivers that formed their chief artery of communication emptied into the Persian Gulf, and beyond that lay the open expanse of the Indian Ocean. As early as the middle of the third millennium B.C., Baby-

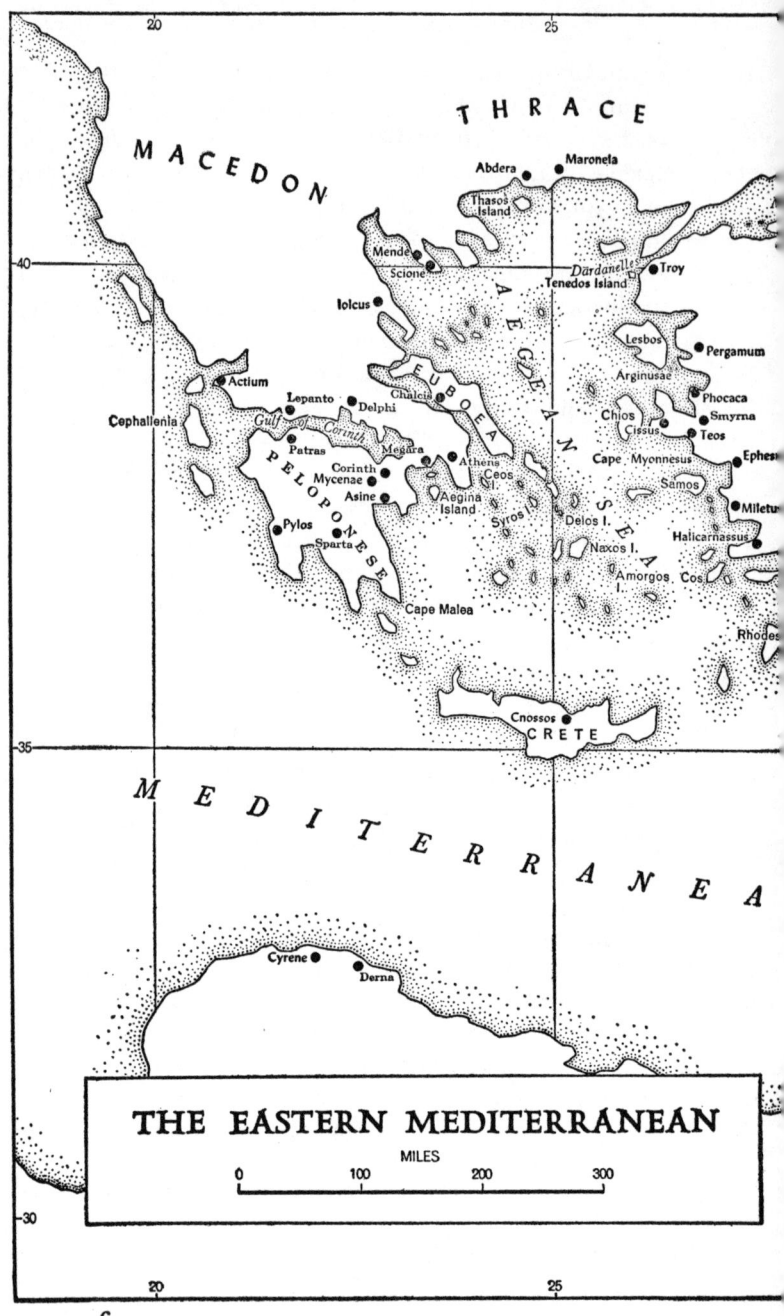

30
35
BLACK SEA
Heracles Pontica
40
ASIA MINOR
CILICIA
Side
Coracesium
Phaselis
Myra
Gulf of Adalia
Seleuceia
Antioch
Orontes R.
Salamis
CYPRUS
Arvad
35
Simyra
LEBANON
PHOENICIA
Byblus
Beirut
Sidon
Tyre
SEA
Gaza
Alexandria
Memphis
Nile R.
30
EGYPT
SINAI
30
35

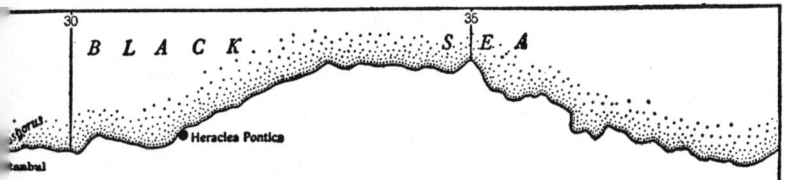

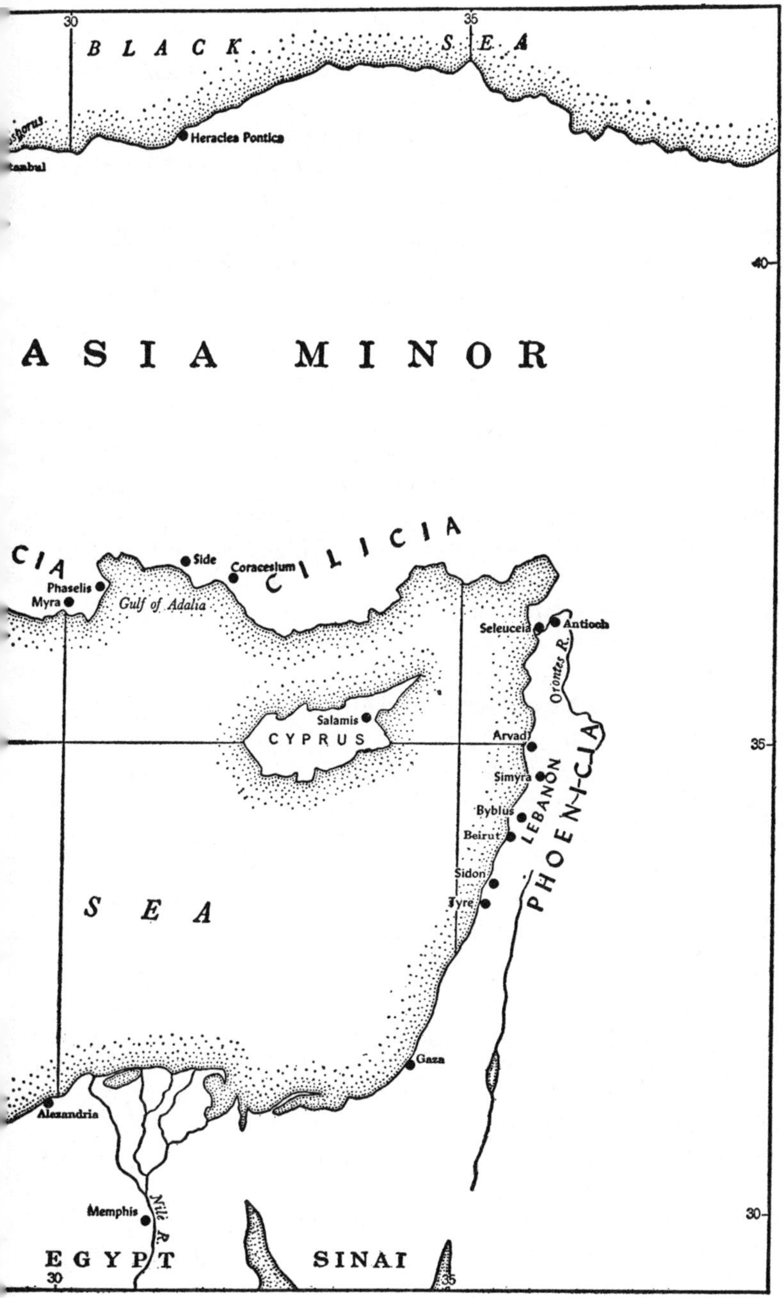

Ionian merchants were either sailing these waters themselves or dealing directly with traders who were.

The rulers of southern Mesopotamia in this age imported for their statues the handsome black stone known as diorite from a place they called Makkan, probably Oman on the Arabian shore of the gulf. Since Makkan had a reputation for shipbuilding, most likely its people provided the freighters and did the carrying. From the same area came timber and, most important of all, copper. By the end of the second millennium B.C., trade in the Persian Gulf was thoroughly organized on a businesslike basis. On the island known today as Bahrein, a full-fledged port of exchange had been created. Merchants from Mesopotamia sailed there carrying cargoes of textiles, wool, leather objects, and olive oil and returned with their holds laden first and foremost with copper ingots but also with finished objects of copper, precious stones, ivory, and rare woods. Bahrein itself is bare; everything shipped out of it had first to be brought there. The copper poses no problem: it came from nearby Makkan where the metal is still mined today. But the source of the ivory opens up interesting speculations.

In the ruins of the cities of Mesopotamia of the third millennium B.C., archaeologists have dug up certain large conchs with a snow-white shell. These are examples of the sacred Indian chank which is found only in the coastal waters of India and Ceylon. They have discovered, too, some seals that could only have been made in India. The implication is clear: traders even in this early period ventured beyond the Persian Gulf and sailed the open waters of the ocean to the west coast of India; the raw ivory and the ivory objects that Mesopotamian merchants exchanged for their textiles and wool came from there. Often ancient cargo lists of the period include a mysterious entry that is literally translated "fish eyes." Can these be pearls from the famous banks off the Indian coast?

A great many details are known about the businessmen of Mesopotamia, for they wrote their correspondence and kept their accounts on clay tablets which are just about indestructible; excavations have yielded hundreds of them. All Mesopotamian import-export transactions were in the hands of individuals, not the state. The chief problem of the merchants, as their records show, was the same that faces their modern counterparts: where and how to get the capital to finance a voyage. Generally a group of partners went into a venture together. They borrowed from a banker the cash to buy a cargo and guaranteed to repay the loan at a fixed rate of interest. Except for the usual hazards of credit, the banker was completely protected: if the vessel went down the partners shared the loss among themselves. But if she arrived safely they divided all the profits; the financier received only his original advance plus interest. Occasionally a less conservative banker took a flyer and had himself included as one of the partners in a venture, thereby sharing in the profits—or the losses. The clay tablets have even produced what is probably the earliest letter extant from a dissatisfied customer, one that dates sometime between 2000 and 1750 B.C. Ea-nasir, a merchant of Ur in southern Mesopotamia, had delivered a consignment of copper from Telmun, as Bahrein was then called. The consignee was outraged at the quality of the shipment. "Who am I that you treat me in this manner and offend me?" he writes. "That this could happen between gentlemen as we both are! Who is there among the traders of Telmun who has ever acted this way?"

For some reason this amazingly far-flung and highly developed trade died out shortly after 1750 B.C. and did not come to life again until almost a thousand years later. One must go back to Egypt to continue the record of what was happening on the sea lanes.

Egypt had need of imports for which she had to turn to countries other than Phoenicia. Every year enormous amounts of incense, myrrh and frankincense, were burned on her altars. These products were available only from South Arabia and the African coast below the Red Sea, an area which the pharaohs' scribes called Punt and which we know today as the Hadramaut and Somaliland. For centuries supplies had come overland, maintained by countless small traders who passed the merchandise along from hand to hand and, presumably, passed along an increase in price at each exchange. The earliest pharaohs set themselves the job of cutting out these middlemen. In so doing they created one of the first great state-operated maritime enterprises.

The task was not easy. The only alternative to the overland route was by water down the Red Sea. But Egypt's centers were all strung along the banks of her great river separated from the Red

Sea at the closest point by an eight-day march across desert. On a barren coast bare of shade and roasted by an ovenlike sun the pharaohs had to set up shipyards, build a fleet, lay out harbors with all necessary facilities and, when all was accomplished, maintain and protect what they had created. The easiest route from the Nile to the Red Sea was along a gorge in the desert called the Wadi Hammamat. On the rocks lining it at one point Henu, minister of Pharaoh Mentuhotep III, some two thousand years before the birth of Christ inscribed an account of his services to the state. In a few bald sentences he reveals graphically the difficulties that faced the founders of such a trading venture. "My lord sent me," he writes, "to despatch a ship to Punt to bring him back fresh myrrh. . . . I left (the Nile) with an army of 3000 men. Every day I issued to each a leathern bottle, two jars of water, 20 loaves of bread. . . . I dug 12 wells. . . . Then I reached the Red Sea, made the ship and despatched it." Henu was clearly a capable man. There was nothing haphazard about his methods: notice how each step was carefully plotted, especially the key one of how to supply three thousand men with water during an eight-day desert trek. In his scrupulous attention to detail he even records the exact dimensions of the wells he dug.

Not very long after Henu had accomplished his mission, sometime in the twentieth century B.C. Pharaoh Senusret took a step that rendered such an assignment from then on unnecessary: he dug a canal from the northern end of the Nile to the Red Sea. Cargoes that came through it were spared the wearying caravan trip and the time and effort lost in transshipping every item from ship to donkey to riverboat and vice versa.

Yet even the opening of the canal did not make the Egypt-Punt trade a sinecure. There was still the long sail down the length of the Red Sea and back. That body of water was tricky to navigate, had few points where a ship in danger could take shelter, and was the spawning ground of a particularly virulent breed of brigand. (Pirates are a problem there to this very day.) It is no surprise that it furnishes the scene for the first report of shipwreck that has been preserved.

The story is told in the first person. The narrator is a sort of Egyptian Sinbad, for his tale is at the same time the earliest sailor's yarn that we have; many centuries must pass before we meet a sober eyewitness' account of shipwreck. "I had set out for the mines of the king," the anonymous storyteller relates, "in a ship 180 feet long and 60 wide; we had a crew of 120, the pick of Egypt." The mines must be those in the Sinai Peninsula, so the departure was made from some Red Sea port. The ship's size is imposing; it was no little coaster but a full-fledged cargo vessel. "A storm broke while we were still at sea," he continues; "we flew before the wind. The ship went down; of all in it only I survived. I was cast upon an island and spent three days alone; I stayed in the shade. Then I set forth to find what I could put in my mouth. I found figs and vines, all kinds of fine leeks, fruit and cucumbers. There were fish and fowl; everything was there. I satisfied myself and there was still some left over. When I had made a fire-drill I kindled a fire and made a burnt-offering for the gods."

So far nothing that we couldn't find in the pages of Robinson Crusoe. But things suddenly change. "Then I heard the sound of thunder and thought it was a wave; trees broke and the earth quaked. I uncovered my face and found that a serpent had drawn near. It was 45 feet long and its beard was 2 feet long. Its body was covered with gold and its eyebrows were real lapis lazuli."

The serpent's looks, it turns out, were deceiving; it was a most considerate and accommodating creature. It took the sailor up in its mouth tenderly, carried him to its lair, listened sympathetically to his story and then comforted him with the news that, after four comfortable months on the island, one of the pharaoh's ships would come along, pick him up, and carry him home. In gratitude the sailor burst out with a promise to bring it thank offerings of all sorts of incense. "Thereupon it laughed at me. And it said, 'I am the prince of Punt and myrrh—that is my very own!'" As if to confirm these words, when the rescue ship as prophesied did come along, the serpent sent the sailor off with a full cargo of incense of every conceivable type. Two months later he was safely home.

Near the famous valley across the river from Thebes where so many of the pharaohs dug their tombs, stands the huge temple of Deir-el-Bahari. It is a monument erected shortly after 1500 B.C. by Hatshepsut, the first great queen of history. On its walls she carved a record, with magnificent illustrations, of one of the great achievements of her rule, a large-scale trading voyage to Punt.

Fig. 1. Hatshepsut's fleet at Punt.

International Trade Begins

Many years before Hatshepsut's reign Egypt had fallen upon difficulties. Civil war had split the country, and the fragments were ruled by upstart princelings or by invaders. None was in a position to maintain a project as sizable as the Red Sea fleet. Senusret's canal was abandoned and gradually silted up. The shipping of incense, as centuries before, was once again carried on overland through middlemen. But by 1570 B.C. a new dynasty arose which reunited the country, established a firm rule, and inaugurated an age that was to be Egypt's most celebrated. The fifth member of the line was Hatshepsut. Her contribution, as befits a woman, was an act of peace: she restored direct maritime connections with Punt.

On one of the walls of the queen's tomb-temple, exquisitely carved in the low relief the Egyptians used so effectively, is a unique series of vignettes (Fig. 1). We see a fleet entering the harbor at Punt: three sleek clean-lined vessels are still under way, their great sails bellying with wind, while two others have doused their canvas and are ready to tie up. Next is the disembarkation: an Egyptian royal messenger heads a file of men and offers a heap of familiar objects of barter—necklaces, hatchets, daggers—to the king of Punt who advances to meet him, followed by an enormously fat wife, two sons, and a daughter. Then ensues a scene of frenetic activity as a long line of Puntites brings the products of the country to the tent of the royal messenger while another file carries jars and trees up gangplanks onto the vessels. Then comes the departure, the ships leaving the harbor under full sail, their decks piled high with cargo. Each scene has a caption to describe it down to the minutest details of action ("Hard to port!" calls the pilot of one of the ships as they maneuver; "Watch your step!" is carved over the stevedores in the loading scene), and from them an almost complete list of the cargo can be compiled. It is imposing: various woods including ebony, myrrh-resin, live myrrh trees (clearly shown in the reliefs with their roots bagged in a ball as carefully as any gardener would want), various other types of incense, ivory, gold, eye cosmetic, skins, 3,300 head of cattle, natives and their children. And some souvenirs: native spears, apes, monkeys, dogs, even "a southern panther alive, captured for Her Majesty." The inclusion of myrrh trees is suggestive. Were they merely to decorate the royal gardens or did Hatshepsut have the shrewd notion of cultivating them in Egypt to reduce her country's dependence on a foreign source of supply?

The vessels shown on Hatshepsut's reliefs represent the high-water mark of the Egyptian shipbuilder. Yet, though they are fine-looking ships, their design had serious weaknesses and for good reasons was not to play an important role in the history of naval architecture.

In Egypt, stretched like a ribbon along the banks of a river which offered a clear course of over four hundred miles, it was natural that the designing and sailing of boats would begin early and develop rapidly. The Nile offered the best and easiest form of transport. It was even blessed with a prevailing wind that blew from the north: one could sail upstream and drift downstream—or row without strain, if in a hurry. The tombs of Egypt have yielded pictures and even models of a bewildering variety of river craft, from tiny rowboats through swift yachts and dispatch boats to enormous barges that were built to carry huge obelisks, weighing hundreds of tons, from the granite quarries far upstream. Life on the ancient Nile must have been every bit as varied and picturesque as on Mark Twain's Mississippi. And as designers of river craft the Egyptians were unsurpassed. This was their weakness: when they turned to seagoing ships they simply constructed oversize Nile boats.

In almost all times and places people have, in building ships, used a framework of keel and ribs. The keel was the spine; the ribs curved upward and outward from it, and to them was made fast the skin of planks. In this way strength and rigidity were imparted. Not so the Egyptians. Building for use on a river where there were no storms, no violent winds, battering waves, or ripping currents, they constructed their vessels, even the largest ones, without keel and with few, very light ribs. Planks were pinned to one another rather than to a skeleton. The only stiffening provided beyond the handful of ribs consisted of beams run from gunwale to gunwale on which the deck was laid. This was adequate for a river. A good deal more was needed for a ship that was to sail the open Mediterranean.

About 2550 B.C. Pharaoh Sahure built a fleet of transports to ferry his troops to some Asiatic coast. To commemorate the achievement he ordered his artists to carve a picture of the scene on the walls of his pyramid and thereby left the earliest clear picture of seagoing ships extant (Pl. 2a). So carefully did the artists execute their assignment that almost every detail of construction appears; we can see precisely what the Egyptian naval architect did to adapt for use on the sea a boat basically built for a river. Around one end of the vessel he looped an enormous hawser, carried it along the centerline above the deck, and looped it about the other end. By placing a stout pole through the strands of the hawser where it passed over the deck, and twisting, one could tighten the whole harness like a tourniquet. This was his substitute for keel and ribs; twisted until it had the proper tension, the hawser held the ends from breaking off when the vessel was forced to batter her way through heavy seas. The architect further added an elaborate netting that ran horizontally about the upper part of the hull. Is this, too, an aid in holding the ship together, a sort of girdle as it were, or is it mere chafing gear to protect the sides from rubbing? The architect could not use the ordinary single mast, for there was no keel in which to sink its end securely (the heel of a mast exerts tremendous leverage against its socket); so he designed a two-legged affair which distributed the pressure, and he stayed it carefully with lines fore and aft. On it a tall slender squaresail was mounted, in a fashion peculiar to Egypt: two yards spread it, the usual one along the head and another along the foot. But the ship was not solely a sailing vessel; when there was no wind or when it was foul, sail was taken in, the mast was lowered and rowers sent her on her way. The Egyptian artists in their scrupulous attention to detail have added a homely touch that permits us to figure out what kind of stroke the rowers used. Oarsmen are always pictured with a special type of loincloth, one made of a netted material with a square patch of solid leather on the seat. This obviously was chafing gear: the rower must have handled his oar the way they did in the Middle Ages, rising to his feet at each stroke and throwing himself on the seat with the pull: without a sturdy patch on his rear, he would have rubbed through his loincloth in short order. We cannot tell how large Sahure's ships were, but the story of the shipwrecked sailor shows that seagoing vessels could reach 180 feet in length and 60 in beam.

A thousand years later naval architects were designing the ships shown on Hatshepsut's reliefs (Pl. 2b; Fig. 1). They are cleaner and faster than Sahure's. Their lines have the graceful curves of a racing yacht. The sail has given way to one much larger but no longer tall, enormously broad instead; it was still spread in the old manner by a yard along the foot as well as along the head. It was so wide that the yards were made of two tapering spars, with their ends fished together, instead of one; this not only gave greater strength but was easier to construct, since a pair of saplings fastened together at their thick ends did the trick. The broad sail has permitted the use of a much shorter mast, one that consequently exerts less leverage, and the architect has accordingly given up the old two-legged arrangement for a single pole. But except for these, improvements rather than radical changes in design, almost everything else is as before. The keel-less vessel with its handful of light ribs must still be held together by a heavy hawser looped about the ends and twisted to the proper tension. These boats were beautiful; unquestionably they were fast; but they sadly lacked sturdiness. We shall not see them outside Egypt.

The peak of Egyptian expansion was reached in the reign of Hatshepsut's successor, Thutmose III, perhaps the greatest of the pharaohs. It was he who extended Egypt's arm over Palestine and Syria and Phoenicia and even beyond to the countries inland, and carried out his conquest and organization of the areas so thoroughly that his successors were able to coast for centuries on what he had accomplished. For the next three hundred years, until about 1200 B.C., Egypt's trade flourished as never before. Vessels from the Levant dumped on her quays everything from ponderous timbers to the finest and most delicate objects of Asiatic craftsmanship. The pharaohs and their courts rode in chariots that had been made in Syria, raised cattle that came from Asia Minor, ate delicacies that were grown on the island of Cyprus, and were served by swarms of Asiatic and Semitic slaves. Their wives dressed in gorgeous stuffs from Syria and scented themselves with the perfumes of South Arabia. Punt provided, as always, its stores of incense, ivory, and rare woods. Copper was brought from Cyprus and silver from Asia Minor. In return Egypt sent out gold that was mined in Nubia, papyrus made into sheets for writing paper or twisted into cordage, linen textiles, and the fine products of her workshops—beads, faience, scarabs, figurines. A king of Cyprus, who had supplied the pharaoh with copper and timber, writes to ask for horses, chariots, a bed of rare wood all gold-plated, women's dresses, jars of oil of fine quality. In another letter he requests an Egyptian specialty which may not have been as unusual as it sounds—a sorcerer; this one had to be an expert with eagles. The tempo of trade was such that merchants from overseas established residences in Egypt. In the great city of Memphis a foreign quarter sprang up complete, as such places always are, with temples to the strangers' gods.

A picture can at times tell more than a bookful of words, and by great good fortune there is one available to illustrate the commerce of this period. The business executive of today orders a photograph of his plant in action and hangs it in his office; the ancient Egyptian functionary commissioned a picture of himself in official action and had it painted on a wall of his tomb. Kenamon was an official under Pharaoh Amenhotep III, in charge of, among other things, commerce with the Levant. So he had painted on one side of his tomb a picture, complete to the last homely detail, of a typical moment in an Egyptian harbor fourteen centuries before the birth of Christ (Fig. 2).

A fleet of ships has just arrived. You can tell where they are from by the dress and looks of the skippers and the mates who wear gaily embroidered ankle-length robes and have full beards and prominent hooked profiles. They are unquestionably Semites; the vessels consequently must be from Syria or Phoenicia, perhaps even from Byblus itself. Are the ships, too, foreign or Egyptian? With their gracefully curved bow and stern and prominent overhang fore and aft they seem very like Hatshepsut's vessels. Yet they lack the telltale looped hawser. Perhaps it is the artist's fault: as an Egyptian he may have unconsciously grafted a native look on to vessels that were really Phoenician or Syrian. He's a bit lubberly at best; no vessel could ride so high out of the water as his ships do. A number of them are already made fast, their sails furled, the boarding ladders lowered from their prows to the shore. Harbors were rough-and-ready affairs in those days; since there were no wharves ships were simply run up on the beach. Other vessels are shown making ready to land. Sailors have sprung aloft to take in canvas, and on one the skipper stands in the bow carefully taking soundings as the ship inches in toward the beach. On shore everything is bustling the way one expects when a fleet comes in. An Egyptian customs official, standing before an officer and file of men from one of the ships, is entering information about them on a tablet. One Egyptian tradesman is busy trying to sell his wares; he points with emphasis to his scale to assure prospective customers that it is accurate. Another is actually transacting a piece of business with one of the ships' officers. The latter is trying to sell a large jar, probably of wine or oil, for no good grade of either was ever produced in Egypt; behind him a file of hands from the vessel unloads more of them. A tradeslady appears to be feeling the heat; instead of hawking her wares she sits under slippers and other articles of clothing she has for sale and lazily fans the flies away. In the upper right-hand corner of the panel a ship's officer leads two women and a child before an Egyptian official. Are they slaves? Note the diaphanous, triple-tiered dress that one of the women wears; we shall have occasion to refer to it later (p. 22). In the lower right-hand corner is the procession before Kenamon himself: men from the ships stolidly file before him with wares of all sorts, while their officers grovel in the dirt before the great man.

Active as Egypt's trade was, it had strict limits. Her lightly built ships raced south to Punt and north to the Levant but very likely not much farther. Many of the products the Egyptians imported and exported were carried in foreign bottoms, like those in Kenamon's picture. The distinction of being the first great traders of the Mediterranean goes to another people, a race of born sea sailors rather than rivermen.

Some decades before Kenamon sat in his office supervising shipments from the Levant, a noble named Rekhmire, vizier of Egypt and second in importance only to the pharaoh, ordered an opulent tomb to be prepared for himself. On its walls he commanded the artists to paint pictures showing all the world paying tribute to his master, the great Thutmose III. As in Kenamon's picture, there appear Semites from Phoenicia and Syria. There are men from the south, Negroes from the Sudan and people from Punt. Alongside

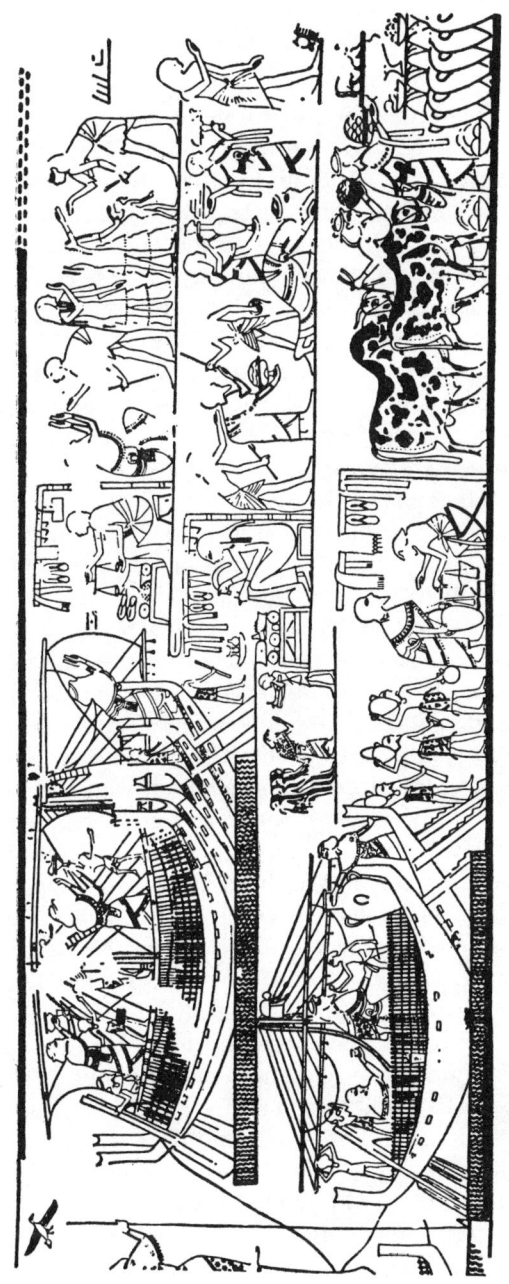

Fig. 2. Arrival of a fleet of Phoenician vessels in an Egyptian port.

these by now familiar faces suddenly appear others who are completely new. They wear unusually decorated kilts and queer sandals, and do their hair in a strange fashion. The bowls and other vessels they carry have unfamiliar shapes. "The People of the Isles in the midst of the Sea," the caption calls them. It has been one of archaeology's prime achievements to identify these figures.

"Minos is the first to whom tradition ascribes the possession of a navy. He made himself master of a great part of what is now termed the Hellenic Sea; he conquered the isles of the Aegean and was the first colonizer of most of them." So wrote Thucydides, one of the most sober and scientific historians who ever existed, in the fifth century B.C., some thousand years after the times of Thutmose and Rekhmire. As late as the nineteenth century, the statement seemed hard to believe: Minos, as far as anyone knew, was a figment of mythology, not a character in history. All that was reported of him seemed pure fancy: that he ruled the island of Crete, that he had built there a trackless maze called the "labyrinth" and kept in it the Minotaur, "Minos' bull," a mythical creature with the body of a man and the head of a bull; that he had the grisly habit of feeding it live mortals and for this purpose yearly levied seven young men and seven young women from Athens; and that Theseus, the legendary hero of that city, volunteered to be sent out, and with the help of Minos' own daughter, who had fallen in love with him at sight, slew the monster and escaped safely.

In 1900 a British archaeologist named Arthur Evans began to dig at Cnossos a few miles inland from Heracleion, the chief city on the north shore of Crete. His results were spectacular. Within a few months he had begun to uncover the remains of a mighty civilization whose existence had hardly been suspected. He laid bare the foundations of an enormous palace, one that had so complex an arrangement of rooms and corridors that in truth it resembled a veritable labyrinth. Everywhere he found the bull's head used as a sacred symbol. He found, too, a symbol in the form of a double-ax and he remembered that Plutarch had once written that there was a non-Greek word *labrys* which meant "ax." In the ruins were thousands of fragments of pottery decorated gaily in a unique style. On the walls were murals done in a charming naturalistic manner. He even uncovered clay tablets with two distinct forms of writing.

International Trade Begins

Here, then, was a people with a fully developed civilization, their own art, architecture, and literature. What they called themselves Evans had no idea, for their writing was indecipherable. But the clues that connected them with the heretofore mythical Minos and his labyrinth and Minotaur were incontrovertible. So he dubbed them the "Minoans" and so they have been called ever since.

As excavation proceeded and more came to be known of these people, two features in particular came to the fore: first, that their pottery, so easily identified by its unique decoration, was to be found in many lands lying overseas, while foreign objects in abundance were scattered through the ruins of their cities; second, that their cities were completely unwalled. The conclusion was inescapable. Thucydides knew what he was talking about: the people of Crete, in an age remote even when he was writing, had been daring and active traders and the possessors of a great navy; Minoan towns needed no stone walls, for wooden ones, their ships, protected the island.

As far back as the days of Snefru and Sahure there was trade contact between Minoans and Egyptians. In the ruins of Crete archaeologists discovered stone bowls which seem like types made in Egypt as early as 2700 B.C. Some seven hundred years later, when Pharaoh Amenemhet II was selecting treasures to be placed in his tomb he included a group of silver bowls of a kind made in Crete. Did Minoan ships bring these objects directly to Egypt or did they carry them to the nearer coasts of Phoenicia or Syria and did they then make their way to the Nile as part of the trade Egypt carried on at all times with the Levant? There is no certain answer. Some of them may have, but not necessarily all. The sailors of Crete traveled to far more distant places; the direct voyage to Egypt could have held no terrors for them.

Minoan traders have left a trail of their pottery in Palestine and Syria and Asia Minor in the east. They reached north as far as Macedonia. Southward they knew other parts of Africa besides Egypt. One of the signs found among their carvings is a representation of a plant, highly prized in ancient days as a medicine and spice, that grew only in one particular spot on the coast of Libya. A tiny seal found in their ruins has a picture of a kneeling camel, another that of an ostrich. In the west they pushed as far as Sardinia, for ingots of copper stamped with the telltale double-ax have been found there. Sicily they knew very well. Objects made of liparite, a rare form of stone originating only in the islets off Sicily, have been found on Crete. Legend had it that Minos himself died on Sicily, and one of the Sicilian towns of later historic times was named Minoa.

Some hold that they made their way farther west still, to the coasts of Spain. Bronze began to be used in the Mediterranean about 3000 B.C. Copper had always been available nearby; there were large deposits in Cyprus and Asia Minor. But the new alloy required tin, and that is a metal in short supply in the eastern Mediterranean. There were, however, rich deposits in Spain. Was it carried in Minoan bottoms from there? Possibly, but only possibly. More likely it was quarried nearer home in the meager deposits so far located and in others not yet discovered.

The picture of what the objects of Minoan trade were is lopsided because the evidence is limited almost entirely to the sort of things the archaeologist can dig up. Yet enough has been found to show that the outside world clamored for the products of Cretan workshops. Among the highly civilized nobles of Egypt and Phoenicia and the semibarbaric chieftains of Greece alike, there were those who preferred to eat off dishes decorated in the Minoan fashion, carry Minoan-style weapons in battle, and wear Minoan jewels and garments of Minoan textiles in court. The women of Crete wore a tight bodice and bell-shaped skirt made up in a number of tiers; in an Egyptian tomb painting a Semitic princess appears wearing precisely such a skirt, and it reappears on one of the women in the harbor scene of Kenamon's tomb (Fig. 2). In return, the Minoans imported a good many things: gold, beads, faience, figurines, and probably papyrus, from Egypt; copper from Cyprus; ivory from Syria; from Greece blocks of porphyry. Amber, following prehistoric routes across Europe from the Baltic, made its way to their workshops.

From about 1800 to 1500 B.C. was the heyday of the Minoans' trade, when they exported to, and possibly even kept up trading stations in, Sicily, Greece, Rhodes, Cyprus, and the Levant. It was in this period that their commercial and political leaders built the magnificent dwelling places, furnished in opulent and beautiful style, which the archaeologists' spades have uncovered.

The inhabitants of Minoan Crete were, then, the first great sea power of the Mediterranean, the first to explore in a fruitful way that great sea and to lay out trade lines that were destined to last for millennia. They were even the first—at least so far as we know—to depict the sea monsters that their sailors, like seamen everywhere, yarned about (Pl. 1d). Must they not, therefore, be the "People of the Isles" on the wall of Rekhmire's tomb? The figures there wear their hair in the same manner as the men that appear in Cretan murals and they carry vases shaped and decorated like those found in Minoan sites. Can we not conclude without further ado that these "People of the Isles" come from Crete? The problem is not quite that easily solved.

No more than a day's sail from Minos' palace in Crete lies the southern portion of the peninsula of Greece. Early in their history Cretan traders had made their way here. The effect of their arrival was startling. The local inhabitants gobbled up Minoan civilization as avidly as Japan in the nineteenth century did that of the occident. Their whole lives were transformed. They decorated the walls of their houses, their pots and dishware in the Minoan manner. They fashioned the same sort of seals and jewelry, wore the same sort of armor, dressed in the Minoan style. The women did their hair *à la minoenne* and looked to Crete for their fashions the way we do to Paris and Rome. Much of what was native disappeared under an overlay of culture from Crete. The phenomenon was so striking that some scholars, viewing it, theorized that Crete had physically conquered the mainland of Greece and ruled it as a vassal.

But they had the facts somewhat twisted. A brilliant stroke of scholarship identified beyond doubt the people inhabiting Greece at this period and straightened out the historical incidents of this remote age. On the island of Crete tablets inscribed in two types of writing had been found. One of the two types reappeared on the mainland. In 1953 a British architect named Michael Ventris, who had as a hobby played about with these inscrutable documents, using pure cryptographic methods capped twenty years of work by breaking the script. They were written, he determined, in Greek.

In a flash the picture became clear: the Cretans had carried their civilization to the mainland Greeks and, not long after 1500 B.C., the latter had repaid them with conquest. That was why in the palace ruins on Crete, along with the tablets—still undeciphered—written in the native Minoan language, excavators found writings in Greek of the new masters.

With this act these early Greeks established themselves as the complete heirs of the Minoans' maritime empire. They held Crete with its fine location at the heart of the trade routes. They set up their own overseas colonies: near Syracuse in Sicily and Tarentum in Italy, on Rhodes, on Cyprus, along the Phoenician coast. Their cities in the homeland grew rich, especially Mycenae where in later days Homer's King Agamemnon ruled; this was the first of their centers to be excavated and as a result scholars refer to the Greeks of this time as Mycenaeans and the period as the Mycenaean Age. From almost the middle of the second millennium B.C. to its end they were the trading nation par excellence of the Mediterranean. "The People of the Isles" of Rekhmire's tomb and of other Egyptian paintings may have been Minoans from Crete, but it is just as likely—the frescoes all date in the fifteenth century B.C.—that they were Mycenaeans. So many of their objects have been found in the ruins at Tell el-Amarna, a city built from scratch about 1370 B.C. by Pharaoh Ikhnaton as his capital, that it is even possible he maintained there a colony of Greek workmen.

A trail of pottery fragments dug up by archaeologists marks the routes these traders followed. Their ships worked eastward to the west coast of Asia Minor, or southward to Crete from where they cut east by way of Rhodes and Cyprus to the cities along the Syrian coast. Here most unloaded and, letting the Phoenicians transship whatever was consigned to Egypt, picked up return cargoes that included whatever the Phoenicians had brought back from there. All papyrus, for example, was manufactured in Egypt, but so much of it came to Greece by way of the Syrian coast that the standard Greek word for the product was *byblos,* reflecting the name of the harbor at which most Greek traders must have taken on their cargoes of it. When traveling westward, the Mycenaeans probably sailed to Crete to pick up consignments of Minoan products, then up the west shore of Greece and across the Adriatic to

International Trade Begins

Sicily. The most crowded ports of all, though, must have been those on the Syrian coast. Here ships from all quarters of the Mediterranean put in: the Phoenician merchant marine shared the quays with vessels from Egypt, Cyprus, Crete, and Greece. The harborside of Sidon or Byblus must have presented a scene every bit as polyglot and bizarre as that of Singapore or Alexandria or any of the modern international entrepôts. In the ruins of Ugarit, a city located just east of Cyprus and whose beginnings antedate written history, archaeologists have discovered the foreign quarter. From about 1800 on, a Cretan colony lived there, as one would expect. About 1400 it was shouldered out by Mycenaean Greeks. In the ruins of the town a foundry was uncovered, no doubt used to process the copper ore which these traders brought in quantity from Cyprus.

Only the Phoenicians have left any real record of what their merchantmen looked like in this age. The ships manned by Phoenician sailors which were drawn on the walls of Kenamon's tomb were deep-bellied freighters with curved ends terminating in short straight stems and sternposts (Fig. 2). Flush decks not only covered over their ample holds but, girt with high railings, permitted them to carry a liberal deck load. They were driven by broad squaresails which in shape and rig greatly resemble the Egyptian type and may have been modeled on it. As on Hatshepsut's vessels, the sail is bent to two yards, one along the foot as well as on top, and there is a web of lines running through the upper part of the mast to raise and hold these spars. But a clay model that was dug up at Byblus shows a different type of merchantman, an undecked affair with sides built up so high that the vessel has something of the appearance of an elongated bowl. It no doubt carried a good deal of cargo, but it also ran the risk of swamping if it got caught in heavy weather and took green water over the side. Probably it was used only for short coastal hauls.

The Minoans liked to engrave pictures of their ships on seals, and archaeologists have dug up a number of them in the ruins on Crete (Pl. 1c, e). But the drawings are so small and sketchy that they tell very little. The hulls seem rounded and roomy, and the number of lines that the artists drew running from gunwales to mast reveals that they carried large-enough sails to need considerable staying. It is disappointing not to know more about the vessels with which this early race of mariners achieved so much. Even less is known of those of their successors: not one representation of Greek merchantmen of this age has survived.

The lords of Mycenae, like their Minoan predecessors, were rich and powerful men. They were able to build for themselves grand palaces to live in and sumptuous tombs to be laid away in. In them excavators have found the fabulously rich trappings of their daily life. They fought in beautifully wrought armor, drove in handsome chariots, wore rich clothes, and dressed their wives in style. They ate off magnificent dinnerware and drank from superbly decorated golden goblets. The age was a great one, great enough to linger in men's memories long after it had come to an end, for it was of the last part of it that Homer sang. But Homer is a poet of warriors, not traders, and his heroes, the soldiers of the sea, deserve their own chapter.

3 War on the Sea

FROM THOSE EARLIEST DAYS when Egyptian merchantmen first sailed down the Red Sea and traders from Crete and Byblus made their maiden voyages in the eastern Mediterranean, the freighter had to share the seas with the man-of-war.

When the warship made its debut in history it was not the stripped-down platform for mounting attacks against an enemy ship that it is today. It was far more prosaic. The first vessels used in warfare were merely an adjunct of the army, transports to ferry troops. There may have been no distinction between ships of the naval arm and freighters at the outset: the general who conceived the idea of water-borne transport almost certainly carried it out by commandeering available merchantmen.

The idea was thought of at least as early as about 2550 B.C. Egyptian records reveal that at this time Pharaoh Sahure used a fleet of transports to ferry an army to some Asiatic shore (p. 14; Pl. 2a). A century and a half later, Uni, Pharaoh Pepi's great commander, rushed troops by boat to quell a rebellion, probably along the Palestinian coast. But the master of the technique of transporting soldiers overseas was Pharaoh Thutmose III (1490-1436), Egypt's outstanding figure in so many of the arts of war. The great general fought eighteen campaigns in Syria and, from at least the sixth on, moved his troops there by water. His first step was to secure undisputed control of the harbors along the Phoenician coast. He then placed them in charge of vassal Lebanese princelings who had strict orders to keep these all-important facilities in top-notch order and fully provisioned. Each year he made a personal tour of inspection to make sure his instructions were carried out to the letter. The details of this enormous project are all lost. From a scanty allusive line such as "Every port town of His Majesty was supplied with every good thing . . . with ships of cedar loaded with columns and beams as well as large timbers," we must imagine the ring of hammers and adzes, the grunting of oxen, the shouts of carpenter and rigger, and the other varied sounds of a shipyard as quays, warehouses, repair shops, and the hundred and one other requirements of a naval base were set up. Thutmose carried it all out so rapidly and successfully that his military victories may have come about more from the quickness and ease with which he got his soldiers to the theater of combat than from their prowess.

But the troop transport was not the only type of man-of-war to sail the seas in earliest times. There were also the ships of the sea rover, slim clean-lined vessels, always driven by oars as well as by sail, and built first and foremost for speed and maneuverability. These actually doubled as both vessels of war and of peace. An attack on an unarmed merchantman or a lightning raid on an undefended coast town could be followed by a voyage of exploration or a rapid run to deliver dispatches when there was not time enough to wait on the vagaries of the winds. The sea rover's ship may be every bit as old as the merchantman; Cretan explorers surely used them in their pioneering voyages of discovery. Yet, curiously enough, it was relatively late when they made their bow on the stage of history, not until the beginning of the fourteenth century B.C.

About 1375 B.C. Ikhnaton sat upon the throne of Egypt, a young man who devoted himself to revolutionizing the religious life of Egypt as intently as his great ancestor had to building up naval bases and extending his military conquests. To break clean with the past, the youthful zealot abandoned the old governmental

War on the Sea

center at Thebes with its traditional associations and built himself a completely new capital on a vast plain farther down the Nile. When, after his death, Egypt reverted to her old ways, his once great city fell into ruins and was forgotten. And so it happened that in 1887, some three thousand years later, a peasant woman, searching for dust to fertilize her garden, came upon what turned out to be part of the official archives of Ikhnaton's Foreign Office, over three thousand clay tablets containing letters that passed between the pharaoh (1380-1362 B.C.) or his predecessor (1413-1377 B.C.) and various rulers of the Near East.

The Tell el-Amarna letters, as they have come to be known from the modern name of their place of discovery, are almost unique in ancient history. Here for once we have before us not some carefully edited records left by a king with an anxious eye cocked on posterity or some second- or thirdhand report by a historian writing years or centuries later, but original documents, the raw material of history comparable, say, to the stenographic record of the Yalta or Potsdam conference.

A large portion consists of letters written by the rulers in those very Phoenician coastal cities that Thutmose III had molded into dependable naval bases. Times are very different now. A religious reformer and not a general sits on the throne of Egypt, and his correspondence is a graphic record of how these cities, once ruled so firmly by the pharaoh, are one by one being picked off by enemies. In this drama Egypt is but the tragic victim; the villain of the piece is the sea rover. As letter succeeds letter, he enters the scene and gradually takes over the lead. Here in these early records sea rovers, formed in fleets, play most of the roles that navies were destined to play from this time on: grouping to enforce a blockade, preying upon maritime commerce, disrupting sea-borne communications.

The chief victim was none other than Byblus, that city whose contacts with Egypt in this age were already over a millennium and a half old. Rib-Addi, a local princeling ruled it and Simyra, its neighbor to the north. "Send me soldiers and provisions!" was the refrain of his earliest letters to the pharaoh, repeated as the years went by with mounting urgency. But then there came a time when the dispatching of mere men and food was insufficient: the enemy had massed a fleet, put it into action, and sea power was exercising its inexorable influence on Rib-Addi. He had foreseen the danger. The ships were being mobilized from the famous old Phoenician ports of Beirut, Tyre, and Sidon. "Put one of your men in each of these cities," he urged Ikhnaton, "and prevent them from using their ships against me!" His plea had as little effect as his earlier ones for military reinforcements, and the inevitable results swiftly became apparent. "[The enemy] has placed ships . . . so that grain cannot be brought into Simyra. We can't enter Simyra," another letter reports. And Rib-Addi sums the situation up with a graphic simile, "As a bird that lies in a net, so is Simyra. The sons of Abdi-Ashirta by land and the people of Arvad by sea are against it day and night." The blockade was complete and Simyra fell. The enemy's forces on the water kept increasing. He grew bolder, and no longer limited himself to blockade alone but took aggressive action. "Two of my ships have been taken," Rib-Addi wrote in desperation on one occasion and, on another, "[The enemy] has seized one of my ships and has actually sailed forth on the sea to capture my other ships." The contact by water between Byblus and Egypt was being severed.

But Rid-Addi wasn't the only one to suffer. Sea raiders were loose all over the high seas. "Ships from the Milim-people," he reported in a worried tone to the pharaoh, "penetrated into the Amurri [north Syria] and killed Abdi-Ashirta [the local ruler]." We don't know who the Milim-people were specifically, but it is clear from Rib-Addi's lines that they were a dangerously successful group of hit-and-run sea raiders. But Ikhnaton soon did not need reports of such activity; he felt the effects of it himself. Raiders from Lycia in southern Asia Minor, a region destined to achieve a great reputation in the grim history of piracy (pp. 201-5), were bold enough to swoop down on the very shores of Egypt. The pharaoh wrote to the king of Cyprus accusing him of collusion, and the latter rushed back an exasperated retort to the effect that, far from aiding the Lycians, he and his island had been suffering their incursions yearly.

The warship, in a word, had come of age. Powerful naval units, massed in north Syria, could blockade nearby ports until they fell, disrupt Byblus' communications with Egypt, and prey on the commerce between the two. Groups of raiders could sack cities on the Phoenician coast, attack the shores of Cyprus, and even harry Egypt. The influence of sea power was making itself felt on history.

Things had not been thus a century before when Thutmose calmly shuttled his troops between Egypt and Phoenicia, and when Rekhmire, his vizier, filled his ledgers with lists of items brought overseas from Cyprus, Asia Minor, Crete, and Greece. Something existed then which was able to maintain peace on the seas and which now, at the opening of the fourteenth century B.C., was gone. It was not the Egyptian navy: their oversize riverboats were never intended for work on the high seas. It could only have been the fleets of Minos and his successors. Crete's bold program of overseas exploration and colonization, its far-flung trade and, in particular, its unwalled cities all presuppose the existence of a great fleet. "Minos is the first to whom tradition ascribes the possession of a navy," Thucydides wrote, and there can be little doubt that he had good reason for saying so. It was a navy that successfully policed the Mediterranean for centuries.

One of the most significant sea battles of the ancient world must have been that in which the Mycenaeans, pupils of Crete in naval warfare as in so many other things, sometime before 1450 B.C. crushed the Cretan fleet and poured over the island to establish their rule there. But it has missed the pages of history altogether; it can only be deduced from archaeological remains. With this victory the Greeks established themselves as the complete heirs of Minoan civilization: they took over its homeland, its trading posts, and its commerce. But, as the Tell el-Amarna letters show so graphically, one thing they did not turn to was the task of policing the seas. As a matter of fact, the new lords of the sea were eventually to become the most renowned sea raiders of all.

"Lo, the northern countries, which are in their isles, are restless in their limbs; they infest the ways of the harbor-mouths." So wrote the scribe of Ramses III as he prepared to recount a great victory of his king in 1190 B.C. Almost three centuries had passed since the Minoan fleet fell before the onslaught of Mycenaean forces and over a century and a half since raiders began to disrupt commerce along the Phoenician coast. The age of flourishing overseas traffic was coming to an end, and the age of the sea raiders was beginning. The Mediterranean was infested with bands of rovers, not only Lycians and other peoples from the coasts of Asia Minor but also people from "the northern countries which are in their isles." They joined the Libyans in a savage attack on Egypt from the west in 1221 B.C. and again in 1194 and were somehow repelled both times. Four years later some re-formed to attack again, by land and sea, from Syria and Palestine. In a great naval engagement, one which stands as the first described and pictured in history, Ramses III threw them back into the sea.

"No land could stand before their arms," Ramses has his scribe write. "They set up a camp in one place in Syria. . . . They came with fire prepared before them, forward to Egypt. Their confederation was the Peleset, Tjeker, Shekelesh, Demyen and Weshesh." Of these names and others, rendered so vaguely by the Egyptian scribes, only one can be identified with certainty—the Peleset are none other than the Philistines. Further Egyptian accounts record still others which suggest tantalizing identifications. Are the *Tursha* Tyrrhenians or Etruscans, in this age still an Asia Minor people not yet having migrated to their historical abode in central Italy? Are the *Akaiwasha* Achaeans, Homer's name for the Greeks?

What faced Ramses was no mere hit-and-run raid such as Egypt had been putting up with since the days of Ikhnaton. These "Northerners of the Isles" had consolidated their forces in North Syria, had sacked the great seaports of the Phoenician coast, and were sweeping down like a flood upon Egypt. It was a veritable migration. And, as the main body moved forward by land, the fleet kept pace along the coast.

Ramses' victory was complete. To celebrate it he erected a great temple near Thebes, and it was on its walls that his scribes wrote the story of his conquest and his artists portrayed, in carefully carved reliefs, its highlights. The encounter on land took place first, and the sculptures depict the pharaoh's troops smiting the northern invaders hip and thigh and breaking through the ranks of soldiers to get to the heavy two-wheeled oxcarts which carried the wives, children, and supplies. Once the land was secured Ramses turned to the enemy fleet. Somehow or other he managed to box it in a corner. As he puts it: "The net was made ready for them, to ensnare them. Entering stealthily into the harbor mouth, they fell into it." The picture illustrating this part of the action is unique (Fig. 3). It is the first and only representation of a historical sea battle that has come down to us from the ancient world. The Egyptian galleys sweep down on the ships manned by the invaders, easily distinguished by their distinctive feathered headdresses. Egyptian archers from ships and shore spray them with a withering fire, crippling them severely before they can get close enough to strike a blow with their swords and thrusting spears; the very lookout in one of the crow's nests has been picked off and hangs dead over the rail. The pharaoh's men then move in with shield and spear to deliver the *coup de grâce*: in the fight one of the northerners' ships has capsized; some of the crew are bound captives in an Egyptian vessel, while others swim to shore only to be pinioned by the waiting Egyptian archers.

But not all the northerners were destroyed in this battle. Battered remnants made their way northward. The Tjeker planted themselves about Mount Carmel, and the Peleset settled to the south along the coast of Palestine. There they remained, not strong enough to try another attack on Egypt but soon sufficiently recovered to resume their old game of sea raiding and to play a great role in the pages of the Old Testament.

Just about the same time, in a different quarter of the Mediterranean, another great action by sea raiders took place. It was, in all probability, much smaller in scope than that which Ramses had thrown back, involving fewer men and ships. Yet its story is one of the best known there is, for it was told not by a scribe or even a historian but by an immortal poet.

On a hill in northwest Asia Minor overlooking the Dardanelles, sometime in the remote past the city we know as Troy had been founded. It grew steadily more powerful through the centuries. It built massive walls to protect itself, engaged in wide trade, especially in silver which was mined in the area, extended its rule over its neighbors, and exacted tribute from them. By the beginning of the twelfth century B.C. its wealth was fabulous. Yet, though it had no fleet of any consequence, its impregnable location and its frowning walls were enough to discourage the ambitions of the ordinary sea raider whose hit-and-run tactics were designed for lightly defended villages. A fortress such as Troy could only be taken by extended siege and full-scale attack.

The sea raiders of Greece took up the challenge. Because some centuries later a great poet decided to use what they did as the subject matter of an epic the world knows of this struggle and the men who figured in it as it does of no other. Homer, of course, got his story not from any set of archives but from popular traditions and he was himself a creative artist, not a war diarist. Yet the tale he tells is so coherent that behind the imaginative poetry can be discerned a skeleton of fact.

For once the major cities of Greece forwent their traditional enthusiastic pastime of preying on one another and joined hands for a combined operation against Troy. Even the romantic cause that Homer assigns to the war may be true: the expedition may very well have been triggered by an abduction of the particularly toothsome wife of some Greek chieftain neatly carried out by an amorous Trojan; wars have been started for less. Each leader contributed ships and men to the great undertaking: Achilles led a contingent from northeast Greece, Nestor from southwestern Greece, Odysseus from a nearby island—the chieftains' names have become household words. Agamemnon, king of Mycenae, one of the most powerful of the contemporary Greek sea lords, received the high command. The fleet rendezvoused in a little barren cove on the east coast of Greece and, after some difficulty with contrary winds—the prevailing summer northeasterlies are foul for a voyage from Greece to Troy—set sail.

The problem that faced Agamemnon and his staff was the same in a very real sense that confronted the American forces in the Pacific a half a dozen times in World War II: he had to ferry his forces safely to the point of attack, secure a beachhead, and then break through the enemy's defenses. He had embarked, in other words, on a full-fledged amphibious operation. It was not the first that had taken place on the Mediterranean. Obviously it was by some form of amphibious attack that the Greeks had conquered Crete some three centuries earlier. But because no Homer chose it as subject matter, it has escaped the notice of history. Yet we can deduce that most likely its naval side outweighed the amphibious.

War on the Sea

On that occasion the key to victory was to defeat at the outset the powerful fleet on which the Minoans relied for their defense; once that was done, the island's unwalled towns couldn't have been much of a problem. The sail to Troy and the landing were the easiest phases of Agamemnon's operation, for Troy had no fleet and the Greeks were the undisputed masters of the seas. His troubles began once he had drawn up his forces on the shore. To lay siege to a strong point in those days was a protracted and costly business, and commanders thought long and hard before undertaking one. Archaeologists have uncovered the walls of Troy, and the visitor even today can take in at a glance the magnitude of the task that faced Agamemnon and his Greeks.

His chief ally was time. He had to keep the garrison bottled up and starve the city out. This meant that he had to secure his own lines of supply, cut off the enemy's, and maintain his forces under rigid discipline in a more or less static position until blockade could ultimately take its grim effect. His fleet gave him uncontested control of the coast, and he sent out constant raiding parties to secure provisions for his men and deny them to the enemy. But his siege was never really complete. The hinterland to the east of the city was always more or less open, and Troy was always able to attract or, with its immense wealth, buy new allies who refilled the ranks and restored the reserves of food and weapons.

Agamemnon had a problem greater even than the leaks in his blockade. He had to keep an undisciplined, highly temperamental gang of sea raiders at the wearing, monotonous job of maintaining a siege. It was like trying to run a music school with a faculty of prima donnas. He didn't even have what we would consider fundamental for his job: absolute power of command. He was merely the chief in a group of leaders who had banded in a loose confederation for this single operation; there wasn't to be another like it for over five hundred years. The Greeks throughout their history have built up an impressive reputation for being resistant to discipline, and the men to whom Agamemnon had to issue orders had a susceptibility to fancied insult of Homeric proportions. It hardly helped matters that, at the very outset, over some ridiculously minor issue a mighty squabble arose, and one of them, in an immortal fit of the sulks, withdrew his forces from the battle line and spent practically the whole of the war in his tent. It was inevitable too that, when large groups of men had to live together under primitive conditions with no knowledge of hygiene, disease would break out. Homer said it came from Apollo; more likely it came from the latrines or the lack of them.

The poet claims that the war lasted ten years. Two probably would be nearer the mark, and that itself is no mean period for a group of sea raiders to have stuck to one project. Even at the end when Hector's death deprived the Trojans of the general who had so brilliantly and doggedly conducted the defense, the city's walls were enough to keep the Greeks, weakened by plague, dissension, and casualties, from victory. They had only one move left: to try a ruse. If the stratagem of the wooden horse had not worked, Agamemnon would have had to retire and the first amphibious operation recorded in detail would have ended in an ignominious admission of defeat.

It was their incomparable fleet that had led the Greeks to try an attack on Troy in the first place. Their fighting ships had no peer in the Mediterranean in that age. Homer is proud of these vessels and describes them with loving detail.

He was most struck by their sleek racing lines, for he cannot mention them without remarking on their slender, graceful appearance and their swiftness. This is, of course, what we should expect in a sea raider's vessel built first and foremost for speed. He often calls them "black"; they must have been kept liberally smeared with pitch. They were "blue-prowed" or "red-prowed"; that is, decorated, as ships have often been ever since, with colored bow-patches. He was impressed, too, by the cunning joints and other careful craftsmanship of the shipwrights; the vessels, in his words, are "well-planked," "well-wrought," and "well-balanced."

There were two types of galleys in the fleet, twenty-oared and fifty-oared. Even the smaller size must have been a full forty feet long: an oarsman needs at least three feet; ten of them on a side totals thirty and we must allow another ten, as we shall see, for decks fore and aft. They were so low that on one occasion when the Greeks, under savage Trojan attack, were driven back upon their beached ships Hector could reach up and grab the ornament atop a sternpost and Ajax could leap from a gunwale to the ground with ease. Homer happens to mention that they were seven feet wide where the steersman sat in the sternsheets, so they couldn't have been much more than nine to ten amidships. They were so light that, when Odysseus was making a fast getaway from the island of the Cyclops, he was able to get his vessel free of the shore with one good shove on the boat pole. The crews ran them up on the beach every night. The fifty-oared craft differed only in being longer, perhaps ninety feet instead of forty, and correspondingly beamier. Either size was ideal for sea raiding, low enough to lie hidden behind some promontory while stalking a prey, swift enough to dash out and overtake a clumsy merchantman handily, and light enough in draught to run, if chased, to the protection of the shore no matter how shallow the water.

Homer calls them "hollow ships"; that is, they were undecked almost throughout, like a dory. Since the slightest chop sent water over their low boards, a latticed spray shield was generally rigged forward. There was a scant deck there, too, for the lookout and for a few marines when the vessel engaged in combat, and there was a slightly larger one aft for the helmsman and captain. Since these ships offered no more in the way of comfort than a racing shell, a skipper did all he could to spend nights ashore; if he had to sail through the night he himself could flake out on the afterdeck under a scrap of sailcloth, but the crew spent the hours dozing on their benches. Gear and provisions were stowed under the decks and the rowing thwarts. When the King of the Winds sent out the south wind and gave Odysseus a bag holding all the others, the only place it could be stowed was under the rowers' seats. The men, seeing the mysterious bundle under their feet night and day, couldn't restrain their curiosity, undid the knot one night when the captain had fallen asleep from exhaustion, and thus inaugurated the much suffering man's long series of mishaps.

Whenever a Homeric skipper could, he sailed rather than rowed. Like a Viking chief, he and his rowers were companions, and using the oars was only a part of their job; they were his fighting men as well. He neither could afford nor was in any position to use them up like the commander of a slave-driven medieval galley. His rowing chief beat only time, never the rowers. When the vessel was under oars, the mast was unstepped and lowered into a crutch aft, and the sailing gear was stowed under the benches. As soon as a favorable wind came along, the crew leaped to make sail. First the mast was hauled up by two forestays, set in the mast-step, locked in with a wedge, and secured aft by a backstay. The one sail with its yard was hoisted and set by braces to catch the wind. The weather sheet was made fast, and the helmsman took his position with the leeward sheet in one hand and the tiller, a bar socketed into the steering oar, in the other. To shorten sail, Homer's sailors used brails instead of reef-points, lines run from the yard, looped about the foot of the sail and carried down to the deck. These rolled up the sail toward the yard just the way a venetian blind is raised. The sail was made of linen, not one piece but patches sewn together for added strength, and the lines of leather strips or of twisted papyrus fibers.

When there was no wind the crew had to run out the oars. They were taken up from below the benches where they had been stowed and placed against tholes, wooden pins which were used instead of oarlocks as the fulcrum against which the oar handle worked. Each oar had a leather strap which was looped about the tholepin; in this way the oar was saved from going over the side if the rower happened to lose his grip.

Whether under sail or oars, working these ships was strenuous, uncomfortable, and dangerous. They were much less sturdy than the robust craft of the Vikings, and the Greeks were correspondingly far less bold than those reckless sea raiders. When Nestor, for example, sailed home from Troy, his first leg was fifteen miles to the island of Tenedos, his second an all-day run of fifty to Lesbos. Here he held a full-scale conference of his captains to plot the next course. With great trepidation he elected to strike out straight across the open sea instead of island hopping, made it safely to the southern tip of Euboea—and, on landing, set up a great sacrifice to Zeus, "thanking him for crossing that vast stretch of sea," all of one hundred and ten miles. Usually skippers stuck to the shore, sailing from one landfall to the next. When they had to travel at night they steered by the stars, but they avoided such voyages as much as possible. They much preferred to put in at evening, running the vessel smartly up a beach or, if there was none handy, throwing over the stone anchor in some shallow protected cove; this gave an opportunity to refill the water jars as well as to provide a night's sleep for all hands. On top of all these precautions, they limited their sailing to the time of year when the weather was most dependable, putting their boats in the water at the beginning of spring, around April, and hauling them out in October or so, when the fall set in. Practically all maritime activity, whether peaceful or warlike, was squeezed into the period between these months, and this remained more or less the case throughout the whole of ancient times.

In a famous passage Homer tells how a boat was made; it is the earliest description of shipbuilding in literature. Very likely the technique described was that used in later days when the poet actually lived, one which he may have observed in a local dockyard. But shipwrights are notoriously conservative, and the method he recounts we may be sure had been in use centuries before as well. Odysseus, in the course of his wanderings, was shipwrecked and wound up with little more than his skin on an island inhabited by a goddess who, rather against her inclination, was ordered by the higher powers to send the much suffering hero on his way. The first step was to enable him to build some sort of craft. The goddess gave him a double-edged bronze ax, an adze, and a drill and led him to a spot where there was a fine stand of aspen, alder, and pine. Odysseus set immediately to work.

He felled twenty trees in all, lopped them clean, smoothed them carefully, and adzed them straight and square. Then he bored them and made them fast to one another with dowels and battens. He laid out the bottom as wide as a good shipwright would for a beamy freighter. He set up close-set ribs, made half-decks fast to them, and finished up by adding the long side-planking. He stepped a mast and yard and added a broad oar to steer with. He fenced the hull about with a latticed bulwark to keep the water out, and he heaped brush upon it. The goddess brought him cloth for a sail; he fashioned a fine one. He rigged braces, brails, and sheets and, putting the craft on rollers, hauled it down to the sea.

What precisely did these seagoing greyhounds that carried the Greeks to Troy look like? Built upon a frame of ribs and keel, they had little in common with Egyptian craft held together by elaborate girding ropes. Homer's heroes lived in Greece about 1200

Fig. 3. Ramses III's fleet defeats the Northerners of the Isles.

B.C. and the general age that he describes came to a close about 1000 B.C. In the ruins of the cities of this period archaeologists have found very few representations of ships. There is only one that is of any help, drawn as decoration on a pottery container probably in the twelfth century B.C. (Pl. 3b). The vessel it shows fits quite well with what we have gleaned from the poet. There is one large squaresail, but that is hardly a distinctive feature. The hull is long and low. More important, the prow, unlike those, for example, of Egyptian craft, rises abruptly without curve from the keel. Homer often compares the shape of his ships to the "straight horns" of cattle as against, say, the curly horns of a ram. This prow is straight but hardly "horned"; its blunt top is finished off with a fish-shaped ensign. But another picture, drawn on a vase about the same time or perhaps a bit earlier, shows a bow profile that neatly fits Homer's simile (Pl. 3c).

The Greeks were not aboriginal inhabitants of their peninsula but most likely made their way there by water. They were, then, a people who knew the sea. Yet they need not have been the inventors of the craft just described. Before the Greeks ever came to Greece, the Minoans had been laying the foundations of a maritime empire and they had navies which sailed the Mediterranean centuries before the attack on Troy. The only pictures of warships of this early age come from the island of Syros in the Aegean north of Crete. Sketchy as they are, one characteristic stands out: the prows rise heavy and straight from the keels and are often topped with a fish-shaped ensign (Pl. 3a). If these are Minoan vessels, then it is not unlikely that the Greeks of the Mycenaean Age borrowed, as they did so much else, their ship designs, down to the very ensign, from Crete.

The most carefully drawn pictures we have of Mediterranean warships of this age are those, drawn on the walls of Ramses' temple, which portray the vessels of the peoples whom he defeated in 1190 B.C. (Fig. 3). Like any sea raider's ship, these are light and lie low in the water. They appear without oars, but this does not mean that they were driven by sail alone, as some writers have hastily concluded; a sea raider could no more depend on a pure sailing vessel than a jockey could on a carthorse. The Egyptian artist has shown them in this way to prove how sagaciously Ramses had seen to it that "the net was made ready for them, to ensnare them." They were taken so completely by surprise that they were still traveling under sail, their oars stowed beneath the thwarts. There are differences in detail between these ships and Homer's. Though the prow rises stiff and straight from the keel, so too does the stern, unlike the Homeric craft whose shipwrights preferred a graceful curving line. Stern and stem end in carved figures of birds, and the mast is sturdy enough to carry a crow's nest, features which Homer never mentions. The Egyptians' galleys in these pictures show some changes when compared with their earlier craft. The heavy hawsers that used to be necessary to hold the frame together are gone, as well as that peculiarly Egyptian feature of rigging, the lower yard on the squaresail, and vertical brails have made their appearance. It looks as if the local naval architects finally had the good sense, in designing ships for the open sea, to copy the sturdy hull and handy rig that their Mediterranean neighbors were using.

To the merchant skipper, anxiously slogging his way to port, it made little difference whether the ominous black shape he spotted on the horizon had the curved stern of a Greek raider or the straight one of the "Northerners of the Isles." Both spelled trouble for him. Centuries were to pass before this condition improved.

4 Raiders and Traders

WHEN ODYSSEUS LANDED at Ithaca after twenty years of war and wandering, alone and helpless, disguised in beggar's rags, an aged shepherd gave him shelter and, in the course of the evening, not knowing his guest's true identity, asked him for the story of his life. (In addition to being conventional courtesy, this would of course give the old fellow a chance of telling *his* in return.) Odysseus naturally had a tale ready. He was a sea raider from Crete, he announced, had served in the Trojan War and had had the luck to come back alive. Then he proceeded to tell the following:

I spent only one happy month at home with my wife and children. Then I got the urge to ready some good ships and crews and lead a raid against Egypt. I had nine ships and it didn't take me long to get them manned.

The men feasted for six days; I had plenty of animals on hand to sacrifice and to eat. On the seventh we slipped our mooring and set sail from Crete. The wind was fair, a fresh northerly, and we speeded along as if we were running downstream in a river. Nothing went wrong on any of the ships. We sat around the decks while the wind and the helmsman kept the course. No one even reported to sick bay. In five days we arrived at the river of Egypt and anchored.

I left men to guard the ships and sent a scouting party to find out what they could and report. But they rashly took matters in their own hands and immediately began to plunder the countryside, killing men and carrying off women and children. The word soon reached a city: the people heard cries at dawn and came out on the run. Soon the plain was full of men and horses: bronze armor flashed everywhere. My men couldn't fight back; Zeus the god of thunder had sent panic upon them and destruction threatened on all sides. Many of us were killed, the rest carried off as slaves.

The incident (as well as the rest of the story, which is irrelevant here) is made up, to be sure, and by a famed liar at that. But Odysseus deliberately chose to tell something the listener would nod knowingly at, something so everyday that his suspicions would never be aroused. This makes it even more valuable than a fragment of history, the factual record of a specific instance. It is the sort of thing that happened in the thirteenth to the eleventh centuries B.C. after the trade of the Mycenaean world had dwindled away. This is piracy as it was in the earliest days of its history.

Our stereotyped conception of a pirate is a swarthy mustachioed ruffian, heading a cutthroat crew, who pounces upon a helpless merchant ship, collects the valuables, singles out the desirable captives for the slave block and offers the rest a walk on the plank. The ancient world, as we shall see, came to know this type all too well in later centuries, complete (except perhaps for the mustaches) even to a version of walking the plank. But Odysseus' story and others like it show that pirates at this remote age were raiders of coast towns, more like tenth century Vikings than like eighteenth century Barbary corsairs. They worked in groups because a single boatload of men would not be enough against even a small village. They plundered on land rather than on sea because the pickings were far more profitable. A town could yield a rich harvest of cattle, furnishings, valuable adornments, perhaps some objects of gold and silver, but above all women and children who would bring good prices in the slave market. And a raid, if pulled off properly—as Odysseus' was not—, was not too dangerous, for all its adventurousness and bountiful return. A stealthy entry into a harbor at night with muffled oars, a few hours of careful professional scouting, a sudden attack at dawn, a rush back aboard, a few hours of grueling work at the rowers' benches—and every surviving member of the crew found himself considerably richer than he had been twenty-four hours earlier. This was much simpler, surer, and more rewarding than taking on a merchantman which might, on capture, turn out to have little of real value on board— a load of building stone, perhaps, or wood, or cheap pottery—or even to be sailing in ballast. Moreover slave dealers were much more interested in young girls and boys who could be trained for household work than they were in weatherbeaten merchant seamen. Nor was there any need to raid shipping to fill up the rowers' benches for, again more like Vikings and unlike Turkish corsairs, each sea raider both fought and pulled an oar. The slave trade was in that era the chief support of piracy and it was to remain so for many centuries thereafter, even, as we shall see, in times when rich cargoes of merchandise were available for highjacking.

Any town was fair game for the sea raiders, but naturally the richer spots were preferred. Odysseus shrewdly locates his incident in Egypt. The land of the pharaohs was no longer the political power it had been in the past, but the Nile which watered and renewed the fields each year guaranteed the country's economic health, and Egypt's prosperous villages were inviting targets. Even in her palmy days Egypt had had troubles: one of the Tell el-Amarna letters, from the files of one of her most powerful rulers, concerns attacks she had suffered at the hands of raiders from Asia Minor (p. 30). Homer at one point provides what amounts almost to a directory of the places the raiders operated in. He has a visitor to the court of Menelaus remark on the richness of the treasures he saw all about the palace. "Ah, yes," Menelaus replies, "I wandered for seven years and suffered much to collect these treasures and bring them home in my ships. I've been to Cyprus, Phoenicia, Egypt; I've seen the people of Ethiopia and of Sidon, and I've been to Libya." Phoenicia, with its cities of Sidon, Tyre, and Byblus that had grown rich as seaports, was bound to catch the raiders' eye. Homer makes one of the nurses in the Odyssey—nurses were invariably slaves in this period—the daughter of a wealthy citizen of Sidon from whom she had been kidnaped by pirates.

But no place near the sea was really safe. On the very first leg of their voyage home from Troy, apparently just to get back into practice, since heaven knows they had loaded enough booty when they left, Odysseus and his men on coming to a town in Thrace "sacked the city and killed the men and, taking the women and plenty of cattle and goods, divided them up." It was an age that men didn't easily forget. Over half a millennium later the great Greek historian Thucydides wrote:

> In ancient times both Greeks and non-Greeks who lived along the coasts or on islands, once they found out how to make their way across the seas, turned to piracy. They would fall upon and plunder the towns, which were either unwalled or mere groups of villages. This was a lifelong pursuit for them, one that hadn't as yet received any stigma but was even considered an honorable profession. . . . So, because of piracy cities long ago, both in the islands and along the coasts of the mainland, were preferably built far in from the sea.

All that we have been saying of life on the sea in this period—the ubiquitous raiders, the difficulties the legitimate trader had, the feeble position of Egypt—comes graphically into focus in one of those unique documents that every now and then time is kind enough to spare for later ages.

The ancient writing material of Egypt and of many of her neighbors was papyrus, a very efficient paper made out of strips of the papyrus plant, the reed that once grew abundantly along the Nile. Of the hundreds of thousands of ancient documents which must have been inscribed upon papyrus, a mere handful survive. The substance disintegrates in any sort of dampness; the few that we have owe their preservation to the miraculously dry climate of Egypt. They lay undisturbed in her arid sands for hundreds, sometimes thousands, of years until some peasant stumbled across them or some archaeologist dug them up.

One day, sixty or so years ago, a group of Egyptian fellahin, rooting around for fuel, unearthed a mutilated papyrus roll. In due course it found its way into the hands of dealers and, eventually, of scholars. Often, papyrus documents turn out to be discouragingly repetitive: many an archaeologist has had high hopes dashed by finding that the well-preserved roll he has just uncovered is only one more copy of the Iliad or of the Book of the Dead, the

Egyptian bible. But this piece was unique. It was the carefully drawn-up report of an Egyptian priest named Wenamon who had been sent by his superiors some time around 1100 B.C. on a business trip to Byblus in Syria. It is like suddenly having a light flicked on in a dark room. Reading Wenamon's account we can for a moment relive a fragment of a trader's life in the twelfth century before Christ.

Wenamon came from Thebes far up the Nile. His official title was "Eldest of the Hall of the House of Amon" (Amon was the supreme Egyptian deity). Whatever his exact clerical position was, it is clear that he stood fairly high in the church hierarchy or he never would have been chosen for the assignment.

Every year during a sacred festival at Thebes an image of Amon was carried on the Nile in a ceremonial barge. This particular year, apparently, a new one had to be built and, since Egypt is practically treeless, the lumber had to be imported. The best and most convenient source was then, as thousands of years before, the famous stand of cedars in Lebanon (see p. 4). Someone had to go to Byblus to arrange the shipment. Herihor, the high priest of Egypt, selected Wenamon.

It was a time when Egypt was at one of the numerous low points of her long history. The country was not even united under one ruler. From the capital at Thebes where Wenamon as a member of the priestly college lived, Ramses XI ruled only upper Egypt; from Tanis, a relatively minor town in the delta area, Nesubanebded, a local prince, controlled lower Egypt. So Wenamon's first move was to make his way down the Nile to the court at Tanis to pay his respects to this prince and his queen Tanetamon and to enlist their aid. He presented a letter of introduction from Herihor, his credentials or passport, as it were, and their majesties received him graciously. They didn't go so far as to order a special ship for him but they arranged passage on a vessel bound for Syria under the command of a captain named Mengebet whom they presumably instructed to pay particular attention to this important passenger. On April 20th, fifteen days after leaving Thebes, Mengebet raised anchor, sailed down to the river's mouth, and the vessel, as Wenamon puts it, "descended into the great Syrian Sea."

So far things had gone swimmingly for Wenamon, and at the

first port of call it seemed that his luck would hold out. They put in at the town of Dor, a little to the south of Carmel, where a tribe of sea raiders called the Tjeker (cf. p. 32) had established a colony less than a century earlier, and the ruler Beder hastened to dispatch to the newly arrived envoy "50 loaves of bread, a jar of wine, and a joint of beef." Wenamon, who, as the narrative makes clear, held a glowing opinion of his own importance, took the gifts in gracious stride as being no more nor less than his due. He probably was genuinely delighted to get something palatable to eat. The ship's galley could have offered him nothing better than biscuit or dried fish, but it's more than likely that, born and bred as he was hundreds of miles up the Nile and away from salt water, he had been seasick every mile of the sail and hadn't had a scrap of food since the moment the ship had left the river. The wine in particular must have been welcome since Egypt produced very little of it, and that not very good, while Syria was the home of renowned vintages.

This was the last time fortune was to smile on Wenamon for a long while. The next lines of his narrative report a horrendous misfortune, one that was to bring a whole series of others in its wake: Wenamon awoke from what we may suppose, after all his fine food and wine, was a refreshing sleep to discover that—but it's better to tell it in his own unvarnished words. "Then," he writes, "a man of my ship made off having stolen one vessel of gold amounting to 5 *deben* [about 1⅕ lbs.], 4 vessels of silver amounting to 20 *deben*, a sack of silver—11 *deben*. Total of what he stole: 5 *deben* of gold, 31 *deben* [about 7½ lbs.] of silver." Every cent the poor fellow had been carrying was gone, his travel allowance as well as the cash Herihor had entrusted to him to pay for the lumber. He had only one valuable possession left. Still hidden securely in his cabin was a small image of Amon-of-the-Road, the patron saint of travelers, which Herihor had also turned over to him to help him in all phases of the assignment. The two priests clearly expected great things of it. Certainly the amount of cash Wenamon had been given was pretty niggardly considering the purchases he had to make. As the sequel shows, their trust in the wonder-working idol was a good deal more than circumstances warranted.

Wenamon did about the only thing he could under the circumstances. "In the morning I got up," he reports, "and went to the king's house and said, 'I have been robbed in your harbor and since you're king of this land you should start an investigation to recover my belongings.'" The Egyptian knew that this line of reasoning was not very convincing, for he quickly added, "For the money belongs to Amon-Re, king of gods, lord of the lands, and to Nesubanebded and to Herihor and the other lords of Egypt and also to Weret and Mekmel and Zakar-Baal, the prince of Byblus [these men were the three lumber dealers who would have received the cash]." In other words this was no mere theft of private property but of state funds, one therefore that demanded international cooperation.

Beder of course was not the type to be bluffed by any such nonsense. At the same time he seems to have been a very decent sort. "Your Excellency," he replied (a little lavishness with titles went a long way with Wenamon), "I don't care how important a person you are, I refuse to recognize the complaint that you've just lodged. If the thief who boarded your ship to steal your money was a citizen of my country, I'd pay you back from my own treasury until I could establish his identity. But he was a man from your own ship. However, wait a few days and I'll do some investigating."

After nine days of waiting Wenamon started to fidget. At this point the papyrus is tattered and we can only try to guess from tantalizing scraps of sentences just what happened. Apparently Wenamon got so officious that Beder could no longer maintain an attitude of quiet courtesy and at one point had to tell him bluntly to shut up. Wenamon then elected to continue the voyage, relying on his sacred image of Amon-of-the-Road to take care of the obviously pressing economic problems that were sure to arise.

The next series of events, however, shows that the Egyptian was not averse to lending his idol a hand in dealing with some of the problems. During the voyage between Tyre and Byblus, probably in the port of Sidon, it looks as if the Eldest of the Hall of the House of Amon saw a chance to recoup thirty *deben* of silver by holding up some Tjekers—and took it. The papyrus is still mutilated at this point, but the sequel shows that something of this sort had happened. Armed robbery is not the sort of thing we should expect from a highly respected Egyptian prelate—and very likely not at all the sort of thing he expected he would be doing in those happy days when he walked up the gangplank of the boat that took him downriver to Tanis. He had no difficulty salving his conscience: his money had been stolen in a Tjeker harbor and this money was Tjeker money; it was probably all just Amon's way of squaring things. "I am taking your money," he told his victims, "and keeping it until you find mine. Was it not a man of Tjeker who stole it?"

If Wenamon thought that his troubles were now over, he couldn't have been more wrong. The moment he dropped anchor in the harbor of Byblus where he intended to buy the lumber, the harbor master met him with a short but unambiguous message from Zakar-Baal, the ruling prince: "Get out of my harbor!" The most reasonable explanation for the unexpected order is that the Tjekers had sent a wanted-for-theft message ahead to Byblus and, since they were his neighbors on the south and had a reputation as formidable sea raiders, the prince was not anxious to start any trouble with them. A man of Wenamon's stamp, however, who had just pulled himself out of a hole by a successful piece of hold-up work, was not going to let a little thing like this stop him. For twenty nine days he hung around the harbor even though each morning the harbor master duly reported with the same message. Zakar-Baal, curiously enough, went no further than this. He had to discharge his obligations to a set of touchy neighbors, but at the same time he wanted to hold on to the chance of a profitable sale if he could. So he chose this interesting expedient of issuing an order and doing nothing to back it up; we shall see later that he had a knack for compromises of this sort.

Finally Wenamon gave up. Mengebet had already left, but when Wenamon found another boat scheduled to leave shortly for Egypt he booked passage on it and put his secretary and all his luggage aboard. He himself hung back, planning to delay until after dark when he could get his precious image to his stateroom without being observed. "I waited for the darkness," he notes, "thinking that when it descended I would get the god on board so that no other eye may see him."

But at this moment the unexpected happened. The harbor master approached with the announcement that Zakar-Baal had scheduled an interview for the following morning. Wenamon, understandably enough, was suspicious. "I said to him," he writes, "'Aren't you the one who came to me daily to tell me to get out of the harbor? And aren't you telling me to stay now just to make me lose my ship so that you can come back and start ordering me to go away again?'" Zakar-Baal met this cogent objection by issuing an order to hold the ship.

Wenamon has a ready explanation for the sudden change of attitude. The previous evening, while Zakar-Baal was conducting sacrifice, one of the young nobles at court suddenly fell into a frenzied fit and started to scream, "Bring the god here! Bring the messenger who is carrying him! Amon is the one who sent him from Egypt and made him come here." Wenamon clearly is out to convince the reader that the influence of his wonderful image had reached the court. Perhaps so. But we are entitled to the conjecture at least that what reached there was perhaps something more tangible, some of the stolen silver that Wenamon was now able to jingle in his pocket, for example. The Egyptian, as we can see by this time, is no man to let Amon-of-the-Road do all the work. He could hardly have spent his twenty nine days at the harbor just taking in the sea air. On the other hand, the fit may have been a device engineered by Zakar-Baal to end a little comedy that he had been directing for almost three weeks. The prince, as the continuation of the story reveals, was a most engaging character with a sharp eye for business and a well-developed sense of humor, a fact that Wenamon never tumbled to. He particularly liked to take his self-important visitor down a peg or two and there is no question that he thoroughly enjoyed keeping the Eldest of the Hall of the House of Amon on tenterhooks and making him cool his heels around the harbor. Besides, it satisfied the requirements of protocol toward his Tjeker neighbors. But it was no time for jokes when a potential customer was on the point of decamping without leaving an order. So Wenamon was suddenly summoned to the palace.

"I found him," he reports, "sitting in his upper chamber, leaning his back against a window, while the waves of the great Syrian Sea beat against the wall behind him." It isn't usual for Wenamon to include circumstantial details like this; the interview and its setting must have burned itself into his memory. "I said to him, 'The blessing of Amon upon you.'" The Egyptian must have been all wound up for an extended exchange of amenities, as at home. If so, he was disappointed. Zakar-Baal, all business, came right to the point: "How long ago did you leave Egypt?" he asked. "Five months and one day," the envoy replied, probably with feeling— the voyage could be done in a couple of weeks at most. Then came the question that Wenamon must have been hoping against hope he would be spared. But he must have seen at the first moment of the interview that a man like Zakar-Baal, who kept one waiting for over a month and brusquely dispensed with all one's carefully thought out phrases, would inevitably ask it. "Where," the prince said next, "is the letter of the priest of Amon which you should have with you?" Wenamon had set out with credentials, of course, but at that moment they were lying in some desk drawer in Tanis: he had presented them there and forgotten to ask for them back. There was nothing to do except play the hand out: "I gave it to Nesubanebded and Tanetamon," he replied, probably with the sort of expression a motorist tells a traffic cop that he has left his driver's license at home. Zakar-Baal saw a fine opportunity for a scene. "He became very angry," Wenamon writes, and we can readily picture the prince working himself into a rage with histrionic art, "and said to me, 'What! you don't have the letter! And where is the ship and crew that Nesubanebded gave you? Didn't he turn you over to this foreign ship captain just to have him kill you and throw you overboard? If that had happened where would people have looked for the god? And where would they have looked for you?'" Wenamon continues: "I said to him, 'What makes you think it wasn't an Egyptian ship? Nesubanebded has only Egyptian crews. He has no Syrian crews.' He said to me, 'There are twenty ships belonging to this harbor which do business with Nesubanebded. And isn't it a known fact that at Sidon, where you have been, there are fifty which do business with Werket-El and are anchored near his office?'" It was a snide remark that hit home: foreign bottoms now carried most of Egypt's trade items; there was little left of the native merchant marine, and Wenamon knew it. He knew it so well that, though rarely at a loss for words and usually ready with quite a flow of them, he had to admit that he "was silent at this critical moment."

Zakar-Baal had had his fun and it was now time to get down to business. "What have you come here for?" he asked. "I have come," was the reply, "for timber for the sacred barge of Amon-Re, King of gods. Your father supplied it, your grandfather supplied it and so will you."

Since the prince held all the cards he could afford to overlook bluster of that sort. "They certainly did," he answered in the best of spirits, "and if you pay me I'll do it too. Why, when my family carried out the former commission, the Pharaoh—god bless him— sent six shiploads of Egyptian merchandise which were unloaded into our warehouses. What are you bringing me?" At this point Zakar-Baal couldn't resist another chance to torture the poor Egyptian: he called for his secretary and ordered him to bring out the old ledgers. Entry by entry he went over them for Wenamon's benefit. And there must have been plenty of entries, for the grand total of receipts was 1000 *deben*.

There had been long periods when Lebanon was an Egyptian possession (p. 28) and the pharaohs didn't have to buy the cedar they needed but just took it. Even less than a century before Wenamon's journey, Egypt had held all the land south of Zakar-Baal's principality and the prince's predecessors had been careful to treat this powerful neighbor with courtesy and respect. Things were very different now, however, and Zakar-Baal, who must have hugely enjoyed the whole interview, gleefully reminds Wenamon of this fact. "If the ruler of Egypt were the owner of my property," he tells him, "and I were his servant, he wouldn't have had to send money. . . . But *I* am not your servant nor your master's. All I have to do is say the word and the logs will be ready on the shore. But where are the ships you should have brought to transport them? Where are the lines to lash them? . . . This really is a stupid trip they have had you make!" At this crack, Wenamon finally lost his temper. "I told him," he writes, " 'Wrong! This is not a stupid trip at all! Every ship on the river belongs to Amon and so does the sea and Lebanon which you call your own. The cedars grow only for his sacred bark, for he owns every ship. It was he, Amon-Re, who ordered Herihor my lord to send me bearing the god with me.

But you, you have kept this great god waiting for twenty-nine days!'" After going on in this way for a considerable time, he wound up with, "Now let a secretary be summoned and I'll send him to Nesubanebded and Tanetamon, the rulers whom Amon has given to the north of his land, and they will forward all the money that is necessary. I will have your men say to them, 'Advance the money until I go back again to the south, and I shall then have every bit of the debt paid to you.' That," he added, "is what I told him."

This was precisely what Zakar-Baal wanted to hear. He must have known through his agents that the envoy had only a niggardly thirty *deben* of silver with him. Now he was being offered whatever price he wanted to set on his product. The secretary was forthwith dispatched to Egypt, and Zakar-Baal, no doubt with most of Wenamon's stolen money in his cashbox as a down payment, let him take along several important timbers: the keel, sternpost, stempost, and four others. Nesubanebded and Tanetamon did just as the envoy had promised: in forty-eight days the secretary returned with a shipment that contained the following impressive inventory:

> 4 jars and 1 bowl of gold
> 5 jars of silver
> 10 garments of royal linen
> 10 bolts of good South Egyptian linen
> 500 rolls of finished papyrus
> 500 cowhides
> 500 coils of rope
> 20 sacks of lentils
> 30 baskets of fish

There were some items for Wenamon personally too: five garments of good South Egyptian linen (he probably needed these badly; he had had no idea he was going to be away for better than a half-year), five bolts of good South Egyptian linen, one sack of lentils, and five baskets of fish. "The prince rejoiced," notes Wenamon, "and detailed three hundred men and three hundred oxen to fell the trees." Eight months after the envoy had left his native land, the timber lay on the beach cut and stacked, ready for loading.

But even then Zakar-Baal had to have a last bit of fun. "You know," he told Wenamon, "you are much better off than the messengers Khaemwaset sent. My ancestors kept them here for seventeen years and they died here.... Here you! [turning to an attendant] Show him the graves!" This was a little too much. "No," was the agonized reply, "please, I don't want to see them." At this point, probably to recover his own spirits, the Egyptian launched into a long disquisition to the effect that Zakar-Baal will be so proud of having done business with Amon and his divine and human associates (these being, of course, the sacred image and Wenamon) that he will not stop until he has rendered the transaction immortal by erecting a permanent stone monument with the whole story inscribed thereon. "That will be just fine," is, in effect, Zakar-Baal's reply.

But nothing was destined to go right for the poor envoy. Just when things looked brightest—the timber was ready on the beach, several payments on account were already in the prince's hands, both sides had agreed amicably that the balance would be remitted later—and Wenamon was on the point of giving orders to load the cargo, suddenly eleven ships sailed into the harbor and delivered a pregnant message to the palace: "Arrest Wenamon and don't let a ship of his leave for Egypt." If the story didn't date six centuries before Greek drama was born, we might think we were reading a typical Greek tragedy with Fate inevitably swooping down on a man at his best moment to exact retribution for wrongs done long before. For the ships were manned by Tjeker sea raiders, there to demand justice for the thirty *deben* of silver that had been stolen from them almost a year ago. Wenamon who, just a little while earlier, had been chattering about seeing his name inscribed on an eternal monument, at this point just gave up: he sat down on the beach and cried. Apparently he carried on so that even the prince became aware of it and sent his secretary down to find out what had happened. "How long will I have to stay here?" wailed Wenamon, pointing to the ships. "Don't you see that those there are coming to arrest me?" He worked himself up into such a state that Zakar-Baal himself got a bit worried. After all, a customer deserved some consideration. His solution has an incredibly modern cast to it: he sent Wenamon a ram, two jars of wine, and an

Egyptian dancing girl. (The envoy, scrupulous reporter that he is, has saved her name for posterity: Tanetnot.)

Let us hope that Wenamon relished his mutton and wine and had a distracting evening with Tanetnot, because there wasn't much enjoyment for him in what he was to go through the next morning. Zakar-Baal was on the spot: he didn't want to lose a customer, especially one with a balance still due, and at the same time he didn't want to get on the wrong side of dangerous neighbors. His decision shows the skill we had observed in him before of coming up with highly original compromises: "I cannot arrest a messenger of Amon in my territory," he told the Tjekers, "but let me send him off and then you chase him." In other words, the prince was going to discharge his obligations to Wenamon by not turning him over to the Tjekers. But he was going to avoid offending the latter by sending the envoy off—with a bit of a head start to give him a sporting chance. Wenamon no doubt had his own ideas about the sportingness of the chance a vessel chartered for hauling timber had of outrunning a crack squadron of sea raiders.

The next portion of the narrative is tantalizingly bald. "He loaded me on board," Wenamon writes, "he sent me away. The wind drove me to the land of Alasia" (Cyprus or the coast of Asia Minor to its north). This wind which took him in a direction almost opposite the one he wanted must have been one of the southeasterly gales that are common along the Syrian coast. Wenamon probably considered it just another item in the list of tribulations his god was unaccountably putting him through, but actually it very likely proved his salvation: the Tjeker raiders, either because their ships were too light or because they figured the gale would save them the job, apparently didn't bother to give chase.

When the vessel landed, unquestionably a good deal the worse for wear, a group of natives promptly descended upon it and hustled Wenamon off to kill him. Their villages had very likely suffered their share of pirate raids and this was looked upon as a welcome opportunity to square accounts. At long last, however, Wenamon's luck changed. He was brought to the palace of the queen and "found her just as she was going from one of her houses and entering into another. I greeted her. I asked the people who stood around her, 'There must be someone among you who speaks

Egyptian.' Someone answered, 'I speak it.' I said to him, 'Say to your mistress—' " but the speech is unimportant and probably represents what, years later at his desk in Thebes, he reckoned he ought to have said rather than what a thoroughly soaked and exhausted and frightened wayfarer actually did say. The important point is that the queen listened. "She had the people called and, as they stood before her," writes Wenamon, "she said to me, 'Pass the night—' " and here the papyrus abruptly breaks off. These are the last words we have from this extraordinary writer. We don't know—and very likely never will, unless by a miracle the rest of the papyrus is discovered—how he got back home, whether the timber arrived safely, or whether Zakar-Baal ever received the balance due him. We only know that he did get back, or else the report would never have been written.

Years after Wenamon had returned to Thebes, vessels continued to make the run between Syria and Egypt, hauling timber and wine from the one in exchange for textiles, papyrus, and hides from the other. In Byblus, Zakar-Baal's children must have kept adding entries to the ledger their father had so mischievously shown the Egyptian envoy. But wherever the legitimate trader was to be found, so was the pirate. To the south of Byblus the Tjekers went on matter-of-factly pursuing their profession of raiding. The shores of Greece, which sent forth the merchantmen that carried among other things the distinctive pottery archaeologists constantly turn up in excavation after excavation on the Aegean Islands and the littoral of western Asia, also launched the plunderers who made life miserable for coastal villages the length and breadth of the eastern Mediterranean. Eventually, raiding came to outstrip trading. The lords of Mycenae and Pylos and other centers in Greece sent out only squadrons of pirates and no longer fleets of peaceful merchant ships. People moved away from the coasts in terror and turned to a new kind of existence inland. By the beginning of the first millennium B.C. what trade was left fell into the hands of the businessmen par excellence of the ancient world, the Phoenicians. But their story belongs to a later age.

5 The Dawn of Maritime Exploration

ONE DAY, SOME THREE thousand years ago, a vessel left the harbor of Iolcus, on the northeast coast of Greece, where Volo stands today, swung its head to the east, and quickly got under way. The world's first recorded voyage of overseas exploration had begun.

The account of this trip is unfortunately not set forth in a matter-of-fact ship's log or a diary, something that would leave as little room for ambiguity as a radio beam, but in a tradition, half sailor's yarn half poetic fancy, that had a leisurely thousand years or more in which to work itself up. The very names involved have an uncomfortable vagueness about them. The skipper's name was Jason "the healer" and his ship *Argo* "the swift." These offer no difficulty. But the far-off country that Jason made his way to was called Aea, which means in Greek nothing more than "land," and its ruler Aeetes, "man of the land." The native woman he brought home from there was Medea "the cunning one." His son is named Euneus, "good man aboard ship," which is almost too apropos. And what can we say of woman-headed birds and movable cliffs and a dragon, all of which he and his crew, the Argonauts, met en route, or of the prize itself that they brought home, a fleece of gold? The task is to distill, from a mass of mythological fancy found in Greek poetry that spans almost a millennium, the sober details that Jason would have entered in his log. It's somewhat like having to reconstruct a naval diary from the stories of Sinbad the Sailor.

The legend of the voyage of the *Argo* goes something like this:

Jason was a young prince who, like Hamlet, was the victim of an unscrupulous uncle: his aged father had been pushed off the throne by a brother, Pelias. Since outright murder of the son (the father was old enough to be left out of the reckoning) would entail unfortunate political repercussions, Pelias availed himself of a time-honored method of getting rid of a popular rival. He set Jason the task of finding and bringing home the fabulous golden fleece. It's as if Ferdinand and Isabella had dispatched Columbus to bring back, on pain of death, the latitude and longitude of Eldorado.

Jason collected a crew to man the 50-oared galley *Argo* that had been specially built for the voyage, and set a course for the east. The vessel sailed swiftly across the Aegean, through the Dardanelles and Bosporus and into the Black Sea, encountering numerous difficulties, including a brush with the Harpies, creatures with bodies of birds and heads of women. Once in the Black Sea Jason was in completely unknown waters; like Columbus he could only cry "Adelante!" and press unremittingly eastward. At last, after a not overly trying voyage, the Argonauts dropped anchor at their destination, a country which they called simply Aea, "land," but which later Greeks identified with Colchis in the far eastern corner of the Black Sea.

Here they ran into troubles of a different sort. Aeetes, the ruler, for obvious reasons showed considerable reluctance to surrender the fleece and was able to back his reluctance with armed force. Moreover, the prize was guarded by a dragon, formidably equipped for dealing with intruders, and discouragingly vigilant. In the nick of time all problems were settled by a stroke of pure luck: Medea, the king's daughter, a handsome girl and skilled sorceress, fell in love with Jason and in short order accomplished what no amount of Greek muscle and bravery could have. Some time later, just before dawn the *Argo* crept out of the harbor with the fleece—and

Medea—safely aboard. In a few hours Aeetes had launched his navy in pursuit.

The trip back was a nightmare. To elude Aeetes Jason laid out a different course home. He lost his way and wandered to the ends of the earth. The ship had to undergo the horror of running the gantlet of the "wandering rocks," two huge cliffs that, when anything tried to pass between, drove together swiftly enough to crush a bird, to say nothing of an object as slow as a ship. At one point the crew had to make a backbreaking portage, pulling the vessel overland on rollers for twelve long days. Much time elapsed before the *Argo* finally was run up on the beach in the harbor of Iolcus and Jason was able to enter the last note in his log.

The aftermath of the voyage tells more of human emotion than of maritime history. Medea again proved invaluable to her lover. Her magical recipes were able to restore his aged father to youth and to do away with Pelias (she gave the youth-recipe to his daughters, simply omitting to tell them of one key ingredient). But success and fame made Jason ambitious. An opportunity came his way to marry the daughter of the ruler of Corinth and ultimately to inherit that rich kingdom. Medea rejected his cold-blooded arrangements for putting her aside and, in a burst of immortal rage, took her revenge by slaying not only his fiancée but the two children she herself had borne him. Of his great days there was but one thing left to Jason and that a mere symbol: the hulk of the *Argo,* which now lay rotting on the beach at Iolcus. He returned there to spend his days prowling dreamily about it. Even this inanimate object turned against him: one day as he lay asleep by it a rotted timber fell and killed him.

So much for what the storytellers and poets made of the voyage of Jason and the *Argo*. What can we make of it?

We must first guess at the date; poets and spinners of yarns are not much interested in strict chronology. When the naval power of Crete had been destroyed and that of Mycenae had degenerated (p. 31), raiders and rovers swarmed over the eastern Mediterranean. To this age, the period between 1200 and 1000 B.C., when Wenamon was sailing to Lebanon and Homer's pirates were raiding Egypt, after the time when Crete had yielded the initiative on the seas to the Greeks and before the time soon to come when the

Black Sea would be as familiar to Greek skippers as their own Aegean, the tale of Jason and his voyage very likely belongs. There is a significant twist in his story that sets him apart from his contemporary sea heroes. Jason was no raider who sallied forth to pounce on the first or best available town for plunder. He was the leader of a carefully equipped expedition whose express purpose was to cross uncharted waters to gain something known only through vague hearsay.

He headed eastward. Why not westward? The golden apples in the garden of the Hesperides, which later Greeks located near the Strait of Gibraltar, would seem just as fair and tangible a prize as a golden fleece. But perhaps not. Later ages knew that the peoples who lived at the farther end of the Black Sea where Jason's Aea was located had a way of washing gold from a river by tying fleeces in the stream so that particles of the dust would adhere to them. It was the earliest known form of placer mining. If we assume that rumors of this had reached Jason's part of the world, the "search for the golden fleece" suddenly comes into focus; it becomes a search for treasure, a completely understandable reason for daring exploration.

There was, too, perhaps another reason for heading eastward: adventure was more quickly come upon. It was a short sail from Iolcus to the Bosporus, probably little more than a week if that, and once that strait had been navigated and his prow was cutting the surface of the Black Sea, Jason was where he wanted to be, passing, along the north shore of Asia Minor, settlements that belonged to strange races. Had he gone west he would have had to slog it out to the seas beyond Sicily before striking unknown territory. For, centuries earlier, Minoan and Mycenaean ships had sailed this far and all the waters up to the straits between Sicily and Tunisia were well known (pp. 21-22, 24).

Jason, then, elected to go east. He could not have had much trouble rounding up a capable crew. There must have been an ample supply of hard-fisted seamen lounging about the wharves of Iolcus and nearby ports waiting around to sign on a voyage that promised to be interesting and profitable—no more trouble probably than Lief Ericsson and other Viking leaders were to have millennia later in gathering crews for their epoch-making ventures westward. Later Greek tradition has it that the Argonauts were an all-star team, that Heracles and Theseus and Orpheus and others from the galaxy of Greek heroes went along, but this is poetic embroidery. Jason's expedition was successful, which meant he had a complement of obedient able-bodied seamen and not a collection of prima donnas. Rowing a galley was a complicated technique that demanded training and coordination; none of the twelve famous labors of Heracles involved pulling an oar. The oldest versions of the legend imply that Jason used only the leaders from his own neighborhood, and this must surely be right.

The *Argo* coasted along the north shore of Asia Minor and met the usual problem that confronted a strange ship in those days: attacks by natives wherever it tried to put in for the night or for provisions. For the *Argo* could not stay at sea any length of time. Roomy merchantmen that could were being built in this age, but the *Argo* was not one of these. Jason wisely chose a fighting ship for his expedition, one which would not be so completely dependent upon the winds as would a sailing freighter and which could either withstand or run away from attack. His vessel could not have been very different from those used in the war against Troy: a slender ship mounting twenty-five rowers on a side, with a sail and mast that could be easily and quickly unstepped (pp. 36-38). When traveling without a break night and day, the crew slept at their oars and there was little room for provisions. Frequent stopovers had to be included in the itinerary.

One of the more unusual encounters on the outward leg of the voyage, according to later legend, was a set-to with the Harpies, creatures who, as drawn in Greek art, have the bodies of birds and the heads of women. They somewhat resemble winged sphinxes, a fact that may account for their presence in Jason's story. Archaeologists have discovered that the winged sphinx is a form that originated and is commonly found in Asia Minor. It occurs in Hittite sculpture, for example. Can the Harpy be the poetic end result of what started as a description by one of Jason's sailors of a picture or bas-relief he had seen somewhere during this trip along the north coast of Asia Minor?

The voyage out was nothing compared with the return, both from Jason's point of view and from that of the historian who tries to track down the nuggets of fact behind the vagaries of tradition. One thing is clear: the *Argo* did not return the way it came. To avoid pursuit Jason charted a different course—and this is where the trouble begins. The various versions of the legend bring him home by different routes, each more fanciful than the next. One actually has it that the crew carried the ship all across Europe, launched it in the North Sea, and sailed it back around Spain and through the Strait of Gibraltar. The poet Pindar, who, writing in the fifth century B.C., is, except for Homer, the earliest author to describe the journey, takes the ship to the western Mediterranean and the shores of Libya before getting it back safely to Greece—but Pindar's virtuosity lies in his glorious imagination, not his historical accuracy. Sophocles, that most level-headed of dramatists, happens in a certain passage to drop the incidental remark that the Argonauts sailed out along the south coast of the Black Sea and back along the north. This makes complete sense, just how complete we shall see in a moment.

If Jason was to return by a different route he had but two alternatives: either to strike boldly across the open sea and follow a straight line from Colchis to the Bosporus, or else to coast along the northern shore. He could hardly have hesitated in making up his mind: an extended sail through open waters in the face of oncoming winter (if he left Iolcus at the very opening of the sailing season, the beginning of spring—see p. 39—, the time spent in the voyage out and at Aea must still have used up most of the summer) was out of the question. Even had his course lain across familiar waters instead of completely new ones, a cramped open galley wasn't the ship for this sort of routing. The Argonauts must have done it the slow way, groping timidly along the strange coast of south Russia. And as they worked farther and farther north, and winter overtook them, they must have inevitably run into a phenomenon completely out of their ken—ice.

It was during this leg of the voyage, the legend has it, that the *Argo* encountered its most nerve-racking adventure, the passage through the "wandering rocks." These became famous in Greek mythology. Homer has Circe carefully brief Odysseus about them when he was taking off on a course that took him into waters the *Argo* had passed through. And well she might. Storms and high winds and shoals or the like were nothing new to Mediterranean sailors. But what must have amazed the Argonauts, or Odysseus, or any other son of Greece who knew only her mild equable climate, were the ice floes off the wintry South Russian shores. A blow from one could easily leave a ship like the *Argo* a mass of splintered wreckage. The high point of Jason's report must surely have been his description of these monstrous formations that floated about so dangerously that only a master hand on the helm could bring a ship safely through them—and then only with luck. The details would become more lurid with each telling, and it should not have taken many generations for the floes to have become Homer's "precipitous cliffs against which the giant swell of Amphitrite breaks with a shattering roar."

What of the grueling portage of twelve days' duration? On the north shores of the Black Sea, the peninsula of the Crimea thrusts downward for some one hundred miles, marking off the Sea of Azov on the east. The Argonauts, following the coast line, would automatically wander into this body of water and find themselves in an icy cul-de-sac. We can easily imagine that a portage across the neck of the peninsula to the open water on the west, despite its obvious hardships, would look to them far preferable to fighting their way south through the floes of the Sea of Azov, running once again the gantlet of the "wandering rocks."

Mankind likes to treasure the names of the men who do things first, who invent or discover, to the point where we even insist on teaching them to our children. Whatever the reasons for which the *Argo* made its journey—whether for gold as I have suggested, whether for commerce with the fleece symbolizing the golden grain of the Crimea that was to become so important later in the Greek economy, whether, as the mythologists suggest, Jason "the healer" traveled east toward the dawn in search of the golden clouds that would "heal" the parchedness of his arid homeland—Jason's name must be added to the list. The expedition he headed was the first we know of that sailed forth to explore new lands. There were, to be sure, maritime explorers of earlier date than he. Cretan skippers, as we have seen, had made their way westward and travelled the waters up to Sicily centuries before the *Argo* set sail. But their names have been lost; they have left merely a dim spoor of potsherds which only archaeologists can follow. History in its wayward fashion has preserved the name of Jason. We don't know who next duplicated his feat, since the second person to do or find something is rarely remembered; but a second there surely was and a third and so on until—it was a long process and took a number of centuries—this once mysterious body of water became in effect a Greek lake. The earlier navigators called the Black Sea the *Pontos Axeinos,* the "unfriendly sea." They soon changed it to *Euxeinos,* "friendly" sea.

6 Westward Ho!

THERE WAS A TIME when sailors, leaving behind the seas they knew, turned their prows toward the west, into uncharted waters, and stumbled upon a new world. The effect was electrifying. Nations rushed men to explore and colonize the new territories, freighters to trade with them, and warships to settle disputes. History in a way was only repeating itself when the Portuguese opened up Africa, and Spain, America. The first great age of discovery and colonization took place almost two and a half millennia earlier, and the principal roles were played by the Greeks and the Phoenicians.

There was a great upheaval in the eastern Mediterranean in the time between 1200 and 1000 B.C. The Greeks of this age ceased to be the wide-ranging traders they once had been. Their cities were now not so secure that they could unconcernedly go off on distant raiding expeditions as in the past. Immigrants from the north, spilling down the peninsula, forced them to turn their attention to defending their own homes. Those who still took to the sea were primarily sea rovers, but there were many other peoples, like Wenamon's Tjekers, to give them stiff competition in this profession. The story of all this is written only in the archaeological record, but it is none the less clear. In the excavations of Greek cities of this age and of the points with which they used to trade, fragments of the pottery once found there in such profusion gradually grow less and less until, by about 1100 B.C., they disappear. Not until several centuries later does Greek pottery show itself again, and this time it is of a different type, belonging to Greeks of a later age, distinct from the Mycenaeans.

Here was a perfect opportunity for an enterprising maritime nation, and there happened to be one such available to seize it with alacrity. The Phoenicians had always been keen and active traders as far back as the days when they sold boatloads of Lebanese cedar to Snefru of Egypt (p. 4). Their geographical location was perfect. From their big cities of Tyre and Sidon main roads led into the hinterland and beyond, connecting eventually with India, and brought to their warehouses the luxury products of the eastern caravan trade. Just south lay Egypt with its own connections with Arabia and Somaliland (pp. 9-13). No other nation was as ideally located as they to serve as middleman in the distribution of wares from all these quarters. But now they could go one step further and expand to take up the slack left by the withdrawal of the Mycenaeans.

It is hard to tell much in detail about the Phoenicians. Even their name is a puzzle. They called themselves Sidonians, from the city that was their greatest center until Tyre outstripped it about the beginning of the first millennium B.C., and their land Canaan. It was the Greeks who named them *Phoinikes,* which some linguists think comes from a root meaning "sea" but which most connect with the adjective *phoinos,* "dark red." The Phoenicians made a specialty of dyeing textiles, using certain species of a sea snail, Murex, that has a glandular secretion which produces various shades of red and purple. (There are actual hills outside of Tyre and Sidon today, made up from top to bottom of the shells of these creatures discarded by the ancient dye factories.) To their Greek customers the Phoenicians probably seemed principally textile traders, "red (-garment)" men. They were businessmen first and foremost, produced no poets or historians to chronicle their accomplishments for posterity—and their business ledgers have gone the way of all such objects. Moreover, being more interested in profits than in publicity, they kept their trade secrets to themselves; they even spread falsehoods to discourage possible competitors. The story is told that once, when a Phoenician merchant was being tailed by a foreign skipper anxious to discover the source of certain trade items, he deliberately ran his ship on the rocks to prevent it. In honor of this heroic act in behalf of the national income, the government rewarded him not with anything trivial like a statue or monument but with reimbursement *in toto* for all loss sustained.

They were sharp traders. The only romantic Phoenician ever mentioned is Dido, the queen who committed suicide after an unhappy love affair with Aeneas, and even she was a canny hand at driving a bargain. The story goes that, when she was founding the city of Carthage, she made a deal with the natives on the site to pay them an annual rent for as much land as a bull's hide could cover. She then skived a hide and managed to encircle with the pieces enough ground for an imposing city. The Dutch—another nation which needed no lessons in trading—hardly did better when they bought Manhattan Island for twenty-four dollars' worth of trinkets. The Phoenicians even perfected ways of handling barter with natives whose language they couldn't understand. Herodotus, the inquisitive Greek of the fifth century B.C., who is called the Father of History but who could just as appropriately be called Father of the Travelogue, had a keen eye for a good story, and reported that the Phoenician colonists of Carthage would arrive at a native village and

unload their wares and lay them out along the beach. Then they would go back aboard their ships and raise a smoke signal. The natives, seeing the smoke, would come down to the shore, lay out the amount of gold they figured the goods were worth, and draw back some paces from them. Then the Carthaginians would come ashore and take a look. If it was enough, they took it and left; if not, they went back aboard ship and waited patiently. Then the natives would approach and keep adding to their gold until the sellers were satisfied.

The reputation for honesty they had, judging by this story, among savages was not always maintained among other customers. Their merchants were always ready to pick up extra money in shady transactions, especially in the slave traffic. Odysseus' swineherd, for ex-

Westward Ho!

ample, born a free Greek, had been kidnaped and sold on the block by a crew that had originally dropped in at his island for legitimate barter.

The Phoenicians were involved in some celebrated business deals. When King Solomon was about to proceed with the building of his great temple about 970 B.C. and needed timber, he naturally turned to Phoenicia with its well-known Lebanese cedar and negotiated a contract. He wrote to Hiram who was king of the great export center of Tyre at the time:

> Now therefore command thou that they hew me cedar trees out of Lebanon; and my servants shall be with thy servants: and unto thee will I give hire for thy servants according to all that thou shall appoint: for thou knowest that there is not among us any that can skill to hew timber like unto the Sidonians. . . .
> And Hiram sent to Solomon, saying, I have considered the things which thou sentest to me for: and I will do all thy desire concerning timber of cedar, and concerning timber of fir.
> My servants shall bring them down from Lebanon unto the sea: and I will convey them by sea in floats unto the place that thou shall appoint me, and will cause them to be discharged there, and thou shalt receive them: and thou shalt accomplish my desire in giving food for my household.
> So Hiram gave Solomon cedar trees and fir trees according to all his desire.
> And Solomon gave Hiram twenty thousand measures of wheat for food to his household, and twenty measures of pure oil: thus gave Solomon to Hiram year by year.

In the days before money was invented, a buyer had the choice of paying in uncoined precious metal, or of bartering. It was because Solomon had no access to gold—he had been forced to exchange Palestinian wheat and oil for his timber—that he entered into his next business operation with the Phoenicians.

For centuries the inhabitants of the northern end of the Persian Gulf had been trading with India and Arabia and Africa (pp. 5-9). The products involved were for the most part luxuries: ivory, silks, and spices from India; ivory and gold from Africa; incense and perfumes from Arabia. The profits were correspondingly large. Solomon, though he controlled a port on the appropriate waters in Ezion Geber at the southern end of the Negeb, ruled a nation that had no merchant marine or, for that matter, no experience with the sea at all, and was consequently in the exasperating position of seeing all this lucrative trade bypass him. What arrived at the Persian Gulf was transported for Mediterranean distribution by caravan to the Phoenician ports, especially Tyre; what came to Egypt was floated downriver to the mouth of the Nile and carried from there in Phoenician bottoms. Even the Phoenicians, though most of the trade in one way or another passed through their hands, were not completely satisfied: they had to share the profits with caravaneers in the one case or Egyptian middlemen in the other. So when Solomon conceived the idea of building a fleet of his own which, working out of Ezion Geber, could trade with Ophir, that is, India, and of manning it with Phoenician sailors, Hiram didn't have to be asked twice:

> And king Solomon made a navy of ships in Ezion-geber, which is beside Eloth, on the shore of the Red Sea, in the land of Edom.
> And Hiram sent in the navy his servants, shipmen that had knowledge of the sea, with the servants of Solomon.
> And they came to Ophir, and fetched from thence gold, four hundred and twenty talents, and brought it to king Solomon.

From Egypt in the south to Asia Minor in the north and westward to Cyprus, Rhodes, and Crete, Phoenicia had practically a monopoly over the trade routes for the three centuries between 1100 and 800 B.C. It must have been some time during this period—no one can date it exactly—that she passed along to the Greeks one of the greatest gifts that the East was to give to the West. The Phoenicians, unlike their neighbors who wrote in clumsy hieroglyphs or cuneiform, used an alphabetic system of writing that some Semitic tribe had invented, probably centuries earlier. In the course of trading operations, most likely in the lower Aegean area, some of their merchants brought it to the attention of Greeks, who immediately recognized its superlative convenience and swiftly adapted it for writing their language. Subsequently they in turn gave it to the Romans who passed it on to the Western World. In this transfer the Phoenicians were not creators but middlemen. Their second great contribution was one which they conceived and carried out completely by themselves.

Even in the great days of Minoan and Mycenaean expansion (pp.

21-22, 24) the western limit of the ancient world had been Sicily and Sardinia. Beyond this lay uncharted seas and terra incognita. Some time later—ancient historians have it 1100 B.C., but it was more likely at least a century or more afterward—daring Phoenician sailors took the plunge and headed their prows into the waters beyond. Within a short time they had put the stamp of success on their venture by planting an outpost, the colony of Utica in north Africa, not far from Tunis of today. Phoenicia never did anything for the sheer adventure in it; something must have drawn her interest in this direction. Judging by what happened next, it looks as if her sailors had picked up rumors that there were lands farther west where they might find silver and, still more interesting, tin, a mineral in short supply in the eastern Mediterranean and of vital importance because, fused with copper, it forms bronze. For they are next reported sailing even beyond Gibraltar into the Atlantic to trade with Tartessus, as the coast of Spain just outside the strait was called. Here the natives mined silver locally; but, even more important, to this place tin was brought by local carriers along the Atlantic coast of Spain. It came from regions farther north and so far out of the ken of the Mediterranean mariner that he long knew them only vaguely as the "Tin Isles"; the best guess is that the source was Cornwall in England. Between 900 and 800 B.C. the newcomers set themselves up permanently by establishing on a fine harbor beyond the strait the key center of Gadir, or Cadiz as we call it now.

This was the first great line of travel the Phoenicians laid down: from Tyre to Utica to Cadiz. Climate and current dictated the next step. The western Mediterranean is swept by northwest winds during the summer months which made up the ancient mariner's chief period of activity. To sail westward along the North African coast from the colony of Utica was to risk a lee shore and buck a a hostile current in the bargain. By working to the north at the outset, and following a general southwesterly slant from there to the strait and using the African shore only for the homeward leg, Phoenician skippers assured themselves favorable wind and current for the round trip. And so they planted way stations at strategic points: on Sardinia for that first leg northward, on Ibiza and the Spanish Mediterranean coast for the long slant to the strait, and in the neighborhood of Algiers or Oran for the homeward lap. No details about any part of this striking achievement are known. The Phoenicians wanted no competitors and they not only were tight-lipped about what they were doing but even surrounded it with an effective smokescreen of sailors' yarns no doubt filled with hair-raising details of shipwrecks and sea monsters.

About 800 B.C., Tyre founded the colony of Carthage a little south of Utica. This is the expedition which, according to tradition, Queen Dido headed. The new settlement, quickly overtaking Utica, became the center of operations in the west. It carried out a program of colonization on its own, sending out expeditions to explore and occupy new sites and to convert former way stations into full-sized communities. By 700 B.C. Carthage had moved into Sardinia, had founded several colonies in Sicily, including Palermo with its fine natural harbor, and had planted Málaga plus a few other towns on the Mediterranean coast of Spain. This took care of the new territory to the west, but there was still the link to the homeland far in the east to think about. So Carthage occupied Pantelleria and Malta which, combined with Phoenician settlements that had long been established on Crete and Rhodes and Cyprus, gave her a set of convenient steppingstones back to the home port of Tyre.

Her work was now complete. The west was fully open—but to Phoenicia alone. Through a wide-flung network of stations, the trade in tin from the Atlantic coast and in silver and lead and iron from Spain was firmly in her hands. She had become one of the great powers of the ancient world. But over three centuries had now passed since the Phoenicians had discovered this new world, and another great nation had entered on a career of colonization. Competition lay just over the horizon.

While Phoenicia was sailing the eastern and western seas with a completely free hand, the waves of immigrants that had swept over Greece and helped to finish off the great commercial activity of the Mycenaean Age (p. 66) finally came to an end. By 800 B.C. Greece had by and large taken the shape it was to have in its heyday three centuries later. It was a conglomeration of independent cities that dotted not only the original peninsula but also the Aegean Islands and Crete and Cyprus and, above all, the western coast of Asia

Westward Ho!

Minor. Their vessels, merchantmen and warships, once again plied the sea in numbers. The time was ripe for Greece to embark on its own program of colonization.

The Phoenicians had picked out a limited number of commercially advantageous sites and exploited them for trade; their impress was only skin deep. The Greeks, between 750 and 550 B.C., in a series of concerted bursts of activity, settled themselves the length and breadth of the Mediterranean and the Black Sea, "like frogs on a pond," as Plato put it. They founded in the neighborhood of 250 colonies, a number of which have had a continuous existence ever since. In a way it was like administering injections of Greek culture into the body of barbarism at 250 points. Most of them took, whether the recipients were Scyths on the shores of South Russia, Italians in South Italy, or Gauls at the mouth of the Rhone. In a very real sense, the boatloads of Greek emigrants that crossed the seas in those two centuries were the advance guard of Western civilization.

Like the Phoenicians, Greek colonists usually picked sites for hardfisted commercial reasons. When they settled Syracuse in 733 B.C. or the site of Istanbul in 658, they took over two harbors that were among the very best in the Mediterranean and that were ideally located for trade. But the people who joined in the founding expeditions were not all merchants or sailors. Often they were poverty-stricken peasants—the soil of Greece is so poor that the threat of overpopulation has dogged the country during almost the whole of its existence—who went out to the colonies in much the same spirit as the south Italians and Sicilians who flocked to America at the beginning of this century. Sometimes they were political exiles from their home; there were even cases when out-of-power parties would quit en masse and join a group leaving to found some new city overseas. Rhegium is a good example of the mixed motives that lay behind a Greek colony. It was planted in a perfect position to command the trade that passed through the Strait of Messina between Sicily and the mainland; yet its founders included one-tenth of the population of the Greek city of Chalcis who were bidden to leave because of famine, as well as a band of political exiles from south Greece. Many men must have signed on simply for the ride, for the sheer adventure of it. The Greeks were wanderers at heart—

it was no accident that the story of Odysseus was one of their national epics—and they were to be found knocking about odd corners of the ancient world at all times. For such roving spirits the age of colonization must have offered unparalleled opportunities.

In some foundations commerce played no part whatsoever. Many of the little colonies that lined the sole and instep of the boot of Italy were agricultural communities purely and simply; the founders had left the old country because of hard times to build homes in a new territory that was a land of milk and honey by comparison. Occasionally a city literally transplanted itself because life had become unbearable, generally for political reasons, in the old site. The people of the little town of Teos, for example, on the Asia Minor coast couldn't stand the thought of living under Persia, a mighty empire that was aggressively extending its way westward, and when that threat appeared the whole populace moved and established itself on the coast of Thrace. Tarentum—Taranto today—was founded as a refuge for a group of political exiles from Sparta. It was the only permanent colony that that ultraconservative city planted, and one of the stories about the Spartans that went the rounds in ancient days offered an interesting reason. Toward the end of the seventh century B.C. the Spartans left for a war that took them twenty years to win. When they returned they found—and viewed with considerable disfavor—a group of almost full grown children, obviously born during these two decades. After some complications these "sons of virgins," as they were called, since they were a little too public proof of the dilution of the pure blood the Spartans were so proud of, were packed off in a group to continue their lives elsewhere, and the founding of Tarentum was the result.

There is a good deal known about the way in which the Greeks went about founding a colony. The initiative always came from a particular city, although outsiders, as long as they were Greek, could and very often were encouraged to participate. A smallish town like Megara, for example, which was responsible for an incredible number of settlements, would have completely drained of its population without help from outside. The first step was to appoint an "oecist" or founder to lead the expedition. Since he played the major role, he was often worshiped in the colony he suc ceeded in planting. Even when all details about the founding of a given place were lost, the oecist's name lived on; they were the William Penns and Roger Williamses of their age. The oecist's first step was to consult the famous oracle of Apollo at Delphi about a site to colonize. Usually the priests of the shrine had got intelligence of the desired location or locations and simply went ahead and confirmed one or the other, provided no conflicts were involved. The Delphic Oracle performed a vital function in this period: it was the priests' job to see that clashes were avoided by, among other things, diverting colonies that looked as if they would encroach on previously established foundations, and on the whole they did their work well. Their role was rather like that played by the Vatican when, at the end of the fifteenth century, it headed off a possible ugly situation by allocating Africa to the Portuguese and America to the Spanish.

All the next steps are lost. No ancient writer ever bothered to tell how the ships were collected, what they were like, how they were loaded, or how the oecist managed to keep his sanity during a voyage, often lasting over a month, in which he had to oversee men, women, and children—and assorted livestock—who were leaving all the certainties of a traditional homeland for the most uncertain of futures. The only hint of detail saved through the centuries is the random mention of a colonist who, en route to found Syracuse, swapped his allotment of land for a home-made cake; whether because he was that hungry or that drunk or that homesick for something from the past is not divulged.

The colonists as a rule were spared the rigors and dangers of landing on an unknown shore. Sailors and traders had long before scouted the site, determined the number and state of mind of the natives, and forwarded reports to the founding city (some of which no doubt found their way into the files at Delphi), and the area had even been apportioned into lots for distribution. Sometimes the natives welcomed the newcomers. When the group that founded Marseilles landed, so the story goes, they were invited to a native bridal ceremony where the chief's daughter, in accordance with immemorial custom, was to go the rounds and hand a cup of water to the one among the young braves she wanted to marry. With an unerring eye, in the best Pocahontas tradition, she picked the newly arrived oecist. Not such charming anecdotes but the sober records of archaeology show that more often than not the Greeks drove the natives out. In most of the cemeteries of the colonies in Sicily and south Italy, for example, the early graves are almost all of Greeks; no native tombs are found there any more than they are in early New England. Sometimes, as was to be expected, whole colonies were lost as completely as Sir Walter Raleigh's ill-starred settlement on Roanoke Island. It took three tries to found Abdera on the Thracian coast; the natives wiped out the first two expeditions and the third only took hold because the entire population of a Greek city decided to emigrate there to escape Persian bondage.

The only allegiance a colony owed its "metropolis," its "mother-city" as the Greeks put it, was sentimental: the fire on the sacred hearth of the new foundation was kindled with flame taken from the hearth at home; familiar place names were applied to the new environment like the "New England," "New York" or "New London" of American colonial days. If, as often happened, the daughter decided to send out a colonizing party on her own, she would give the metropolis the privilege of supplying an oecist, and if the mother city got involved in a war the daughters usually could be depended upon to support her.

Practically every established Greek city took part in the movement overseas to some extent and boasted one or more colonial offspring. But there were two key figures, particularly from the point of view of commercial expansion. The one, Corinth, concentrated her attention on the west, the other, Miletus, on the east.

Eastward of the Mediterranean lay the Black Sea. It was outside the orbit of the Greeks, and their ships had not cut its waters since the pioneering voyage of Jason and his Argonauts. A formidable pair of gates barred it, the straits of the Dardanelles and the Bosporus. During the summer months, the greatest period of activity for the ancient mariner (p. 39), a ship going through had to sail almost into the eye of prevailing northeasterlies and buck a current which spilled out of the sea beyond like a millrace. Yet once through, not only was the sailing clear but the returns were substantial. On the north shore the rich fields of the Crimea produced surpluses of wheat which could be sold at good prices in the grain-poor cities of Greece; the shallow waters teemed with fish; and on the south coast there were gold and silver and iron to be mined.

On the lower part of the west coast of Asia Minor, less than two hundred miles from the Dardanelles, stood the city of Miletus. It is a pile of ruins now; the harbor has silted up and the focus of trade moved elsewhere so completely that today the whole region is a backwater and the sightseer has to fight his way for days over battered roads to get a view of the deserted site. But in the eighth century B.C. and long thereafter it was a great commercial center. Its merchants sent their ships southeast to Phoenicia, south to Egypt, and west to Italy, and enticed caravans with products of the Asia Minor hinterland and beyond to their warehouses. Its sheep breeders developed a prize quality of wool that commanded a market everywhere and its cabinetmakers were known for the fine furniture they turned out. The city, by mingling its native Greek culture with the rich foreign influences that rode in on its far-flung trade, acquired a reputation for intellectual distinction as well. Two of its natives haunted the bustling quays, listened to the reports of returning sailors who had scouted sites or founded colonies or sailed on trading voyages, and, collating this material, launched the twin sciences of cartography and geography: Anaximander of Miletus around 550 B.C. drew up the first map of the inhabited portion of the earth; half a century later, Hecataeus of Miletus published an improved version along with the first work of geography, a book (now lost) entitled *Circuit of the Earth* which described the known world from Sparta to India. Thales, the first and one of the greatest of the Greek scientific philosophers, was a native, and along with his fundamental work on the nature of the universe found time, like a good Milesian, to work out a geometrical procedure for determining the position of a ship at sea and even, one year, to make a financial killing by cornering the olive-press market.

It was the skilled mariners of Miletus who found the key that unlocked the doors of the Black Sea. They discovered that favorable southwesterlies were to be picked up along the Dardanelles and Bosporus during the early weeks of the spring, that the hostile current created favorable eddies along the shores, and that even in summer a ship could go through on the night breeze that blew up the straits. By 800 B.C. Miletus had planted a colony on the south shore of the Black Sea and within two centuries or so her establishments—tradition says eighty of them—dotted its circuit as well as the coasts of the straits and of the Sea of Marmora. For some reason she overlooked the site of Istanbul with its superb harbor, the famous "Golden Horn," perfectly located on the European side of the Bosporus, and left it for the little town of Megara to plant a colony called Byzantium there. Even Megara needed two chances, for the first colonists she sent out passed up the site and settled on the Asiatic shore opposite instead; this so exasperated the priests of the Delphic Oracle that, when a second expedition was readied seventeen years later, they waspishly instructed the oecist to settle opposite the city "of the blind." But the Black Sea was almost a Milesian lake; the tons of wheat and fish shipped out annually were financed by the traders and bankers, and hauled by the skippers, of Miletus and her colonies. To make things perfect, her ships did not have to return in ballast. They arrived loaded with Greek pottery and bronze manufactures which had a ready sale among the natives, as well as with wine and olive oil for the Greek colonists of the north shore who never acquired a taste for the local beverages or learned to cook with the local butter and were eager customers for these reminders of life in the old country.

The city of Corinth had a unique location. It commanded the isthmus that separates the northern portion of Greece from the Peloponnese. Its ships could take off from a harbor on the east of the isthmus into the Aegean and, from one on the opposite shore, could proceed straight through the Corinthian Gulf to the west; every other Greek city had to send its freighters the long way around the Peloponnese to get to the west.

In the days of the Minoans and the Mycenaeans (pp. 21-22, 24), colonies had once flourished on the shores of Sicily and south Italy. But they had long since died away and now, a half millennium later, uncivilized tribes inhabited the areas, while north of Naples the peninsula of Italy was controlled by a powerful and warlike people called the Etruscans. The first Greek ships that in this age sailed through the strait between Sicily and the mainland and entered the Tyrrhenian Sea quickly discovered two things: that the Etruscans held the waters from this point northward, and that they would buy practically any Greek manufactures offered them. And so it was natural that the first settlement in this new Greek penetration into the west, founded probably about 750 B.C., was on the little island of Ischia off Naples, a strategic location for an entrepôt to serve Greek and Etruscan. Within twenty years Corinth had entered the field: in 733 she planted the colony of Syracuse on the site of one of the finest harbors in the eastern Mediterranean. In the next few decades a dozen towns sprang up along the coasts of Sicily and south Italy, but Syracuse's position and her harbor, backed up by Corinth's trade, guaranteed her preeminence. In the earliest finds on all these sites archaeologists have uncovered the products of various Greek states; within a generation, the finds are prevailingly Corinthian. A monopoly had begun that was to last for a century.

Other cities had established colonies on both sides of the Strait of Messina. Corinth negotiated treaties to give her right of way and, with Syracuse recognized as the distribution point for most products from Greece, her trading position was set. But only in the east of the island. When the Carthaginians decided to move into Sicily (p. 72), finding the whole eastern part firmly in Greek hands, they laid hold of the west. The Greek colony nearest them, one established by Rhodes and called Selinus, as a result of its location was always in a tight spot. It traded with its Carthaginian neighbors as well as with their home base on the African coast opposite and, when Greeks and Carthaginians eventually came to blows, it could never be trusted to put sentiment before business.

Corinthian ships arrived loaded with fine pottery, oil and perfume, Egyptian work such as faience, amulets and scarabs, and heavy loads of marble (the local rock was too soft for first-rate building stone). What wasn't distributed from Syracuse to east Sicily continued through the strait to the Naples area for sale to the Etruscans. The latter paid for their imports in refined metals, while Sicily paid in the product so all-important to the Greek economy, wheat. Around 600 B.C. Corinth's trade was so great that she found herself faced with a real problem: her superb location on an isthmus, which made commerce in both directions possible, also forced her to maintain duplicate navies and merchant marines—on the eastern side a fleet of freighters to carry, and of warships to guard, the trade with Asia Minor and Syria and Egypt, and on the western side another for that with Sicily and south Italy. Periander, who was on the throne at the time, toyed with the idea of cutting a canal but gave it up as too big a project (one wasn't actually attempted until the time of Nero, who had the vast resources of the whole Roman Empire at his disposal; see p. 226). Periander did the next best thing: he built an ancient version of a marine railway over three miles long. It was a road, carefully paved with limestone slabs and so engineered that all grades were held to a minimum, which spanned the isthmus; vessels were hauled out of the water at one end, rolled onto a wheeled trolley which ran in tracks cut in the stone surface, pulled—probably by oxen—to the other side, and there set afloat again. The road was wide enough, and the power available strong enough, to handle all warships and ordinary sized freighters; and it provided a quick way of transferring the cargoes of ships too heavy to be hauled out. It must have been tremendously costly, but this was the heyday of the city's prosperity and she had the money to pay for it.

About 550 B.C. Corinth began to lose her tight monopoly in Sicily and south Italy. From this point on, Athenian and not Corinthian pottery prevails in the archaeological excavations. It was just about this time, too, that the Sicilian cities began to coin their own money. Barter was all right for the strict exchange of wheat for Corinth's manufactures, but money gave a town more latitude in its choice of commercial contacts. The versatile Corinthian merchants shrewdly met the changed conditions: they sold the cities the silver needed for coinage and they supplied Athens with bottoms to haul its newly acquired trade in pottery.

Beyond Sicily lay the far west, a vast and vital area that the Phoenicians had turned into their private preserve. If a story that Herodotus tells can be believed, it was a sheer fluke that first brought the Greeks into this quarter and opened their eyes to its value. A certain Colaeus, skipper of a vessel from Samos, an island off the west coast of Asia Minor, on one occasion had particularly bad luck with the winds. Headed for Egypt, sometime about 650 B.C., he was first blown off course and forced to land far to the west of his destination at Cyrene on the north African coast, a little west of where Derna now stands. He took on fresh provisions,

Westward Ho!

raised anchor, shaped a course once more for Egypt and this time was caught in an easterly gale, probably the same sort that seven hundred years later was to carry St. Paul from Crete to shipwreck off Malta. Colaeus scudded before it the whole length of the sea and even through the Strait of Gibraltar, and finally reached land in Tartessus, the Spanish coast just beyond the strait, whose natives had never seen Greek products, much less Greeks. He was able to turn in his cargo, probably chiefly Samian pottery and wine, for a fabulous amount of silver and returned home a multimillionaire.

It was neither his home port on Samos nor any of the other great commercial centers of Greece that capitalized on his discovery, but a relatively small Greek town whose sailors had a reputation for skill and daring even in this age of maritime enterprise. The city of Phocaea stood on the west coast of Asia Minor, the easternmost edge of Greek civilization. But it was to play in the far west the role that Corinth had in Sicily, and Miletus in the Black Sea.

The Phocaeans had the sagacity to take to the sea not in merchantmen but in warships, swift galleys called penteconters, or "fiftiers," because of the number of oars they carried (p. 85). Moreover, they probably traveled in packs and not singly. The Phoenicians may have closed the western seas to freighters, but a flotilla of Phocaean galleys, stripped for action, was a different matter. The Phocaeans were friendly with the powers that controlled the Strait of Messina and had even been granted the privilege of toll-free passage. Beyond, they carried out a skillfully organized program of colonization. By planting a series of stations on Ischia off Naples, Sardinia, Minorca, Majorca, Ibiza, and along the Spanish coast—warships needed provisioning points at far smaller intervals than merchantmen, which were able to hold the sea for days at a time—they carved out a route that led them past the Strait of Gibraltar into the tin and silver depot of Tartessus. There are even vague rumors that a pair of their skippers ventured farther into the Atlantic, one along the Spanish coast toward the source of the tin, and the other southward along the Moroccan coast.

But another accomplishment of the Phocaeans was more significant if not as spectacular. They explored the Gulf of Lion to the south of France and, about 600 B.C., planted a colony called Massilia, the Marseilles of today, at the mouth of the Rhone, a door through which the culture first of Greece and then of Rome was to pass to the whole of France. From here they spread east and west. When they had finished, the Spanish and French coast from a little east of Málaga, which the Phoenicians held, to Nice was firmly settled by Greeks.

The Phocaeans had not only carried out their colonizing in an aggressive and orderly manner, but they had picked a perfect time, about 600 B.C., a period when Phoenician hands were tied. Tyre was busy with wars back home and Carthage with running help to its colonies in Sicily to fend off attacks from the neighboring Greeks. Once the Phoenicians were free of these entanglements, clash was inevitable. The first took place in 535 B.C. Spurred on by troubles with Persia back home in Asia Minor, the Phocaeans elected to move out lock, stock, and barrel and establish a new home elsewhere. As always, they picked a spot with care: the expedition landed on the strategically placed island of Corsica. Neither the Carthaginians nor the Etruscans, who held the seas north of the island, could afford to overlook this. The result was the first of a series of great naval battles. Despite heavy odds—the enemy fleet was precisely twice as large—the Phocaeans held their own, but the victory was a pyrrhic one: when the day ended two-thirds of their vessels had gone to the bottom and the rest were badly damaged. The remnants of the expedition abandoned the attempt to colonize Corsica and transferred to a site in south Italy well in Greek territory. The Carthaginians had taken the first step toward closing the Strait of Gibraltar to competitors. Two more naval engagements were fought in the next fifty years, and the Greeks won both. But they were defensive actions: victory meant that they could maintain their hold on the eastern portion of Sicily, south France, and northeast Spain; the rest of the western Mediterranean belonged to Carthage, and by 480 B.C. she had bolted the gates of Gibraltar. The situation in the west was now fixed in the form it was to have until the coming of the Romans centuries later. The vital trade in tin from the Atlantic and in silver and lead and iron from Spain was an acknowledged Carthaginian monopoly.

In these days there was no one state which had the naval strength to police the seas. Every city involved in trade had to maintain its

Westward Ho!

own fleet, not only to protect its merchantmen against the ubiquitous pirates (whose calling now as before had the status of a recognized profession) but also to repel attacks delivered by commercial rivals since such attempts were an acknowledged means of discouraging competition. Carthaginians preyed on Greek shipping, Greeks on Carthaginian, and independents on both. The perfecting of men-of-war and the building up of navies went hand in hand with the planting of colonies and the opening up of trade routes.

When the fleets of Carthage and Phocaea clashed off the shores of Corsica in 535 B.C., it was no mere set-to of a pair of packs of Homeric rovers. The ships that fought that day were the result of centuries of improvement. Ever since the era of colonization had begun, the art of shipbuilding had not only been constantly refined but had become a major industry as shipyards worked to meet an ever expanding demand. As one would expect, Corinth took the lead and her ship designers during this period achieved a reputation they were to hold for years.

The old undecked sea rover, efficient enough for raiding and piracy, was no vessel to protect the new long trade routes now flung across the Mediterranean. By 800 B.C. Greek shipbuilders were taking the basic steps toward creating the craft that was to serve as the standard ship of the line for the next thousand years (Pls. 3d, 4). A revolution in design was carried out, every bit as sweeping in its time as the mounting of guns on shipboard in the fourteenth century or the introduction of ironclads in the nineteenth.

As in the case of so many other key changes in the ancient world, there are no written records to tell how this one took place. But the course can be followed thanks to the Greek's characteristic of insisting on artistic and interesting decoration for his pottery—whether used to hold his ancestor's ashes or to carry slops. The vase painters in this age of colonization, as was natural, included among the scenes they favored pictures of vessels in action, some drawn with exquisite care.

The very earliest, painted probably between 850 and 800 B.C. (Pl. 3d), shows that a new type of warship had already come into existence. It is one clearly derived from those used in Homer's day and before, for it has the high rounded stern and straight prow of the earlier craft, and the two give the "horned" effect that Homer had noted (p. 41; Pl. 3c). But a revolutionary new feature has been added. The vessel has been given an offensive weapon: from its prow juts a powerful pointed ram. This must have inaugurated a new era in naval tactics. No longer was a sea battle simply a match between the archers and spearsmen carried as marines, a sort of land fight, as it were, transferred to shipboard, as in Ramses' successful attack on the sea raiders (p. 32). The ram changed all that: it shifted the emphasis to the men that manned the oars. Victory would go to the crew so trained that it could respond instantly and accurately to command and drive its ship to that position from which a blow of the ram could be launched at the enemy's vital point. A fight now became a contest in maneuvering, the captains using their oars as, centuries later, frigates were to use their sails to attain the proper position for a broadside. Since the ram first appears on Greek vases, its invention is generally credited to their account. Perhaps the Phoenicians thought of it earlier but there is no way of telling, for they never pictured their ships on their pottery.

Homer's vessels had been open, undecked affairs. The new age required something more efficient and protected. A second radically new feature was added, a fighting platform from which the marines—archers and spearsmen—could function (Pl. 4a-d). It took the form of a deck that covered most but not all of the ship; it ran over the centerline from stem to stern but not from board to board. A space along the side was left open and, when the vessel was merely cruising, the rowers sat at the level of the deck and worked their oars from there (Pl 4a, b). In action such a position was dangerously exposed. The naval architects met this weakness by an ingenious device: they inserted a complete series of rowers' benches at a lower level. When a ship engaged in combat the oarsmen took their places down there; with their heads well below the line of the deck they were protected from enemy darts and the only exposed personnel were the marines on it, directing fire against the opponent (Pl. 4d). Oarsmen placed deep in the vessel for shelter during combat was a fine idea but hardly helpful if they suffocated; so the architects left the area between the upper and lower thwarts open as a low waist covered only with a kind of lattice (Pl. 4c). This not only provided ventilation but also an escape hatch for emergencies. Panels probably closed in the open spaces between the slats when the water was choppy.

The ancients, instead of using rowlocks, worked their oars against tholepins which they called "keys," and in the vase paintings these have just that sort of shape (Pl. 4c). The oars were made fast by a leather strap looped loosely over the pin so that they could not go over the side if a rower lost his grip.

In the sixth century B.C. warships saw still more improvement (Pl. 5). The prow was straightened and lost its swept-back curve. The stern was finished off in a plume- or fan-like adornment which became thereafter the distinguishing mark of the warship and was looked on, along with the ram, as a sort of naval scalp: victors cut them off vanquished vessels and took them home as trophies. The low waist and its lattice was almost completely eliminated and, as a result, the hull took on a sleeker, trimmer look (Pl. 5c). Though ships manned by twenty rowers, as in Homer's day (p. 36), were still in use (Pl. 5a), larger types were favored because the more powerfully a ram was driven, the more damaging was its blow. Thirty-oared craft, triacontors, were now built for lighter work, and the ship of the line was the fifty-oared galley, the penteconter (Pl. 5b). Twenty-four rowers lined each side, and two steering oars at the stern filled out the complement. A single bank of oars was the only arrangement naval architects had heretofore used. It was not always completely successful. In the case of the penteconter it made for an excessively long and slender vessel, expensive to build, difficult to maneuver, and dangerously unseaworthy. Yet to shorten it was out of the question since this meant giving up some of the essential oar power.

Alternative seating of the rowers gave the clue for the next improvement in the penteconter. If the vessel could be driven either from the deckline or from some lower point, why not from both at once? And so the naval architects designed a new type of hull, one in which the twenty-four oarsmen were split into two superimposed banks, twelve along the gunwale and twelve along lower thwarts, rowing through ports in the hull. To fit everybody in, the oars were staggered so that each one of the upper bank was placed over the space between two of the lower (Pls. 6b, 7a). The new craft were shorter than the old by at least a third. They were more compact, far sturdier, far more seaworthy—and offered 33⅓ per cent less of a target to an enemy ram. Yet not a rower had been sacrificed. The stage was now set for the last step, the introduction of a third bank, but that was not taken for a century or so.

The earliest picture preserved of the new two-banked galley is in a relief carved on an Assyrian king's palace that was built between 705 and 681 B.C. (Pl. 6c). The vessel must be Phoenician because the Assyrians, having no navy of their own, used the fleets of the Phoenician cities which they controlled at this time. It is a lofty craft with a full upper deck girt by a bulwark; clearly the designers were interested in providing space and protection for a good-sized complement of marines. Shortly thereafter two-banked galleys, lower and lighter than the Phoenician type, appear on Greek vases (Pls. 6b, 7a). It is anybody's guess which of the two nations deserves credit for the invention. Whichever it was, the other quickly followed suit.

Greeks and Phoenicians were conservative when it came to rigging their vessels. The new warships carried the same rig that Mediterranean craft had for centuries, a single broad squaresail. But this was almost exclusively for cruising. In battle a vessel had to be able to move in any direction in its efforts to get into position for a ram attack, so it was impossible, even dangerous, to depend on the wind. A captain, on going into action, generally ordered mast and sail unstepped and left ashore—he had no space aboard to store such bulky gear—and, from that moment on, depended solely on the muscle and reflexes of his oarsmen (Pls. 3d, 6b). Pirates, who had to carry sail at all times in order to chase down merchantmen, to meet their particular requirements actually worked out a special version of the two-banked galley, the *hemiolia* or "one and a half-er." It was so constructed that, when the quarry was overtaken and the boarding action ready to begin, half the rowers in the upper bank, those between the mast and the stern, were able to secure their oars and leave the benches; this left not only an ample space in the afterpart of the ship into which mast and sail could be lowered and stowed away, but a dozen hands or so available to carry out the work (Pl. 7a, b).

Westward Ho!

Although many Greek cities designed and made their own craft, others found it easier to turn to great shipbuilding centers. When, in 704 B.C., the island of Samos decided to create a navy, she applied to Corinth and the latter sent her a topflight architect who superintended the construction of four vessels of the latest design, probably two-banked galleys. There is no telling how many units made up a fleet at this time. When the Phocaeans fought against Carthage off Corsica in 535, they managed to put sixty vessels into action and they had a reputation for having a powerful navy; the Carthaginians, together with the Etruscans who joined them in the fight, had a force of 120.

Along with the pictures of the new warships on the Greek vases are a handful showing merchantmen (Pl. 6a, 7). In a way these are even more to be prized because they furnish the only clue to what a freighter looked like for a period that extends a full fifteen hundred years, from the Egyptian wall paintings of the fifteenth century B.C. to the beginning of the Roman Empire. Whatever the Greeks made they made with beauty, and this was just as true of so prosaic an object as a cargo vessel as it was of their proud temples. To that which in other hands became a clumsy tub, the genius of the Greek designer gave graceful form and superb lines and, as a master stroke, added a bow with the same concave curve that lent so much distinction to the famous American clippers (Pl. 7). The rig as always is the single broad squaresail, but it is in these boats a great billowing spread that needs a complicated system of brails (p. 38)—the ancients knew nothing of reefpoints—to shorten sail. These vessels had to work hard. There were few convenient quays in the ports where they put up; most of the time they ran right up on the shore. And so they always carried, lashed on deck, two types of landing ladder: a short one for beaches that dropped abruptly and steeply, where they could come in quite close, and a longer one for those occasions when they had to stand farther off on a beach that shelved gradually.

By 550 B.C. the vast movement from homeland to colony came to a halt. The Mediterranean was now a far different place from what it had been almost a half millennium earlier when the Phoenicians embarked on their pioneering voyages or when the Greeks entered the field two centuries later. Shores that had been uninhabited or populated only by barbarian tribes were now dotted with flourishing colonies. Trade routes crisscrossed the whole of the sea from Cadiz beyond the Strait of Gibraltar to the far eastern shore of the Black Sea, from the mouth of the Po to that of the Nile. Scholars, digesting the mass of information brought back from all these quarters, compiled it and constructed maps from it and inaugurated thereby the science of geography. A half a dozen Greek states had become significant maritime powers, backing their commercial interests with powerful navies. The fifty-oared galley of Homer's day, redesigned to carry a ram and with its rowers split into two compact banks, had emerged as a first-rate fighting ship. It had seen action in some sharp clashes, especially in the west between Greeks and Carthaginians.

But this was just the dawn of a great age of naval warfare. Within little more than a half-century, battles were to be fought whose names may be found in every history book; and the fine new two-banked galleys were to lie rotting in the yards, rendered obsolete by still another ingenious advance in naval architecture.

7 The Wooden Walls

ON THE MORNING OF September 23, 480 B.C., Xerxes, ruler of the great Persian Empire, "king of kings," walked up a hill just west of Athens and sat down on a golden chair set there by his servants. Behind him smoke rose from the city: his soldiers had capped a successful march through north Greece with the sack of Athens. At his feet glistened the waters of a narrow sound, a mile wide and somewhat over three long, which separated the island of Salamis from the mainland. Against the farther shore lay the whole of the Greek fleet, a mélange of groups from the chief cities. It was tightly corked up in the sound by Persian squadrons stationed at each entrance. The king gave the order to his admirals to move in for the kill and relaxed in his chair for a bird's-eye view of the impending destruction.

Ten years earlier Persia, a nation that covered as much territory as the United States, under Xerxes' father had attempted to conquer Greece, a land smaller than New York State. The attack had been repulsed—much to the surprise of both sides. Now the son was on the point of finishing the job. His land forces had fought their way through north Greece to Athens; all he had to do was wipe out the enemy's fleet and he could just about write finis to the war. Everything was in his favor: his troops controlled most of the neighboring shores, his ships outnumbered the Greeks at least two to one, and, to top it all, a message received at his headquarters the day before had convinced him that one of the key Greek commanders, Themistocles, was ready to turn traitor. It was Xerxes' great misfortune that this particular figure was one of the wiliest and most gifted admirals in the history of naval warfare.

Themistocles had commanded the Athenian sea forces since the outbreak of the war, some months earlier. He was more than merely a naval tactician; he was a statesman of rare vision. Two years before, when Athens had received an oracle that "the wooden wall would be safe," he convinced the populace that this meant a wall of ships. This wasn't all. The treasury had just received a windfall in the form of a rich strike in the government-owned silver mines, and the voters were on the point of passing the appropriate legislation to divide the money among themselves. Themistocles accomplished the almost miraculous feat of talking them into spending it on the fleet. Thanks to his foresight, when the Persians began their offensive Athens had an imposing navy of two hundred ships. Stiffened by these and guided by Themistocles' generalship the entire Greek fleet, though terribly outnumbered, had fought the enemy to a draw off Cape Artemisium in northerly waters two months earlier. And it was thanks to his generalship that the fleet was now hemmed in in the narrow waters of Salamis Sound.

This was precisely the way Themistocles wanted it, the only way the Greeks had a chance to win. It came about solely as a result of his subtle and untiring efforts. The whole Greek fleet totaled somewhere between three hundred and four hundred craft. The Persians, of course, had no ships of their own—Susa, their capital, lay eight hundred miles east of the sea—but, since they controlled the eastern coast of the Mediterranean from the Dardanelles to the Nile, they had commandeered squadrons from Phoenicia, Egypt, and even from some of the Greek cities of Asia Minor. They had at least over seven hundred ships and perhaps many more; some estimates ran as high as fourteen hundred. Themistocles recognized that a fight in the open sea where the enemy could deploy

PLATE 1
Early Boats

a. Clay model of a sailing (?) skiff found at Eridu in southern Mesopotamia. Ca. 3500 or 3400 B.C.

b. Drawing of a sailboat on pottery from southern Egypt. Ca. 2900 B.C.

c. Merchantman on a Minoan seal. Ca. 2000 B.C. The high end is the prow.

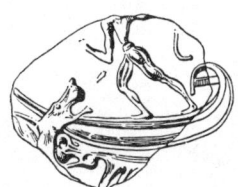

d. Sailor fighting a sea monster. On a Minoan seal, ca. 1600 B.C.

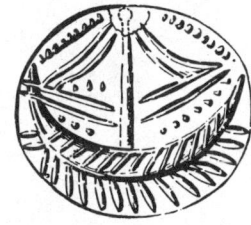

e. Galley on a Minoan seal. Ca. 1600 B.C.

PLATE 2
Egyptian Seagoing Ships
a. Model of ship of Pharaoh Sahure. Ca. 2550 B.C.

b. Model of ship of Queen Hatshepsut. Ca. 1500 B.C.

PLATE 3
Aegean Warships, 2000-800 B.C.

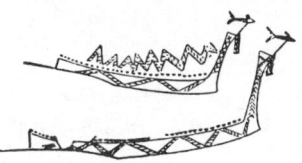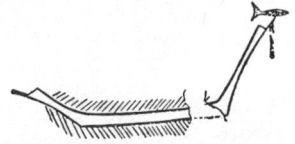

a. Warships drawn on the backs of mirrors found on Syros in the Cyclades. Ca. 2000 B.C.

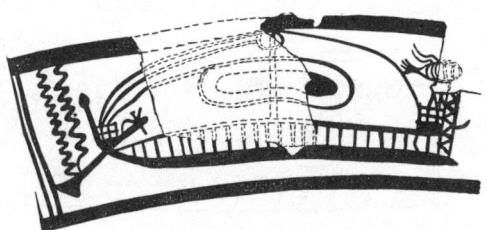

b. Galley, probably 50-oared, on a cylindrical clay box found at Pylos. Ca. 1200–1100 B.C.

c. Galley on a vase found at Asine. Ca. 1200–1100 B.C.

d. Galley on a cup found at Eleusis. Ca. 850–800 B.C.

PLATE 4
Greek Warships, 800–700 B.C.

a. Galley, probably 20-oared, cruising.

b. Galley, probably 50-oared, preparing to shove off. The vessel has only one bank of oars: the artist, wanting to include both port and starboard rowers but not able to handle the perspective involved, naively portrayed the one above the other.

c. Forward part of a galley showing the keylike tholepins.

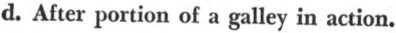

d. After portion of a galley in action.

PLATE 5
Greek Warships, 600–500 B.C.

a. Galley, probably 20-oared, cruising.

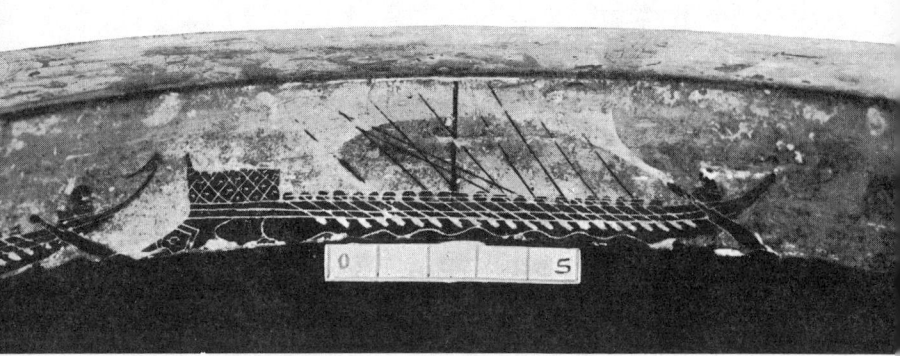

b. Galley, probably 50-oared, cruising.

c. Galleys cruising under sail; note the ports in the gunwales for the oars.

PLATE 6

Merchantman and Two-Banked Warships, 700–500 B.C.
a. Merchantman on a vase from Cyprus. Ca. 700–600 B.C.

b. Two-banked galley, probably 50-oared, in action. Ca. 500 B.C.

c. Two-banked Phoenician galley.
    Ca. 705–686 B.C.

PLATE 7
Merchantman and Pirate Craft. Ca. 540–500 B.C.

a. Hemiolia, 50-oared, overtaking a merchantman traveling under shortened sail. From an Athenian cup.

b. A second scene from the same cup. The hemiolia has secured the upper bank of oars abaft the mast preliminary to lowering it (it already leans slightly aft). The merchantman now has all its canvas drawing in the effort to escape.

PLATE 8

The Greek Trireme

a. Reconstructed cross-section of a fifth century Athenian trireme showing the arrangement of the rowers; flat platform at right represents the waterline.

b. A fifth century Athenian trireme cruising.

all his forces would be disastrous; his only chance lay in waters where the Persians could bring to bear at any one time only a limited portion of their fleet. He chose the cramped Strait of Salamis.

Themistocles' first job was to convince his own allies. Although the heart and brains of the Greek defense, officially he was only the commanding officer of the Athenian contingent—a Spartan held the over-all command—and it took all his diplomacy to sell his fellow officers the idea that the only way to win was to crawl into a bottle and allow it to be corked. Next he had to snare Xerxes into the trap. His guile was equal even to this: on the 22nd of September he dispatched one of his slaves to Xerxes' headquarters with the message that the Greek fleet was making ready to slip out of the channel and scatter, thereby depriving the king of the chance to destroy it at one blow. Xerxes rose to the bait: that night his squadrons moved into position and blocked all avenues of escape.

So far Themistocles had made all the preparatory moves with superb artistry. He conducted the battle with equal brilliance. Most of the Persian fleet was gathered outside the southern entrance to Salamis Sound, their prows pointed toward it. The first step was to suck them in. Themistocles waited patiently until the usual sea breeze, which would tend to move the enemy gradually into the channel, sprang up before he went into action. As soon as he had led out his vessels to face the Persian lines, Xerxes' admirals gave the signal to attack—and Themistocles' first command was to back water, as if afraid of contact. Only when he had in this way enticed the enemy well within the channel did he give the order to charge. The Persians' front line, pressing forward into a narrowing space, gradually contracted until ship began to foul ship. Worse was at hand. First its forward motion was checked by the charging Greeks; and then the supporting Persian lines, rowing ahead hard to get into the action and unable to stop in time, broke into its rear. Themistocles' forces under his rigorous discipline had maintained their ranks and now they were ready for the kill. In line of battle they slammed into their opponents, by this time in utter disorder, ramming with deadly effect. One enemy ship after another, foregoing any attempt to withstand attack, turned to extricate itself and flee. The battle ended in a rout; Greece was not only saved but a Persian fleet was never to challenge her supremacy on the sea again.

Not one penteconter was to be seen in the two lines as they faced each other across the waters of the sound. No more than fifty years earlier a dramatic development had taken place in naval design which had completely changed the complexion of Mediterranean fighting fleets. When Themistocles talked the Athenians into creating a modern navy he asked for much more than the building of additional units; whatever penteconters lay in the slips of the navy yard had to be replaced with ships of the new design. The vessels that fought on both sides in the Persian wars were almost all of a type called by the Greeks *trieres,* "3-er," more commonly known to us under the Latinized name trireme. With the ships came new ways of fighting; decades before Greeks and Persians clashed in the Battle of Artemisium admirals had learned the handling of the new craft and devised intricate tactics for them.

The trireme was the logical offspring of the two-banked penteconter. When naval architects centuries earlier sought to increase the power and speed of the original long ship with its single line of rowers, they found the solution in dividing the oarsmen into two levels, the lower rowing through ports in the hull, the upper over the gunwale (p. 85). How could the power of such vessels be increased still further? One possibility was the addition of a third bank. But there was no longer room for such within the hull itself and to redesign to make room would result in a much deeper, heavier ship, one so much slower that it would cancel out most of the advantages of a third line of rowers. Between 550 and 525 B.C. some architectural genius came up with the answer: he added on either side an outrigger *(parexeresia,* or "by-rowing apparatus" as the Greeks called it) above and projecting laterally beyond the gunwale. In this way he made room for a third bank of oarsmen without drastic changes in the general lines of the hull (Pl. 8; cf. Pls. 10, 11a, 13c). The result was a ship with all the speed and maneuverability of its predecessor but with vastly increased power. The new design spread like wildfire: in the dockyards of Tyre and Sidon among the Phoenicians, at the mouth of the Nile in Egypt, at Corinth in Greece or off in Syracuse in Sicily, penteconters were left to rot or were cannibalized for their timber while shipwrights worked feverishly to turn out triremes. During the whole of the fifth and most of the fourth century B.C., they were the unchallenged queens of the sea, and they were to be found in the fleets almost until the end of ancient times.

No good pictures or models of triremes have survived, but much miscellaneous information about them has in one way or another been collected. The official records of the Athenian navy yard, for example, fortunately for posterity were carved on stone and they have been dug up; they list the exact amount of gear of various types issued to these ships. Several of the slips where triremes were docked in the Athenian navy yard are still visible, and archaeologists have examined and measured them. The longest is a little under 125 feet and the width between each pair is under twenty feet; these then must be the dimensions of the largest ships. Triremes lay low in the water: their total freeboard was probably not much over eight feet and they very likely had a draught of about three, shallow enough to enable them to be drawn up on a beach or portaged on rollers. The lowest bank of rowers, the thalamites as they are generally called, worked their oars through ports that were not over a foot and a half above the waterline (Pl. 8a); a leathern bag fitted snugly about the oar and its opening to keep out the sea, but in any sort of chop these oars were secured and the ports completely sealed with coverings. A form of punishment in the fleets was to lash a man to a thalamite thwart with his head sticking out the port: in harbor this was probably not much worse than the pillory but under way it could be severe. The dockyard records show that there were twenty-seven rowers in this bank on each side. The next higher row, the zygites, had the same number. Each sat above and slightly forward of the corresponding thalamite and worked his oar over the gunwale. On special benches built on top of the gunwale sat the highest row, the thranites, each slightly forward of and higher than the corresponding zygite; the thole pins for their oars were set in an outrigger that projected about three feet from the side of the ship. Their stroke was the most wearing, for their oars, pivoting so high up, struck the water at a relatively sharp angle. Since the hull curved up at each end into long overhangs it squeezed out the lower banks there but left some room for the highest; consequently there were four more thranite oars, a total of thirty-one on each side. All in all, a trireme mounted 170 oars, not including the pair used for steering.

The rowers were so cunnningly arranged that the oars of the three banks were almost all the same length, fourteen feet, four inches, just about the standard used on some navy cutters today. Slightly shorter ones, thirteen and a half feet, were used at bow and stern where the sides curved inward. Thus, not only the manufacture of oars but the stocking of spares was simplified enormously. The dockyard records show that each ship was issued two hundred; one hundred and seventy for the three banks and thirty of the two sizes for reserve.

If one looked at a vessel's side the oars seemed to make a quincunx pattern. The important cluster, however, was the group of three in an oblique line; the thranite, zygite, and thalamite oars in such a segment was the unit that counted and gave the vessel its name, *trieres*, "3-er" (cf. Pl. 10b). There were twenty-seven units in all on each side plus two thranites rowing alone fore and aft. The distance between rowers is a constant, three feet, set by the size of the human body, so that a trireme was not too much longer than an early penteconter with its twenty-four men to a side. But it was infinitely more powerful, more maneuverable, more adaptable. In calm weather it could be rowed easily from the thalamite bank and, in a choppy sea, comfortably from the thranite. In action, driven by all three it could sprint at a seven-knot speed or spin about in little more than its own length. Despite its size and power, it was light and shallow enough for the crew to run it up on a beach at night.

The complement of a trireme, when fully manned, amounted to two hundred excluding marines. In addition to the 170 rowers there were twenty-five petty officers and miscellaneous hands, and five officers. In the names of some of the latter one can discern the duties on the original long ships that required personnel with authority: *kybernetes*, "helmsmen"; *proreus*, "lookout"; *keleustes*, "timebeater." The names were traditional; they hardly reflected any longer the duties of these officers aboard a trireme. The *kyber-*

netes carried over some of his original function, for he was the ship's navigating officer and in battle or storm might even handle the steering oars himself, although at other times he turned them over to enlisted personnel. This was only a part of his duties. He was the equivalent of the executive officer of today. If the captain was absent or lost, command devolved upon him. Moreover, in the Athenian navy at least, because the captain was by standard procedure a political appointee the *kybernetes* actually ran the ship. The Athenians had an arrangement whereby a rich man of the community for one year assumed the expenses of fitting out and maintaining a galley and also took over its command; obviously if the trierarch, as this captain was titled, had any naval experience it was only by sheerest coincidence. Next in line to the *kybernetes* was the *proreus*, "bow officer," who had immediate authority forward, was answerable for maintaining a proper lookout, and probably supervised such activities as beaching and dropping anchor. Also, like the first lieutenant of today, it was his job to keep a constant eye on hull and gear. The *keleustes* was responsible for the oarsmen, their equipment, provisions, training, and morale. Under way he set the stroke on orders from the *kybernetes*, but the actual beating of time for the rowers was done by the monotonous tootling of the ship's flutist, the *trieraules*, "trireme flutist" (or simply *auletes*, "flutist"), who could be a foreigner hired for the purpose or even a slave. The fifth officer, the *pentecontarchos*, served as a junior assisting the others and in particular was the trierarch's administrative aide. He kept the ship's records, hired and paid rowers, took care of all disbursements. These five made up, as it were, the commissioned personnel. In addition there were petty officers, including a ship's carpenter, deck hands to take care of lines and sail, marines—ten or so soldiers and two to three bowmen—and the complement of rowers.

To man the benches of a trireme was almost as difficult and as expensive as to build one. The Athenian contingent of two hundred ships at Salamis, for example, required no less than 34,000 men. Such a number was too much to be met by the populace alone, which among other things had to fill the ranks of the land forces at the same time. Moreover, the army, not the navy, was the senior service. Anyone who could afford a soldier's armor and weapons understandably preferred to fight in the field rather than to sweat on a bench in a hot and foul ship's hold; he only submitted to it in emergencies when his city had no other recourse. Slaves in great enough numbers were hard to come by and even when enough were available, being untrustworthy and very expensive (they had to be supported forever instead of just for a given campaign), they were not often used; Athens turned to them only when she had run out of all other sources of manpower, and offered them their freedom as a reward at that. The core of the rowing crews was the lowest class of citizens, those who couldn't afford to equip themselves as soldiers. The rest simply had to be hired, and the chief source of supply was the Aegean islands and the coastal towns of Asia Minor whose people then as today lived off the sea. Since the service was both arduous and dangerous, it commanded attractive salaries; thranites, who had the hardest stroke, could even receive a premium. A state needed money to maintain a fleet. Moreover, skippers could not be as cavalier with these hands, citizens or well-paid foreigners, as the commanders of slave-driven medieval galleys; no lashes were used aboard Greek triremes. At times, especially after severe losses, bringing crews up to full strength was not always possible. So, vessels occasionally went to sea undermanned and admirals were forced, on going into action, to leave some ships behind and use the men from them to fill out the rest.

Since a fleet of triremes not uncommonly numbered one hundred vessels and at times half that again or more, commanders were faced with the task of provisioning twenty thousand to thirty thousand men. Incredible as it may sound, Greek navies of this period never worked out an organized system of supply. Only a few days' rations at most were carried on board because the sole storage available was some scanty space under the bow and stern decks and this was ordinarily assigned to gear. In an extended fleet movement supply ships might be taken along. But most of the time the admirals simply put into shore near some town and the men, quitting the ships, hustled to the local market and bought food. Somehow the system must have worked, for we never hear of crews going hungry. We do hear of canny admirals who won victories cheaply by the simple expedient of lurking out of sight until the enemy commander beached his ships and let the men go off to market; they then would run in and destroy or tow off the empty vessels.

Greek navies had no admirals as such, just military chiefs who were expected to be competent on land or sea. A man in command of an army one month might expect to find himself at the head of a fleet the next. Moreover, in Athens, where the citizens pushed democratic procedures just as far as they could, they assigned commanders themselves, picking them from a board of ten annually elected by popular vote. Somehow the system worked as well as most: by and large it succeeded in getting the fleet into competent hands, even at times into those of a naval genius like Themistocles; on occasion it turned it over to men of monumental pigheadedness (p. 106).

The crews had to be rigorously trained. Their job, from the point of view of timing and coordination, was probably as exacting as any aboard a modern ship and incomparably more taxing physically. In 494 B.C. the Greek cities of Asia Minor, in an attempt to throw off the Persian yoke, began to organize a fleet. They turned over the training of the rowers, citizens who had volunteered, to a hard-bitten officer from Phocaea, that city of gifted seamen (p. 81). The men were able to take just three days of the punishing régime he put them through; after that they quit. Anyone who has nursed a set of blisters and sore muscles from a few hours in a rowboat can appreciate how they felt.

In general the oarsmen were saved for battle. For cruising a mast was stepped and braced with wedges, and a large squaresail raised on it. But this rig was useless during battle since a vessel had to be ready to turn in any direction at a moment's notice and simply couldn't depend on the vagaries of the wind (cf. p. 86). Moreover, since there was no place aboard to stow such bulky gear, it was generally left ashore when the ship went into action. All that was taken along was a smaller mast and sail, a "boat sail" as the Greeks called it. When a ship turned to flee this was raised; to "hoist the boat sail" was Greek sailor slang for "run away." Warships of the much later Roman navy are depicted with the *artemon,* a small sail set over the bows on a short raking mast (p. 213). It has been suggested that this is the "boat sail" of the Greek triremes of the fifth and fourth centuries B.C., but it is far more likely that the "boat sail" was simply a replacement for the regular-sized gear and was used because, being of convenient size, it could always be kept on board.

It was as expensive to maintain a fleet as to man it. A trireme was such a lightly built thing and subject to such severe strain that its life was short. Most had to be scrapped after twenty years of service, many earlier, and any that lasted twenty-five was a veritable Methuselah. The Athenian navy carefully divided its galleys into categories: the newest were assigned to the "reserves," that is, to be kept home for emergencies and not sent out on routine duties; the others were rated first, second, or third class, depending upon age and condition. Ships that failed to measure up to even the last category could get a stay of execution by being converted into transports to ferry the cavalry's horses (p. 102); those that had outlived their usefulness for service of any sort were declared obsolete and struck from the records. Most of the discards were probably cannibalized, although there is at least one case on record of a "war surplus" sale: early in the fourth century B.C., when states were going in on a large scale for the use of mercenary soldiers in their armies (p. 124), an enterprising Athenian bought up a discarded trireme, put it into commission, collected a crew to man it, and hired out as a naval mercenary. Though the replacement of obsolete ships accounted for far and away the bulk of the moneys spent on a navy, the purchase and upkeep of the miscellaneous gear each vessel carried involved no inconsiderable expense. The sails came in two grades of linen, heavy and light. Running rigging included two halyards, two sheets, two braces, and eighteen loops of brails. Standing rigging consisted, as in Homer's day (p. 38), only of a double forestay and a backstay. Since no shrouds are ever mentioned, the double forestay must have been run to each rail somewhat abaft the prow to provide some lateral bracing; deck hands used it to raise and lower the mast and, from incidental remarks dropped by ancient writers, it is clear that it was considered the key item of rigging. There were four heavy and four lighter cables for mooring lines and for the two anchors that were carried. The latter, made of iron, were very light, under fifty pounds, but additional weight could be added by clamping on stones or pieces of lead. An unusual item that formed part of the regular gear was a set of girding cables; each ship normally carried at least two, often a few more as spares, and, when converted to transport the extra weight of horses, four. These were heavy hawsers which, strapped over the planking, girdled the ship horizontally from stem to stern and helped to keep the planks from starting under the shock of ramming or under the strain of the working of the oars. To counterbalance the weight of the extensive superstructure, ballast —rocks or gravel or sand—was distributed over the hold.

The trireme carried two weapons. The first was its ram, a massive timber jutting from the forefoot that was sheathed in an envelope of bronze tipped by a three-pronged barb with subsidiary spurs above, a much more efficient instrument than the single-pointed device of earlier times. The second was the marines on its decks. The Greek vessels that fought at Salamis, like the pentecontors, were not fully decked. There was decking at prow and stern and corridors ran lengthwise over the gunwales and probably down the center. This was enough for the fourteen spearsmen and four archers that the ships carried as marines at the time and, although it left the rowers not completely protected, made for a lighter ship. In the ensuing half-century more decking was added. The corridors were extended laterally to project well over the outriggers. Screens, too, were fitted along the sides so that, all in all, the oarsmen received a maximum of protection. Such ships, protected on top by a deck and on the sides by screens, the Greeks called cataphract, that is, "fenced in" (cf. Pl. 10a); smaller open deckless craft were aphract, or "unfenced."

Not all triremes were alike; there were differences between those of one state and another just as there are between ships of the same class in modern navies. These arose from the tactics favored and lay chiefly in the height of the vessel and the extent of its decking. The Phoenicians at Salamis, although their ships were light and fast for maneuvering and ramming, preferred a good complement of spearsmen and archers—they had thirty to the eighteen aboard the opposing vessels—so the triremes they used had ample deck space and were built higher than those of the Greeks in order to give their marines a chance to shoot down on an opponent; even in the earlier days of the two-banked galley they had gone in for vessels of this type (p. 86). Certain Greek states, such as Corinth, also favored a ship that was heavy enough and had the decks to carry a powerful force of marines. The goal of all such ships was the destruction of the enemy's personnel rather than his vessels. The Athenians, on the other hand, went in for speed and maneuverability. In their heyday, the seventy years after Salamis, they limited the marines to fourteen and relied chiefly on the efficiency of craft and crew to deliver lightning-like ram attacks. They used their vessels as projectiles and, disregarding the enemy's personnel, aimed for a quick decision by destroying his ships.

Ramming was a most delicate maneuver. Only a skilled crew and a commander of fine judgment and keen sense of timing could bring it off. For one thing, it was a one-shot or at best a two-shot affair. A captain couldn't afford to miss more than twice, for by then his rowers were too exhausted to go through the grueling procedure all over again. At the moment of impact his ship had to be traveling at an intermediate speed: if too slow, the enemy could back water out of range; if too fast the thrust would embed the ram too deeply in the enemy hull and his men couldn't back water in time to get clear before the opponent's marines could grapple and board. If the first thrust missed or wasn't mortal, his men had to be ready to back water at full speed just enough to get into proper position again and then resume forward motion at the appropriate ramming speed. It was this need to fight a battle in a sort of slow motion as it were that made marines an essential part of the complement of all vessels, even those designed chiefly for the use of the ram. Without such fighters to rake the opponent's deck during the approach or to stand by to repel boarders after the impact, the attacked vessel's marines could grapple, board, and stand a fair chance of taking over the attacker. Themistocles used fourteen spearsmen and four archers per ship at Salamis; fifty years later Athenian admirals were able to cut the spearsmen to ten.

Those navies which, because of the slowness of their vessels or the poor quality of their crews, could not depend on the ram were forced to rely more on marines. In battle their captains' prime concern was to avoid destruction from a ram stroke, and the standard method of accomplishing this was to keep, at all costs, the prow toward the enemy and give him no chance to get at the flanks or stern. If a captain could do this successfully—it most often involved constant and careful backing water—until the enemy crews were exhausted, he could then bring the fight down to one between marines, in which the advantage lay on his side. If he could destroy enough enemy personnel in this phase, he might even be in a position to attack with the ram himself or, failing that, to grapple and board.

A navy trained in the use of the ram favored two maneuvers in particular, the *diecplus,* the "break through," and the *periplus,* the "sailing around." In battle, opponents generally faced each other in two long lines. The one carrying out the *diecplus* would at a given signal dash forward so suddenly and swiftly that his ships were able to row through the enemy's line before the latter was able to take countermeasures, wheel when through and ram the unprotected quarters or stern. It was a deadly maneuver but it demanded the utmost in coordination, response to command, and cleanness of execution; only fast ships and finely trained crews, taught to work in unison, could carry it out successfully. The *periplus* was simpler; it was an "end run" around the enemy's flank to take his line in the stern.

An admiral could avoid the *periplus* either by extending his line —though not so much that he would open himself up to the *diecplus*—or, if the locale permitted, by keeping one flank close to shore. The *diecplus* was a tougher nut to crack. It probably was invented by those fine sailors, the Phoenicians; at any rate they were the first reported to have used it. They tried it out on Themistocles at the battle of Artemisium, two months before Salamis, but that astute commander had a countermeasure ready: he arranged his fleet in a circle with prows pointed outward and sterns toward the hub and literally left the attackers no line to break through. Another defense was to draw up a fleet in two lines; the second, held in reserve, could pounce on whatever enemy ships broke through the first. This was only feasible when an admiral had some superiority in numbers; otherwise his lines would be so short that the enemy could turn his flanks with the *periplus*. In a battle near the Arginusae Islands off the coast of Asia Minor in 406 B.C., the Athenians successfully used this tactic with a fleet of 150 ships against a Spartan fleet of 120; by picking a locale where there were a few islets so conveniently placed that they could be incorporated in the formation, the Athenian admirals were able to draw up a double line that was wider than their opponents' single one.

When the Athenian navy was in its prime, the only smaller

variety of warcraft it used was the triacontor (p. 85), useful no doubt for scouting and chasing pirates. The penteconter was a thing of the past, completely replaced by the trireme. The latter was far from being only a ship of the line, designed solely for use against enemy units. It was a general workhorse and carried out a multitude of tasks. Stripped of many of its rowers it transported troops; with the oarsmen reduced to sixty it carried horses, thirty to a ship. It was ideal for amphibious operations since it was light enough to be drawn right up on a beach; many a so-called naval engagement was merely a semipiratical attack for plunder by a squadron of triremes on a coastal settlement. They performed convoy duty, escorting freighters to protect them from an enemy or pirates or both. Since there was nothing faster afloat, they served as dispatch boats; the Athenians had a famous pair, the *Paralus* and *Salaminia,* the swiftest units in the fleet, which they constantly used to carry messages or transport important personages.

The trireme had the two drawbacks of all ancient galleys, lack of space and excessive lightness. It was useless in any sort of heavy weather and, unable to carry provisions in any quantity, had to have bases readily available. Sailing freighters could strike across the open sea, but a fighting squadron had to follow the coast so that each night the men could beach the ships and cook, eat, and sleep ashore; naval actions always took place in sight of land. Since operating in waters where the enemy held the seaboard was out of the question, commanders were never able to maintain a true naval blockade; they might bottle a fleet in a harbor as Xerxes did Themistocles at Salamis, or cut a port from seaborne supplies, but they could not patrol an extended shore line that was securely in an opponent's hands. This limitation on cruising range made the open sea a sort of no-man's-land and particularly hindered the cleaning up of piracy; the job was never really done properly until the Romans came along with enormous forces at their disposal and the whole of the Mediterranean coast line more or less under their control (p. 205).

The Peloponnesian War, the great conflict between Athens and Sparta which began in 431 B.C. and lasted for twenty-seven years, was the heyday of the fleet trained in maneuver and the use of the ram. The Athenians, getting off to a flying start in their battles against Persia, had in the ensuing half-century built up the finest navy the Mediterranean had yet seen. Their ships were the fastest afloat; their crews were trained to a razor-edge, especially in the complexities of the *diecplus* and the *periplus;* and in the early days of the war they had a gifted admiral named Phormio who was well able to carry on the tradition started by Themistocles. Their navy was so powerful an instrument that they depended chiefly on it during the whole of the war. Athens deliberately allowed Sparta and her allies to throw a cordon on the landward side about the city. It made no difference: under the besiegers' eyes, freighters convoyed by Athenian triremes brought in all the supplies the populace needed. Like Persia, Sparta was principally a land power and had no ships. Some of her allies, notably Corinth, had sizable navies, but none were particularly enthusiastic about taking on the Athenians except in circumstances where the odds were unquestionably favorable.

During the first years of the war the Athenian navy carried the art of fighting with the ram to heights never to be reached again, and the zenith was achieved at the battle of Patras, fought in 429 B.C. in the waters of the western end of the Gulf of Corinth. Here Phormio with twenty triremes signally defeated an enemy fleet of forty-seven, one which, despite the odds, he had to force to come out and fight. When the opposing admiral—a Spartan, although most of the ships under his command were Corinthian—reluctantly decided to engage, in order to prevent the Athenians from carrying out the deadly *diecplus* he adopted the countermeasure of the circle. Putting five ships as reserve in the center, he rayed the other forty-two in a ring around them, prows outward; after all, Themistocles had used the same maneuver at Artemisium and it had worked then.

But the ships and crews of the Persians were not in a class with those that Phormio now commanded, nor was their admiral. Phormio tried a daring measure: proceeding in column he formed a ring around the Spartan formation and kept circling steadily about it. He thereby put his vessels in the most dangerous position possible—their broadsides exposed to the enemy's rams—but he figured he could rely not only on the quickness of his crews to spin and get out of danger in case of a charge but also on the sluggishness of the enemy in mounting one. Moreover, like Themistocles at Salamis he cannily included the wind in his calculations. It was just after dawn and dead calm. But there was usually a morning breeze from the east in these waters and he reasoned that when it set in it would throw the dense Spartan formation into confusion. He had reckoned perfectly. As soon as the wind sprang up the enemy ships started to foul one another and had to be fended off with boat poles. Soon they were so close that the oars couldn't be worked. At that moment Phormio signaled the attack, and his ships turned from column to line and drilled in. In the very first charge they sank a flagship, and before the enemy could shake free and scuttle away they had seized a dozen prizes.

The Spartans prudently waited until they outnumbered Phormio's little squadron by four to one before they set out to even the score. Again they lost, but this time only because of a single piece of Athenian seamanship that was extraordinary even for Athenians. The Spartans, with their overwhelming numbers, practically had the fight in their hands; they had captured nine ships and were savagely pursuing the remainder. One of their vessels pressed forward at the heels of a lagging Athenian craft. As it happened, a merchantman was anchored just ahead in an open roadstead. The Athenian captain headed his vessel for it but, instead of passing it, made a lightning turn around it which put him in perfect ramming position, and struck the pursuer square amidships. This was too much for the Spartan crews. They sat at their oars stunned and, before they could get under way again, the Athenian squadron stopped its flight, wheeled, charged and sank six craft.

No more than sixteen years after Phormio's spectacular victories a bitter fight took place whose outcome presaged the end of the light fast trireme's undisputed reign as queen of the seas. The locale was the harbor of Syracuse, far from Athens.

The Peloponnesian War was halted for a while by an indecisive treaty in 421 B.C. but erupted again a few years later. In 415 the Athenians took the first of a series of steps that was to lead to their defeat. Their navy was incomparable and they knew it. In an access of cocksureness they voted to send an enormous armada—134 ships and 27,000 men—overseas to capture Syracuse in Sicily. Before the attempt was over, two years later, it had not only cost them 200 ships and 50,000 men but had produced a new style of ship and fighting that spelled the end of their naval supremacy.

When the huge fleet, including the finest units in the Athenian navy, sailed into the harbor of Syracuse in the summer of 415 there were probably few people on both sides who didn't think that the campaign would be over shortly. The Syracusans had a good-sized fleet; but nobody in it, from the admirals to the deck hands, reckoned that it had a chance against the Athenians.

But an important clue to the direction in which victory lay was supplied the Syracusans by what at the time must have been reported as merely a minor naval engagement. In 413, in the narrow waters of a bay near the western end of the Gulf of Corinth, a squadron of Athenian ships engaged one from Corinth. There were no more than thirty-three units in each, a far cry from the great fleets over one hundred strong that were facing each other at Syracuse. When they finally disengaged after a long struggle, three Corinthian craft had gone to the bottom and seven Athenian had been put out of action. To the Corinthians, to have come off this well was tantamount to a victory. The reason for their good showing was clear: before the battle they had taken pains to reinforce their ships with extra timbers on the bows as well as on the catheads forming the front face of the outriggers and, during the battle, they had stuck to narrow waters where their opponents, with no room to maneuver, had to ram prow to prow. As a result, seven Athenian craft bashed in their outriggers against the newly installed massive foretimbers.

Taking their cue from this engagement, the Syracusans reinforced all their triremes in this way. The locale of the fighting was all in their favor. Their harbor was an oval about two thousand by four thousand yards in extent and they had succeeded in plugging the entrance with a line of sunken merchantmen. The Athenians were securely bottled up. They had to battle in waters where there was no room for the style of fighting they had been trained in, their slender prows faced the heavily armored fronts of the newly reconditioned fleet, and their sterns pointed to a shore that was mostly in enemy hands. Ramming could be only prow to prow, in which they had everything to lose and nothing to gain. The Athenian commander tried one last measure: he stationed extra marines in the bows with irons to grapple the Syracusan ships as they surged in; if the crews could back water quickly enough to ride out the first blow, the grapplers could hold the attackers fast, keep them from backing off for a second attempt, and give their own men a chance to board. It was plainly a measure of desperation, for these were the very tactics Athens had never bothered with and had no competence in. As it happened, the Syracusans got advance word of the plans and covered their foredecks with hides so that the grappling irons would rip harmlessly through and not embed in the planks. When the fleets finally engaged, the Athenians fought gallantly but it was in a lost cause. Not one of the 210 ships that, in the course of the campaign, had made their way into Syracuse Harbor came out of it.

The Athenians had incredible stamina. Even this disaster didn't finish them off. In the following years, virtually starting from scratch, they were able to build up new powerful fleets and even win several victories, though their ships and crews were now often inferior to their opponents'; during these years, in a complete reversal, it was the Athenians who defended against the *diecplus* and *periplus* and the Spartan fleets which executed them. The final defeat was almost anticlimactic. In September of 405 B.C. Athens sent her entire navy, 180 units strong, to the Dardanelles to make sure that freighters carrying grain from south Russia to the city got through safely. The commanders drew the entire force up on a bare beach on the north shore of the straits near Aegospotami, "Goat's River." Because there was no settlement nearby, the crews had to straggle off to Sestus, the nearest market, almost two miles away, to get food. The enemy fleet camped on the opposite shore in front of Lampsacus, a well-stocked city. The next morning both sides manned their ships and the Athenians rowed up to the enemy formation and offered battle. The Spartan admiral, however, shrewdly held off and, after his opponents turned to go back to their beach, sent scouts to keep an eye on them and kept his own men at battle stations. The same procedure was repeated for four days. On the fifth day, when his scouts signaled (by shield, hoisted aloft to reflect the sun) that most of the Athenians had beached

The Wooden Walls

their ships and gone off for food, he pressed in at full speed and, without losing a man, seized 171 prizes, probably the most spectacular victory in the history of naval warfare. Only nine Athenian craft escaped. They happened to be under the command of Conon, a gifted naval officer, who managed to man the banks and raise sail on his tiny flotilla quickly enough to make a getaway. The enemy, stripped for action, had no sailing gear aboard (p. 97), so Conon, boiling along toward the Aegean with the prevailing northeasterlies at his back, was able to show his heels to any pursuers. He had so much of a head start that, in a move which reminds one of the bandits in a Western film who turn loose their victims' horses to forestall chase, he took the time to cross the strait, stop at the Spartan anchorage for a few minutes, and cart off all the sails that had been left there.

A few months later Athens, with no fleet to secure her lines of supply, was starved into submission.

In the Mediterranean where states of any size had to depend on overseas sources for food and the only feasible long-distance communications were by water, sea power was paramount. Her superb ships and tactics had given Athens unchallenged rule of the eastern sector for almost a century, from the moment Themistocles had brought them on the stage at Salamis to the ludicrous curtain at Aegospotami. When she tried to extend her arm farther, to the west, she lost everything. Complete control of the Mediterranean was something that had to wait until the Romans came along.

In the years after Aegospotami Athens succeeded in rebuilding her fleet more or less on the old model. But changes were in the wind. For one, the weakness in cramped waters of the light trireme, built primarily to ram, was now apparent. For another, after the vast losses during the war on both sides adequate crews in sufficient number were harder than ever to find and because of certain factors remained so. Another major development in naval design and tactics was soon to take place.

8 The Merchants of Athens

ONE DAY, SOMETIME TOWARD the end of the Peloponnesian War, a pair of Athenian bankers made their way to the slave market in front of the temple of Castor and Pollux at Athens. They needed another employee, and the personnel of their bank was mostly slave. That day they bought a young foreigner named Pasion—perhaps "Pasion" was as near as they could get to a name unpronounceable on a Greek tongue. This new purchase, who trotted dutifully behind as they tramped the five miles from the city to the office at the Peiraeus, Athens' harbor, was eventually to take over their bank, become a key figure in the business circles of the port, and end up one of the richest men in Athens.

Pasion was lucky. He might have been bought by some estate owner and spent the rest of his life in the farmhand's unvarying round of chores, or by some contractor for mine labor and died after a few years of backbreaking work underground. Instead he landed as an employee of the Antisthenes and Archestratus Banking and Loan Company, a position that turned out to be uniquely suited to his talents. He probably started at the bottom as a porter who handled the heavy bags of coin but rose quickly to chief clerk in charge of a moneychanging table at the port. He was quick, accurate, honest and, above all, had a keen eye for spotting undesirable clients and bad credit risks. As the partners grew older they relied more and more on him; they granted him his freedom—it happened often in those days to slaves who had served their masters faithfully and well—and finally, when age kept them from playing an active part in the business, he took the bank over.

Pasion prospered. Some of the biggest men in Athens, military and political leaders, were his clients. With shrewd business sense and scrupulously kept books, he carried on all the multifarious activities of a banker of the fourth century B.C. He received money from his clients and kept it on deposit for them. He supplied the ancient equivalent of a safe-deposit box by storing their valuables. He provided convenient methods of payment for them: although the written check had not yet been invented, a depositor could appear with a person to whom he wanted funds paid and Pasion would transfer the appropriate sum on his books or, if the payee came from another city, arrange to have a business contact there hand over the money and debit the bank's account. This was no ordinary advantage, for it spared the client the risky business of transporting cash, especially overseas.

With his own money as well as that on deposit as working capital, Pasion fattened on the profits from moneychanging, on the conservative interest from well-secured loans, and on the juicy returns from speculative loans to shippers. As time passed and his capital grew, he branched out: he bought ships to charter, and even went into the lucrative munitions business by founding a factory to manufacture shields. He was always keenly aware of the debt he owed the city which had opened up such unique opportunities to him. Once he gave the army an outright gift of a thousand shields. A rich man was often called upon to serve as trierarch, to equip and maintain a trireme for a year (p. 95); Pasion on one occasion voluntarily signed up for five. His service on behalf of the state was finally rewarded by the highest gift she had to offer, citizenship. And this helped business too, since Pasion could now add investment in real estate to the bank's activities. Aliens were not allowed to own property in Athens, and for a banker who wasn't a citizen to take on mortgages was too risky; he couldn't foreclose in case of nonpayment.

Eventually Pasion got too old to play an active part in the business. When he had to make the five-mile walk from his office at the Peiraeus to Athens on business he found it a little too much for his aged legs. At this point he ran into the problem that so often faces a successful businessman. Of his two sons, one was still a minor and the other was too interested in his horses, clothes, and courtesans (the ancient equivalent of chorus girls) to be trusted with the business; the firm just couldn't become Pasion and Sons and prosper. So he did what his former masters had done years before: he turned the bank over to his general manager, Phormio, whom he himself had bought off the slave block, trained in the business, and freed. And, to make sure that the assets stayed in the family, he did what quite a few bankers did in those days: he stipulated in his will that Phormio was to marry his widow. The bank under its new management flourished as it had under Pasion and maintained its reputation for service and square dealing. Phormio, too, became one of the richest men in town.

Athens of the fourth century B.C. was just the time and place where a Horatio Alger career like that of Pasion or Phormio could happen. Commerce was more vital to the city's existence than it ever had been before. In the fifth century Pericles, a soldier and statesman, had led Athens in his office as a member of the board of generals; one hundred years later her destinies were guided by men like Eubulus and Lycurgus, financial experts serving her in the office of chancellor of the exchequer. A web of trade routes crisscrossed the waters between Marseilles and Kertsch, and bankers and shippers and shipowners cooperated in sending over them every conceivable sort of product, especially the basic commodities of the ancient world: wine, oil, and grain. Traders in Byzantium on the Bosporus cocked a wary eye on the crop in Sicily eight hundred miles away; rumors of a bad harvest in Egypt sent prices soaring on the exchanges of half a dozen Greek cities. At the center of this hectic commercial activity stood Athens with its seaport town, the Peiraeus.

When a skipper steered his vessel into the port of the Peiraeus in the fifth or fourth century B.C., he headed for a narrow opening between two moles that closed the entrance of a capacious harbor.

The Merchants of Athens

Here he was hailed and boarded by customs officials who looked over his cargo, checked the valuation, and levied a toll of 2 per cent. Going and coming, ships paid this even on transit goods destined for a further port. It was not a protective tariff but simply a source of revenue; many a conveniently located Greek seaport was able to base a large part of its budget on the collections from harbor tolls. The officials kept such precise records that their ledgers could be produced in court as evidence of the exact nature and amount of cargo a ship had carried. After customs had taken its cut, agents came aboard to collect dues for the use of the port facilities. There was a way to avoid both tolls and dues if one wanted to run the risk: to the north of the port and outside its jurisdiction was a quiet cove so well known as a mooring point for smugglers that it was called "Thieves' Harbor."

Once clear of all the red tape, a skipper steered for the right-hand side of the harbor. The other side, as well as two smaller bays farther on, belonged to the navy and were given over to the long roofed sheds that housed the triremes and other war craft. But on the right stood the *emporion,* the commercial part of the port. All along the water's edge ran a stone-paved quay where freighters made fast. Just behind, parallel to it, were no less than five colonnades. This is where business was done.

If the newly arrived skipper had a cargo of grain he unloaded at the "Long Colonnade," the most extended of the five even as grain was the most important item in Athens' import-export business. Here he was met by the local grain wholesalers who came up bawling out the prices they were willing to offer, as well as by official supervisors who were on hand to make sure that governmental regulations were observed. Alongside the grain exchange were the colonnades where other products were dealt in: jars of Athenian olive oil or crocks of her honey or just empty vessels decorated in the inimitable Athenian style, for export; jars of wine imported from Asia Minor or of preserved fish from the Black Sea, timber and pitch from Macedon for the shipyards, and so on. One colonnade was known as the *Deigma,* the "sample market" or "bazaar," and from here rose a babel in every language of the Mediterranean seaboard as traders laid out miscellaneous wares from all quarters and bickered with officials or bargained with dealers. Here one could buy carpets and pillows from Carthage, seasonings and hides and ivory from Libya, flax and hemp for rope and papyrus for writing paper from Egypt, rare wines and incense and dates from Syria, furniture from Miletus, figs and nuts from Asia Minor (slaves, too, from the same area), pigs and beef and cheese from Sicily and Italy. There was usually a seller's market, for, with all the intensity of the traffic, it was still the age of the small businessman and the organization of supply was haphazard. Hundreds of small traders dumped their wares on the docks and haggled over prices with hundreds of dealers. Spotted here and there among the bewildering varieties of stalls were the tables of the moneychangers, and amidst the clamor of hawking and bargaining could be heard the clink of coins as sharp-eyed clerks exchanged Persian darics or staters from Cyzicus or the coinages of Sicilian cities for Attic four-drachma pieces stamped with the old-fashioned picture of Athena and her owl that Athens kept using since it was accepted everywhere as the trademark of a trustworthy currency.

From April through the summer the hurly-burly went on at the Peiraeus. With the coming of October, winds and weather put a close to the sailing season (p. 39). Moneychangers folded their tables, shippers from abroad sailed for home, shipowners hauled out their craft onto the beach or bedded them down at the quays, stevedores wandered off to the city. Like a summer resort, the harbor closed down to wait for spring.

It was the Persian wars that launched Athens on her career as a center for shipping. Before this time cities on or off the coast of Asia Minor, such as Chios or Miletus, played the key roles in the trade of the east and Corinth in that of the west (pp. 76-82). Aegina, a little island right at Athens' door, had a merchant marine that tramped all over the Mediterranean; when King Xerxes was organizing his attack on Greece and was scouting the Dardanelles, the first thing that met his eye was a convoy of ships from Aegina going through loaded with South Russian grain. But when, in the wake of the victories over the Persians, Athens created an empire which ensured her special privilege in the Greek cities of the Aegean, filled her treasury, and enabled her to build up a navy that could police the seas, the Peiraeus was gradually transformed

The Merchants of Athens

into an international entrepôt. And Athens maintained her commercial domination despite the stunning defeat in the Peloponnesian War. Geographically she stood in the center of the Greek world: any trader who put in and unloaded would be sure to find a return cargo and not have to go home in ballast. She had one of the few good natural harbors in the eastern Mediterranean; her coinage was still one of the best there was and was accepted in every port; there was capital available among her businessmen for investment in maritime ventures. So the Peiraeus hummed with activity.

Far and away the biggest business in Athens was the importing of grain. The ancient Greek lived principally off bread and porridge; if supplies weren't unloaded regularly on the quays of the Peiraeus the populace faced hardship. The same was true of most of the larger Greek cities. Intense commercial competition took place in this age, with many a clash of interests; it was not over markets in which to sell surplus products but over access to supplies essential for keeping a city going: grain for food, wine to drink, and olive oil which, by itself, did in those days what soap and butter and electricity do for us. Athens grew olives; wine could be got nearby; but the most important, grain, was available in quantity in only three places, all of them far overseas: Egypt, Sicily, and South Russia. In the Peloponnesian War Sparta starved Athens into submission by destroying her fleet and blockading her port; a little over half a century later King Philip of Macedon, the able father of Alexander the Great, went about achieving the same result by occupying the city of Byzantium and closing the gates of the Bosporus, thereby cutting access to South Russian grain.

So, to feed themselves, Athens and the other major Greek cities required trade on an international scale. But it is necessary to get the nature and extent of their commercial activity in proper focus. The history of the Greeks in the fifth and fourth centuries B.C. is so important for its great contributions to the civilization of the West that we tend to lose sight of the actual size of the nations and the number of people involved. Athens, by far the greatest city of Greece, was politically and culturally a mighty place, but her population was certainly not more than 300,000, slaves and foreign residents included—in other words what in the United States would qualify as a center of quite moderate size. Less than 100,000 tons of grain, some 800 average-sized boatloads, were enough to feed her for a year, and some of this, though relatively very little to be sure, was grown in her own fields. The activity in importing grain was intense—the actual shipping had to be crowded into the summer sailing season—but the totals involved were small. The day of huge corporations and government in business on a large scale lay ahead. Most of the commerce was in the hands of small traders who operated with partners when they couldn't scrape up enough cash on their own, who handled one cargo a year, and who traveled on the ship along with their goods to make sure that everything went off without a hitch. But though the operations were small in scale, they were widespread. The banker or merchant at the Peiraeus had business contacts in Marseilles or Syracuse or Byzantium. Once, during a period of acute grain shortage around 330 B.C., Cleomenes, Alexander the Great's governor in Egypt, cornered the market on his country's supplies. In Rhodes, a port of call for all ships from Egypt, he was able to establish a headquarters where his agents could collect, from contacts all over, the latest quotations and, as the loaded freighters arrived, divert them to whatever spot was offering the highest price.

It usually took four men of business, each playing a specific role, to bring a cargo from the wheatfields of South Russia or Egypt or Sicily to the miller at Athens: shipper, shipowner, banker, and wholesaler; in many cases it took a pair or group of partners to provide the capital for each of the roles. The shipper practically always worked on credit and generally with a chartered vessel. He contracted with a shipowner for a ship or space on one and then borrowed money from some banker like Pasion to pay for the freight charges and a load of merchandise. Those who owned their own ships pledged them as security, but most put up the cargo they intended to buy. Obviously they must have been by and large men of integrity, for the banker never saw his security until months after the loan was made, when the vessel with its load finally docked at the Peiraeus. Interest for this service ran high, $22\frac{1}{2}$ to 30 per cent for the four to five months of the sailing season, that is, between $67\frac{1}{2}$ and 90 per cent per annum; but that was only natural. There was no insurance in those days; the banker

The Merchants of Athens

assumed total responsibility—if the vessel failed to come back he, not the shipper, lost everything—so his reward had to be big enough to compensate for all risks. And these were considerable because, alongside the purely maritime ones, there was the ever present possibility of seizure by hostile men-of-war (cf. pp. 82-83) or attack by pirates. The same risks plus the lack of any system of insurance made the shippers and shipowners anxious to work as much as they could with borrowed funds even when they had some of their own; in this way they limited their personal loss when a venture ran into trouble.

Whether a shipper hauled grain to Athens from Sicily or the Crimea or Egypt, the voyage was difficult and slow one way, quick and easy the other. This is because of the prevailing winds in the eastern Mediterranean and Black Sea, which during the ancient mariner's sailing season are prevailingly from the north; in the Aegean, for example, summer northerlies were so constant that the Greeks called them the Etesian, "annual" winds (the *Meltem* of the Turkish sailors today). A skipper leaving Athens on the Black Sea run had to fight his way out there but could boom home with a following breeze. For those who handled Egyptian grain, the reverse was true: they sailed downhill before northerlies from Athens to Rhodes and before northwesterlies from there to Egypt but had to work into them all the way back, and the best course they could lay was a roundabout one by way of Cyprus; it helped somewhat that between Egypt and Rhodes they were willing to sail all year round. A skipper headed for Sicily had the wind behind him only as far as the southern tip of Greece and from that point on he had to tack; conditions were, of course, just the reverse on the homeward leg. An ancient freighter could make between four and six knots with the wind, only two or a bit more against it. This meant that the round trip to Egypt or the Crimea involved about three weeks at sea, to Sicily about two.

After a vessel arrived at the Peiraeus and the customs and port charges were paid, a shipper unloaded in the "Long Colonnade" and stood by while the wholesale grain dealers, who in turn sold to millers or consumers, bid for portions of his cargo. He had to get a good price, for this was his one chance to make a profit: what with the time consumed at sea and in loading up, generally only one round trip was fitted in the short sailing season; if the price had fallen between the time he purchased his cargo and the day he arrived at the Peiraeus, he had to swallow the loss and wait until the following year to recoup. When he finally collected from the wholesalers, he paid principal and interest to the banker and chartering charges to the shipowner and pocketed as profit what was left.

In a system of credit such as this, a great deal depended on the integrity of the shipper. The Athenians realized this and, though in other fields they were free and easy in making loans, even to the extent of turning over cash without papers or witnesses, when it came to maritime loans they nailed everything down hard and fast in a written contract that tried to anticipate all contingencies. But businessmen are the same in all ages and places, and the Peiraeus saw its share of shady operations. One favorite was to pledge a cargo for a loan from one banker and then, by repledging the same security, collect further loans from others. If a man could load, transport, and sell a cargo quickly enough to pay off the creditors in short order, there was a fair chance the fraud would never be discovered. If a shipper, after negotiating a series of loans in this way, could inveigle a shipowner into entering a deal to arrange a convenient shipwreck, either real if the boat wasn't worth much or pretended if it was, both could clear in one season more money than they could possibly make in years of legitimate business.

The great orator Demosthenes is best known for the fighting political speeches he made before the Athenian Assembly. In private life he was a lawyer, and his clients included a number of bankers who had lent money at one time or another to shippers who turned out to be unfortunate credit risks. In the gallery of rogues whom Demosthenes sued, the most lurid without question were a pair named Zenothemis and Hegestratus. Zenothemis was a shipper and Hegestratus a shipowner, a partnership which, if dishonest, could prove disastrous to a banker. Both came from Marseilles; like so many of the men who did business at the Peiraeus they were foreigners. The transaction involved in the case began as a perfectly legitimate one. Protus, a shipper of Athens, got a loan from a banker named Demo, putting up as collateral a cargo of

Sicilian grain which he was to buy at Syracuse. He chartered space on Hegestratus' ship, left Athens, arrived at Syracuse, bought his grain, loaded it aboard, and was ready to leave. So far everything was fine. But at this point Hegestratus and Zenothemis swung into action. Each made the rounds of the local bankers, raising as many loans as he could; when asked about collateral each would glibly describe the cargo of grain that lay in the ship at the quay, merely omitting the slight detail that it wasn't his. When they had collected a sizable amount of cash in this way they sent it off to be cached in their home town of Marseilles.

This was one of those swindles in which a shipowner had to take part, since it was essential to the scheme to get rid of the grain: if that ever arrived at Athens and was sold by Protus, in the normal course of events the word would get back to the lenders at Syracuse and they would sooner or later catch up with the culprits. Zenothemis and Hegestratus laid their plans carefully. They waited until the ship was two or three days out of Syracuse en route to Athens and was coasting along not too far from the island of Cephallenia. On a dark night Hegestratus, leaving his partner to chat on deck with the passengers, stole down to the hold clutching a handsaw, made his way to the ship's bottom planking, and started to saw away energetically. Apparently Zenothemis' diversion on deck wasn't loud enough, because some of the passengers heard the noise below, went down to investigate, and caught Hegestratus redhanded. He rushed on deck and, without breaking his stride, went straight over the side, intending to grab the ship's boat, which was being towed behind, and cut loose; obviously he and his partner had in mind to use this means of saving their skins if the scuttling had gone off as planned. In the dark he missed it and, as Demosthenes comments, "met the end he deserved." Zenothemis, who was a quick thinker, tried a last-minute tactic: he raced about the deck hollering that the ship was going to go down at any minute and exhorting officers, crew, and passengers to climb into the boat and abandon ship. This might have worked except that Protus called to the crew that he would reward each one of them handsomely for bringing the vessel in and they stuck by their posts. When the voyage finally ended at the Peiraeus, Zenothemis was far from through. At Athens he decided to claim that the grain was really his and, when Protus and his banker took it over, hired a sea lawyer to sue the two of them for return of "his property." It's clear that Demosthenes, who represented the Athenian banker, had a tough case on his hands, especially since the creditors at Syracuse, realizing that they had been swindled and that they could recoup only if Zenothemis could acquire some assets, were zealously supporting the latter's story. What is more, it seems that at the end even Protus made a deal with Zenothemis, since the price of grain had dropped by the time he arrived and, after paying off his debt and interest and the rewards to the crew, he faced a good-sized loss on the whole transaction. We don't know what the court's decision was, for all that is preserved is the speech Demosthenes wrote for his client.

Another case that Demosthenes took for a banker was against two Lycians who, like Zenothemis and Hegestratus, turned out to be lamentable credit risks. This pair made a loan, offering as collateral both a cargo of wine which they were to pick up in north Greece and deliver to the Black Sea area, and a return cargo of grain which they were to load out there. The contract between the parties is still extant, and since it is the only document of its kind preserved it is worth quoting (I have added the rubrics and parenthetical notes):

parties: Androcles of Athens [this was Demosthenes' client] and Nausicrates of Carystus
have lent to
Artemo and Apollodorus of Phaselis [in Lycia, in Asia Minor]

amount: 3,000 drachmas,

purpose: for a voyage from Athens to Mende or Scione [both in north Greece] and thence to Bosporus [in the Crimea], or, if they so desire, to the north shore of the Pontus [Black Sea] as far as the Borysthenes [Dnieper], and thence back to Athens,

interest: on interest at the rate of 225 drachmas on the 1,000—however, if they should leave the Pontus for the return voyage after the middle of September [that is, run the danger of hitting equinoctial storms], the interest is to be 300 drachmas on the 1,000—

security: on the security of 3,000 jars of wine of Mende

The Merchants of Athens

which shall be conveyed from Mende or Scione in the ship of which Hyblesius is owner [that is, a chartered vessel].

They provide these goods as security, owing no money on them to any other person, nor will they make any additional loan on this security.

They agree to bring back to Athens in the same vessel all the goods [certainly grain] put on board as a return cargo while in the Pontus.

time of repayment and permissible deductions:

If the return cargo is brought safely to Athens, the borrowers are to pay the lenders the money due in accordance with this agreement within 20 days after they shall have arrived at Athens, without deduction save for such jettison as the passengers shall have made by common agreement, or for money paid to enemies [the inevitable pirates] but without deduction for any other loss.

provisions in the event of nonpayment:

They shall deliver to the lenders all the goods offered as security to be under the latter's absolute control until such time as they themselves have paid the money due in accordance with the agreement.

If they shall not pay back within the time stipulated the lenders have the right to pledge or even to sell the goods for whatever price they can get,

and if the proceeds of the sale fall short of the sum the lenders are entitled to in accordance with the agreement, they have the right to collect [the difference] by proceeding, severally or jointly, against Artemo and Apollodorus and against all their property whether on land or sea, wherever it may be.

After several further stipulations the agreement closes with the signatures of the parties and witnesses.

Artemo and Appollodorus neatly managed to break every provision in the contract. First they loaded aboard only 450 jars of wine instead of the specified 3,000. Next they proceeded to float another

loan on the same security. Then they left the Black Sea to go back
to Athens without a return cargo. Finally, on arrival they put in
not at the port but at the smugglers' cove, the Thieves' Harbor
(p. 111). Time passed, and the creditors, seeing no sign either of
their money or of any merchandise which they could attach, confronted the pair and were blandly told that the cargo had been lost
in a storm and hence all obligations were off. Fortunately the
creditors were able to produce sworn depositions from passengers
and crew that no cargo of wine or grain had been aboard. Again
we don't know how Demosthenes made out because all we have is
the speech he wrote for his client.

One of the more surprising features of commerce in Athens at
this time is that so many of the men involved were not Athenian.
The citizen of Athens traditionally invested his capital in land, and
the law protected this field for him by disqualifying foreigners from
owning real estate. Occasionally he would take a flier and speculate
by lending money to a shipper on the security of a cargo, running
all the risks of losing his investment in a shipwreck or in the shady
dealings of an unscrupulous borrower on the gamble of a juicy
return of better than 25 per cent after a few months. Even in the
frank commercial atmosphere of the fourth century B.C., when
financial considerations often determined governmental policy and
the state went out of its way to encourage shippers and brokers, the
citizen preferred to put his capital in farms and houses. Syrians,
Phoenicians, Greeks from Marseilles or Syracuse or the seaports of
Asia Minor, some of them ex-slaves, took care of much of the banking, and practically all of the shipping and wholesaling. Many of
them became "metics," aliens who had established permanent residence at Athens. The Athenians, like all Greeks, were too close-
knit a community to share readily any of their privileges as citizens; but to mark the metics as a class a cut above out-and-out
foreigners they magnanimously extended to them the questionable
joys of partaking in paying taxes and serving in the army. Despite
this, the metics had a genuine feeling of devotion toward the city.
For one thing, they were businessmen first and foremost and there
was money to be made at the Peiraeus. It was one of the few places
in the ancient world where, like Pasion and Phormio, a man could

pull himself up by his own efforts from the bottom of the ladder; there were many other metics besides these two who, though they started out as slaves and never learned to speak Greek without an accent, ended up well-to-do and respected members of the business community. For another, these metics and their business contacts were a vital link in the city's food supply, and Athens went out of her way to look after them. She had to make sure, for example, to provide swift and efficient justice for them. So, she opened her courts to their cases between November and April when the sailing season was over and they had the spare time to bother with legal proceedings. She passed a law that cases involving shippers had to go on no later than one month after the original complaint had been lodged; no trader was to be lured away to sell his grain at Corinth or Samos just because Athens had kept him waiting around for justice until his name came up on some overcrowded court calendar. And, whereas in other cases the penalty usually was a fine, those involving shippers carried prison sentences. This helped both parties: if a native Athenian won a case against a foreigner, the prison sentence guaranteed that the latter couldn't settle matters in his own way by taking off in his ship without paying judgement; conversely, if the Athenian lost, the fear of prison made him pay up promptly and not compel the foreigner, whose home might be hundreds of miles away, to hang around Athens and go through all the red tape involved in collecting on the judgement.

The city was even prepared to grant some of the privileges of citizenship, or even the citizenship itself, to those businessmen who had demonstrated over the years their loyalty and dedication to her interests. This was the way ex-slaves like Pasion and Phormio got to be citizens. It took a special act of congress to do it, but Athens found it prudent to be liberal with such acts. She had to be: there were plenty of other cities ready to come across, particularly when bad harvests gave the grain-shippers even more leverage than they normally had.

The grain trade of Athens was too vital to the city's well-being to be left completely in the hands of private businessmen. Yet the government had neither the administrative machinery nor the desire to take over any part of the actual operations. It did the next best thing: it exercised careful control. The Peiraeus, because of its location and facilities was, like London or New York, a central clearing point: loads of merchandise came into the harbor which were simply in transit, destined for consignees farther on. The government passed a series of stringent decrees to make sure that enough grain to feed the city resisted the lure of higher prices elsewhere. Of any cargo that entered the port, only one-third could be transshipped; the rest had to stay on the dock. No Athenian, either citizen or metic, could import grain to any place other than Athens: in other words, only out-and-out foreigners could handle transit grain. No Athenian, citizen or metic, could lend money on a grain cargo destined for any place other than Athens: in other words, Athenian capital was to be used for Athenian benefit. The regulations didn't end with the shipper. When the cargo arrived each wholesaler was allowed to buy only fifty measures (probably about seventy-five bushels); this kept ambitious dealers from cornering the market at any time. There were, of course, dealers and shippers who were willing to break the law, but it was risky business since the penalties were severe. At times even all these precautions didn't ensure an adequate supply, and then the city was forced to step in and take an active part. She appointed special boards of grain purchasers to buy supplies at any cost in the open market which they then sold at normal prices to the citizen. The princelings who controlled the rich grainlands of South Russia were always collecting statues and elaborate expressions of thanks from the Athenian Assembly by giving the city cargoes of wheat gratis, by granting loading priority to ships headed for Athens, or by canceling the port dues for them. A sure-fire way for a foreigner to get honors at Athens, or at any Greek city that lived off imported grain, was by contributing to her grain fund, by giving her a gift of grain, or by just selling some to her at the normal price during a scarcity. Here, for example, is the text of a resolution that was moved and passed by the Athenian Assembly in 325 B.C. (the Athenian government recorded the bills it passed on imperishable stone instead of paper and archaeologists have dug up hundreds of them):

> Motion put by Demosthenes, son of Democles:
> Whereas Heracleides of Salamis [the town in Cyprus] has continuously shown his dedication to the interests of the People of Athens

and done for them whatever benefactions lay within his power, viz.

> on one occasion, during a period of scarcity of grain, he was the first of the shippers to return to the port, and he voluntarily sold the city 3,000 *medimni* [4,500 bushels] at a price of 5 drachmas per measure [the market price was probably in the neighborhood of 16], and
> on another occasion, when voluntary contributions were being collected, he donated 3,000 drachmas to the grain purchase fund, and
> in all other respects he has continually shown his goodwill and dedication to the people,

be it resolved that official commendation be extended to Heracleides, son of Charicleides, of Salamis, and

> that he receive a gold crown for his good will and dedication to the interests of the People of Athens,
> that he and his offspring be declared an Accredited Representative and a Benefactor of the People of Athens,
> that they have the right to own land and buildings, subject to the limits of the law, and
> that they have the right to undertake military service and the payment of property taxes in common with Athenian citizens.

Be it further resolved that the secretary currently in office have a record of this motion and others ancillary to it inscribed on a stone slab and set up on the acropolis, and that the treasurer provide for this purpose 30 drachmas from the appropriate funds.

The stone, as the last section indicates, also records a companion motion passed by the Senate which includes two additional interesting pieces of information, that the crown is to cost five hundred drachmas and that once, when the ruler of the town of Heraclea on the Black Sea tried to keep Heracleides from sailing to Athens by confiscating his sails, the Athenians stepped in immediately and dispatched a representative (with fifty drachmas officially voted for expenses) to lay down the law.

Obviously Heracleides was a man to cultivate. In the cases Demosthenes took, the cargoes involved were never worth more than 9,000 drachmas and usually half that; here was someone who handled cargoes worth 15,000 drachmas and, on behalf of the city, was willing to forego a clear profit of 33,000. No wonder Athens sent an official representative at government expense when he got into trouble.

Heracleides' little incident at Heraclea reveals another and very important problem that the government had to contend with. The grain did nobody any good until it arrived at the Long Colonnade, and there were unscrupulous competitors, like the Heracleote ruler, and pirates loose all over the seas. One of the reasons the Peiraeus was so important a center for the grain trade was that Athens had a navy large enough to supply escorts to convoy fleets of freighters, especially those that sailed from South Russia through the Bosporus and Dardanelles. Although no serious battles took place during a large part of the fourth century B.C., the Athenian navy at this time counted more units than it ever did during the bitterly fought Peloponnesian War. No less than four hundred warcraft of various sizes lay in the naval base at the Peiraeus. To keep this armada in repair, the city controlled the trade in timber and naval supplies as carefully as grain. Because most of the wood and pitch came from the pine forests of Macedon and Thrace, Athens forced the local rulers to sign treaties guaranteeing sale of their products to her and no other state. They had very little choice in the matter inasmuch as Athens' fleet controlled the waters right up to their shores. A tiny island named Ceos had only one exportable product, ruddle, a substance used in paint; she was bound by treaty to turn her total output over to the city. The Athenians were thorough.

The size of Athens' naval forces is deceptive. Of her four hundred vessels, many were not in shape to put to sea and of those that were, many had to be left in their slips because there were no crews to man them. Athens and every other Greek city that maintained a navy was plagued by a shortage of rowers. The Greek citizen of the commercially minded fourth century wasn't as willing as his fifth century ancestor had been to spend the better part of his days in military service. Athens' military leaders now included hired professionals, like the condottieri of fourteenth and fifteenth century Italy, who signed on along with their own following of mercenaries. This meant that the labor force which used to be available only to

The Merchants of Athens

the fleet now had a chance to enroll in the army, and they seized it with alacrity; the life was far easier than on the rowing benches and a man stood a fair chance of fattening his salary with loot or booty. The trierarchs, those rich men who were required to equip and keep a trireme in fighting condition for a year (p. 95), were hard put to keep the rowing benches filled. "Many of my crew," complains a trierach in 360 B.C., "jumped ship; some went off to the mainland to hire out as mercenaries, some went off to the navies of Thasos and Maroneia which not only promised them a better wage but paid them some cash down in advance. . . . There was more desertion on my ships than on those of the other trierarchs since I had the best rowers. . . . My men, knowing they were skilled oarsmen, went off to take jobs wherever they figured they could get the highest pay." The situation grew so serious that it ultimately resulted in one of the greatest changes in fighting ships that took place in the ancient world. For the details we must leave Athens for a moment and turn westward.

Just about the time when Sparta and her allies were closing in on Athens for the kill that was to end the Peloponnesian War (see p. 106), off in Syracuse an astute, hardheaded political opportunist was taking the first steps in building up a powerful and sizable empire. Dionysius was a canny statesman, a practical and unscrupulous politician and, above all, a soldier who regarded warfare as a science. In the field he reorganized the traditional army unit and devised new tactics for it; he learned the techniques of oriental siegecraft from his Carthaginian enemies and bettered them by designing enormously powerful catapults. And, on the sea, he revolutionized naval design by launching in 398 B.C. the first ships in which one man no longer handled one oar as in the trireme, but four or five rowers pulled at long sweeps. With such an army and navy he was able to fashion an empire that covered nearly all of Sicily and much of south Italy. His galleys swept the Tyrrhenian Sea and the Adriatic free of pirates; traders from the Peiraeus were able to import Sicilian grain without molestation.

The new type of warship—we shall treat the details later (p. 145) —did not catch on immediately. Although Athenian naval observers must have kept a careful eye on what was going on in the Syracusan shipyards, there was no need for them to urge any quick changes. Dionysius was too occupied in the west to be any threat himself, and Athens' enormous fleet of triremes had no serious rival in the east; there was no pressing reason to undertake the expense of immediate wholesale conversion. But the new types were gradually introduced into the squadrons: the inventory records of the Athenian dockyards are preserved for the year 330 B.C. and they list 392 triremes and 18 quadriremes, ships with four men to an oar; by 325 B.C. the number of triremes had dropped to 360, there were 50 quadriremes and, in addition, 7 quinqueremes, vessels with five men to each oar. Within a few decades the new types had become standard in all navies.

There was a practical reason for the introduction of such units: it was one way of meeting the growing shortage of skilled rowers. It took 170 men to fill the benches of a trireme, and each had to be a trained oarsman. But on a ship where a number of men handled a single oar, only one had to be skilled; the others followed his lead and were needed only for their muscle.

Changes were in store for the ancient merchantman, too, but they were not to come to pass for another century (p. 174). In this age freighters were much as they had always been, beamy vessels propelled by one large squaresail, although now they began to reach respectable size. Those that brought grain to Athens or were the standard carriers for the bulky cargoes of wine and oil very likely held 130 tons on an average, and vessels capable of hauling 250 were not uncommon. (What their dimensions were is anybody's guess; the smaller American coastal packets of the first half of the nineteenth century, which had a carrying capacity in the neighborhood of 250 tons, ran 80 to 85 feet long, 23 to 25 wide, and 11 to 12 feet deep in the hold.) These were, of course, the queens of the sea: they made their runs with a minimum of stops en route, they sailed in fleets, and they were often given an escort of warships which, besides protecting them, would throw over a line when the wind was foul and tow them to make sure they got through. The ordinary workhorse freighter of the Mediterranean was not so large nor so well treated: it probably carried about eighty tons or so on an average; it tramped leisurely from port to port picking up and delivering any and every sort of cargo, and it took its chances on wind, weather, and pirates.

The speed of ancient merchantmen depended on the wind: when it was favorable, blowing over the stern or quarters, a ship could do between four and six knots; against it, only about two or a bit more. A shipowner generally accompanied his vessel on voyages but left its handling to the *kybernetes*, his hired captain, and a crew of slaves. Skippers still navigated by stars at night and by landmarks and wind direction and "feel" by day, but now they had one new useful aid: sometime about the middle of the fourth century B.C. a geographer named Scylax the Younger published the first *Periplus*, "Coast Pilot," a volume that described the circuit of the Mediterranean, naming ports and rivers, giving distances between points, telling where fresh water was available, and so on.

In 322 B.C., the year after Alexander the Great died, Athens fought two major actions in the Aegean. The shortage of rowers was fatal for her: though there were four hundred craft in her slips, she couldn't man half of them; she entered the second, the battle of Amorgos, outnumbered 170 ships to 240. Her navy was shattered and, with startling abruptness, her career as a great seapower came to a close forever.

The victor was Alexander's fleet, now under the control of one of his successors. Alexander's blazing career profoundly changed the world of the fourth century B.C. His conquests almost overnight brought into existence new great nations and with them new trading centers and routes. Business went on at the Peiraeus—the city, after all, had an excellent harbor and its populace still had to eat. But Alexander's work shifted forever the focus and nature of commerce and left Athens on its edge and no longer at its center.

9 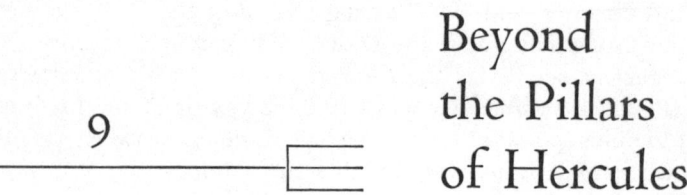 Beyond the Pillars of Hercules

JUST ABOUT THE TIME that Athen's sea power was disintegrating in battle in the Aegean (p. 127), far to the west, in the harbor of Marseilles, maritime history of a different kind was being made: Pytheas, the most gifted of the ancient mariners, was setting off on a voyage of exploration that for daring and length was not to be matched until the days of Da Gama and Columbus.

Pytheas' expedition did not come out of the blue. It came, as a matter of fact, toward the end of a series of bold ventures out of the Mediterranean into the ocean.

After Jason had led the way to the Black Sea (pp. 58-64) and the Phoenicians had opened up Spain (p. 71), the tide of exploration ebbed for a while. Skippers busied themselves investigating the nooks and crannies of the newly opened areas. In the west, Phoenician and Carthaginian traders in tin from Cornwall poked their noses past the Pillars of Hercules, those landmarks that flanked the Strait of Gibraltar, only as far as Cadiz (p. 71) and left the ocean portion of the transport for native craft; in the east no one tried to challenge the monopoly of Indians, Arabs, and other locals who plied the Indian Ocean (pp. 5-9). Then from the beginning of the sixth century on, seamen, as if bored with the Mediterranean, turned their attention to the waters that lay outside it.

Early in the seventh century B.C. Egypt, which up to then had gradually become suspicious of foreigners, opened its doors to Greek and Phoenician traders. Pharaoh Necho (610-594 B.C.) went further and dug out the old canal between the Nile and the Red Sea (p. 10), which had silted up over the years, in order to facilitate communications between the Mediterranean and southern waters. Then, with his eye no doubt on profits in new sources of trade from this quarter, he made a bold move: he fitted out an expedition to undertake nothing less than a circumnavigation of Africa from east to west, from the Red Sea clockwise around the continent, through the Strait of Gibraltar and back to Egypt. He entrusted it to Phoenicians, presumably the best qualified to carry out such a voyage.

Homer had described the world as an island encircled by a river called Ocean, and Greeks in Necho's day were convinced that water surrounded Europe and Africa; it is hard to say whether this was deduced from sailors' reports or whether, since Homer was their bible, they just took his word for it. However, they had no idea Africa extended as far south as it does; they conceived of it as a rectangle running east-west, and thought that once a ship got a little south of Ethiopia it could make a right turn and skirt, along the bottom of the continent, a shore that paralleled the Mediterranean coast along the top. No doubt Necho's Phoenicians believed this too, and agreed to attempt the expedition partly, at least, because they considerably underestimated its length. (One of the reasons for Columbus' confidence was that he reckoned the circumference of the globe one-quarter less than its true size.)

There was only one ancient writer to describe this remarkable voyage, the sharp-eyed Greek traveler Herodotus (p. 68) who somewhere or other during a tour of Egypt picked up the story. His account doesn't amount to much more than a paragraph; here are his words (with modern equivalents substituted for his geographical names):

Africa, except where it borders Asia, is clearly surrounded by water. Necho, Pharaoh of Egypt, was the first we know of to demonstrate this. When he finished digging out the canal between the Nile and the Red Sea, he sent out a naval expedition manned by Phoenicians, instructing

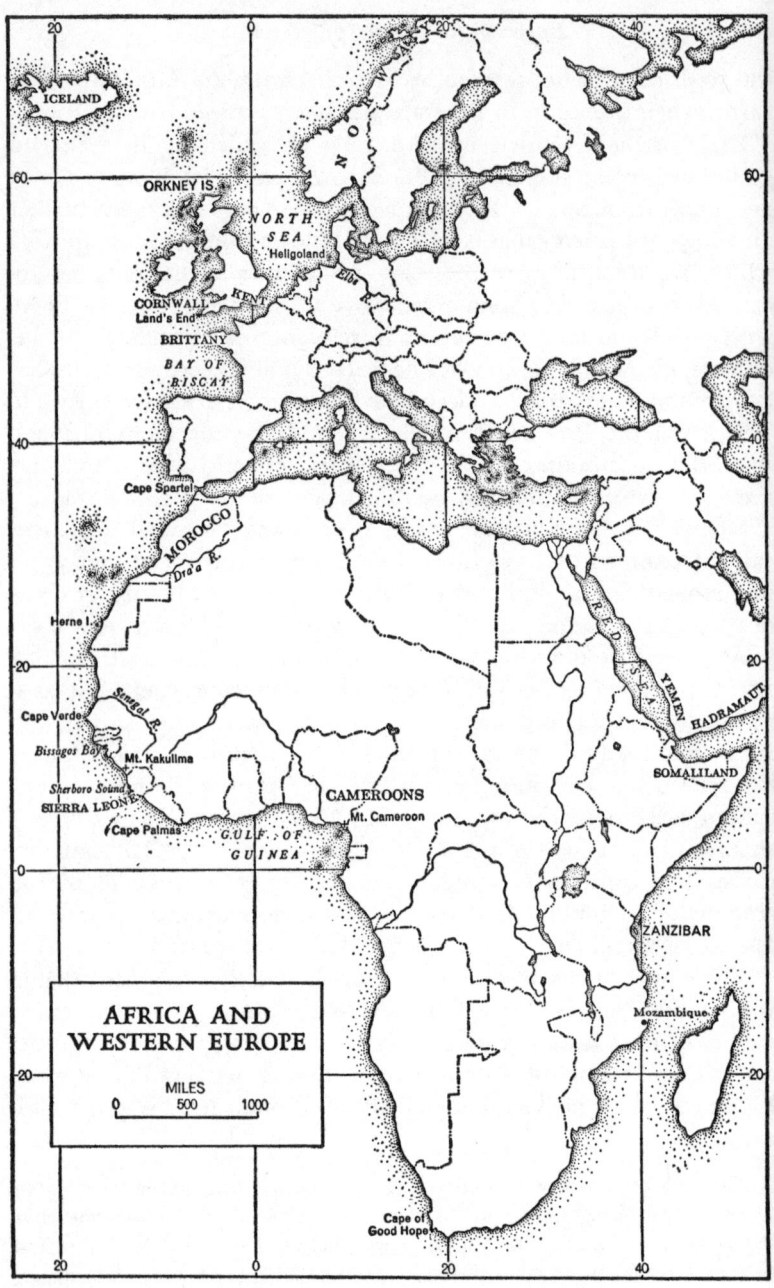

them to come home by way of the Straits of Gibraltar into the Mediterranean and in that fashion get back to Egypt. So, setting out from the Red Sea, the Phoenicians sailed into the Indian Ocean. Each autumn they put in at whatever point of Africa they happened to be sailing by, sowed the soil, stayed there until harvest time, reaped the grain, and sailed on; so that two years went by and it wasn't until the third that they doubled the Pillars of Hercules and made it back to Egypt. And they reported things which others can believe if they want but I cannot, to wit, that in sailing around Africa they had the sun on the right side.

Hundreds of pages have been written about this bald paragraph, debating the truth of the story, questioning whether such a tremendous feat had actually been accomplished. Two centuries after it was written, Polybius, one of the finest ancient historians and an African explorer himself, registered his doubts. Many, perhaps a majority, of modern scholars are also unconvinced.

On one point most agree: a voyage such as Herodotus describes was feasible. There is no reason why a crew of Phoenicians could not have carried it out in the span of time and in the way he said they did. They could have started late in autumn and, after rowing against the northeast monsoon and the current of the Red Sea, turned south beyond Cape Guardafui where wind and current would be favorable. Soon they would have picked up the Mozambique current, then the Agulhas current around the Cape of Good Hope. Here they could have stopped, sown wheat in June and harvested in November, just a year after starting. Favorable current and south winds would carry them up the west coast of Africa, and the current would be in their favor along the Gulf of Guinea to Cape Palmas, although they would be held up by calms and troubled by torrid heat in this stretch. From Cape Palmas they would have to row against the northeast tradewind and the Canaries current to Morocco where they could land and sow again, at this point near the end of their second year out. They could reap in June, head for the Strait of Gibraltar and, once inside, the homeward leg helped by wind and current would go quickly.

Even if the skeptics are right and Necho's Phoenicians did not actually circumnavigate the continent, some sort of expedition must have been launched and, judging from Herodotus' details about crops sown en route, a carefully planned one at that. What is more, it must have made its way beyond the tropic to a point where the crew was able to report they had the sun on the right side, that is, to the north of them as they worked southwest and west. The very item Herodotus singles out for disbelief is the most convincing element in his account.

The next attempt to sail around Africa was made the other way, from west to east, and there is no doubt whatsoever that it was a failure. Again Herodotus tells the story and this time he mentions his informant, although he is reticent about his name: when the explorer died, one of his eunuchs absconded to Samos with a lot of his money and there, writes Herodotus, "a certain Samian got his hands on it. I know the man's name perfectly well but I shall willingly forget it here." The voyage, it seems, started as the result of a scandal at the court of King Xerxes (485-465 B.C.), the same one who spent that unsettling day watching the defeat of his fleet off Salamis (p. 89). His cousin Sataspes had violated one of the court ladies. Xerxes was ready to carry out the appropriate punishment, namely impaling, but the boy's mother suggested he be sent on a trip around Africa instead. The king had no objection to this—he probably figured the end result would be the same—so

Sataspes went to Egypt, got a ship and crew there, and made for the Straits of Gibraltar. Passing through them and doubling Cape Spartel, he headed south [all the ancient geographers were convinced that the Atlantic coast of Morocco trended south, even southeast, instead of southwest]. After sailing for many months over a vast amount of water and always finding that he had to keep going further, he put about and made his way back to Egypt. From here he returned to Xerxes and reported that, at the farthest point he reached, he sailed by a dwarfed race who wore clothes of palm leaves and left their villages to flee to the mountains whenever the boat put in at the shore, and that he and his men did them no harm but only went in and took some of their cattle. Moreover, the reason he didn't sail all around Africa was that the ship stopped and just couldn't go any further.

This turned out to be most unfortunate for Sataspes personally since, on the grounds that he had not completed the assignment, Xerxes went ahead with the original sentence and had him impaled.

It sounds very much as if Sataspes got south of the Sahara, as far as Senegal or even Guinea, where he saw Negro tribes, perhaps

Beyond the Pillars of Hercules 133

Bushmen living farther north at that time than they do today, and then either ran into the calms and hostile current of the Gulf of Guinea or the adverse winds and currents beyond. As a matter of fact, wind and current make the circumnavigation of Africa from east to west, the way Necho's Phoenicians set out to do it, far easier; although a number of ancient mariners after Sataspes tried the west to east voyage, they all failed. Vasco da Gama in the fifteenth century was the first to turn the trick.

Necho's expedition and Sataspes' were purely voyages of exploration, probably launched with an eye to opening up new trade routes. About a century after Necho—some scholars think before 500 B.C., others after 480—another venture outside the Strait of Gibraltar along Africa was made, this time as part of a grandiose scheme for colonization; perhaps word of this journey, reaching the Persian court, induced Xerxes to send out Sataspes. It is the best known voyage of discovery made by the ancients and there is no doubt about its genuineness, for we have the exact words of a report submitted by the commander, Hanno of Carthage. He had it inscribed in bronze and set up in his home town, and years later an inquisitive Greek made a copy which has come down to us.

"The Carthaginians commissioned Hanno to sail past the Pillars of Hercules and to found cities of the Libyphoenicians [Phoenicians residing in Africa]. He set sail with sixty vessels of fifty oars and a multitude of men and women to the number of thirty thousand, and provisions and other equipment." So begins Hanno's report, a document of less than 650 words which over the centuries has provoked several hundred thousand of explanation, comment, and argument.

If the whole expedition had been put aboard sixty penteconters, the ships would have quietly settled on the harbor bottom instead of leaving Carthage; a penteconter barely had room to carry a few days' provisions for its crew, to say nothing of a load of passengers with all the equipment they needed to start life in a colony. The pentecontors were only the escort of warships and scouting craft; the colonists must have tagged along in a good-sized fleet of merchantmen. Very likely there were far less than thirty thousand. The Greek manuscripts that we have today are all the result of successive copyings over the centuries by scribe after scribe, and numerals, since they can rarely be checked by the context, are particularly liable to miscopying.

In following Hanno's narrative, the prime difficulty lies in identifying the places he records. Almost all the names he uses mean nothing to us today; there was no system available to him of identifying points by latitude and longitude (not used by geographers until over two centuries later); and the physical details he records are not always numerous and specific enough to make identification certain. He had clear sailing at the beginning and so do we: there is no question that his first leg was through the strait and southwest along the Moroccan shore where he kept dropping off batches of colonists who founded half a dozen settlements. At the mouth of the Draa River he made friends with a local tribe of nomads, probably Berbers, and, since they were familiar with the coast further south, he took some aboard as guides and interpreters.

His very next step brings us to the knottiest point in the narrative. Some time after the interpreters joined him, Hanno led his fleet into a deep easterly gulf at the head of which he came upon "a small island with a circuit of five stades (about half a mile). Here we founded a colony named Cerne. We estimated from the distance traversed that it lay in a line with Carthage; for the distance from Carthage to the Pillars and from there to Cerne was the same." Most modern commentators think that Hanno's Cerne is Herne Island, a little north of the Tropic of Cancer; the relative distances, from Carthage to Gibraltar, and from there to Herne Island, are just about the same. But some argue that Hanno's estimate of the mileage he covered, being based solely on elapsed sailing time and his best guess as to his average speed, was off and that Cerne is a good deal farther along, at the mouth of the Senegal River. For, from Cerne Hanno "sailed through the delta of a big river, named the Chretes, and came to a lake containing three islands larger than Cerne. From there we accomplished one day's sail and arrived at the head of the lake. . . . Sailing on from that point we came to another deep and wide river, which was infested with crocodiles and hippopotami. Thence we turned back to Cerne." The crocodile-filled river can only be the Senegal. The question is how far does it lay from Cerne and, if Cerne is really Herne Island, which is a good five hundred miles north of the Senegal, why did Hanno backtrack that much? It sounds rather as if Cerne was at the mouth of the Senegal and that Hanno did not retrace any steps but simply left off coasting for a while to investigate the interior, sailing inland by one arm of the Senegal and returning to Cerne at the mouth by another. The identification doesn't fit in too well with the number of days Hanno mentions that it took him to get from point to point, but none of the identifications offered does so completely; moreover, as mentioned above, figures are always the least trustworthy element in these accounts.

Leaving Cerne a second time, the expedition resumed its voyage along the coast, passing Negro tribes who fled at their approach and whose speech the interpreters couldn't understand. They took two days to double a promontory marked by wooded mountains, probably Cape Verde, the westernmost point of Africa. Then they came to

a great gulf, which according to the interpreters was called the West Horn. In it lay a large island, and in the island a marine lake containing another island. Landing on the smaller island, we could see nothing but forest, and by night many fires being kindled, and we heard the noise of pipes and cymbals and a din of tom-toms and the shouts of a multitude. We were seized with fear, and our interpreters told us to leave the island.

We left in a hurry and coasted along a country with a fragrant smoke of blazing timber, from which streams of fire plunged into the sea. The land was unapproachable for heat.

So we sailed away in fear, and in four days' journey saw the land ablaze by night. In the center a leaping flame towered above the others and appeared to reach the stars. This was the highest mountain we saw: it was called the Chariot of the Gods.

Following the rivers of fire for three further days, we reached a gulf named the Southern Horn. In the gulf lay an island like the previous one, with a lake, and in it another island. The second island was full of wild people. By far the greater number were women with hairy bodies. Our interpreters called them Gorillas. We gave chase to the men but could not catch any, for they all scampered up steep rocks and pelted us with stones. We secured three women, who bit and scratched and resisted their captors. But we killed and flayed them, and brought the hides to Carthage.

This was the end of our journey, owing to lack of provisions.

Hanno was the first to record the sort of things that today are commonplace in explorers' reports from Africa: the jungle, the beating of tom-toms, the enormous grass fires that natives kindle to burn off stubble and help the following year's crops, the ubiquitous monkeys. Hanno's Gorillas can't be what we know by that name; his men were tough but they weren't up to catching gorillas, even females, alive. Chimpanzees or baboons are the best guess. (It was an American missionary, Thomas Savage, who in 1847 applied Hanno's term to what we now call gorillas.)

Just how far did Hanno get? Most geographers hold that he stopped short of the calms and heat of the Gulf of Guinea and pushed no further than Sierra Leone, that the West Horn is Bissagos Bay, that the Chariot of the Gods is Mount Kakulima in French Guinea which, although relatively low (ca. 3000 feet), stands out in the midst of low-lying ground, and that the Southern Horn is Sherboro Sound. Others take him as far as the Cameroons, arguing that the Chariot of the Gods is better identified with Mount Cameroon, the tallest peak in West Africa (13,370 feet) and a volcano to boot. In either case, the voyage was a milestone in geographical discovery. Hanno, in one summer—he seems to have spent less than fifty days under sail on the outward leg—penetrated farther than anyone was to get for two thousand years, carried out his original mission of founding colonies, and got back without mishap. Nor did his work die with him: the settlements he planted lasted for centuries and were only abandoned probably after Rome had destroyed Carthage itself in 146 B.C. Scylax the Younger in his "Coast Pilot" (p. 127) reports that at Cerne, Hanno's furthest outpost, Phoenicians were conducting a thriving trade in his day. One of the tasks for archaeologists is to investigate the sites in question to see if any traces of these merchants can be found. They probably lived in jerry-built houses which would leave no vestige, but there is a good chance they buried their dead in typically Carthaginian tombs which would remain and are easy to identify.

For over a century after the return of Sataspes and Hanno, no further attempts were made outside the Mediterranean. The Carthaginians were satisfied to exploit the settlements Hanno had founded, and their hold on the Strait of Gibraltar kept others out of the Atlantic. Then, as the fourth century B.C. drew to a close, Pytheas of Marseilles entered the picture. He slipped through the blockade and was off on a unique and daring voyage of discovery.

"In fact there is no star at the pole but an empty space close to which lie three stars; these, taken with the point of the pole, make a rough quadrangle, as Pytheas of Marseilles tells us." It is only through such stray notices as this, scattered among the writings of ancient astronomers and geographers, that we know of this remarkable mariner, so accomplished a navigator that he was the first to observe that the polestar did not mark true north, and so skillful a seaman that he sailed to a quarter of the globe as unknown then as America was in Columbus' day, and returned safely.

Pytheas was a native of Marseilles, the city which those doughty seamen the Phocaeans founded (p. 81) and which grew and stayed rich through overseas trade. He made an epoch-making voyage, but nothing written by his own hand survives, just excerpts made by those who had access to his writings, many of whom were convinced he was an out-and-out liar and only mentioned what he said to scoff at it. They would have done better to take him seriously. Pytheas was no charlatan but the most scientific seaman of the ancient world.

Besides determining the true position of the polestar, he calculated the latitude of his home town and came within a shade of getting it right (43° 3′ instead of 43° 17′ N). He took observations of the sun during his voyage which helped later geographers to establish a number of parallels of latitude. He was the first to notice the connection between the moon and the tides. He was the first to use the name "Britain." For centuries, whatever was known of the northern regions—Brittany, Ireland, the British Isles, and the North Sea—was derived from his observations.

Sometime during the decades before 300 B.C., Pytheas sailed out of the harbor of Marseilles, headed his prow westward, and got under way on a voyage that was not to end until he had gone around Spain to the British Isles and beyond. One of his reasons for going was certainly scientific, to explore and to collect astronomical data, but this cannot be the whole explanation. He was not wealthy enough to finance such a voyage on his own, so he must have got backing from the merchants of Marseilles. Yet it's hard to imagine that they would put up hard cash in return for some abstruse geographical findings. It is more than likely that they did it in order to get information about the source of tin. This was one of their prized objects of trade. It reached the city from somewhere up north but only overland through France; the cheap sea route around Spain was a monopoly of the Carthaginian merchants of Cadiz (pp. 71, 82). If Pytheas could come up with some way to circumvent them or somehow to increase the supply, his trip would be worth every penny it cost.

Like all ancient voyages of exploration, Pytheas' is full of problems and the very first is how he managed to evade the Carthaginian blockade at Gibraltar. Possibly his timing was right: he may have picked one of the years between 310 and 306 B.C. when Carthage, locked in a bitter struggle with the Greeks of Sicily, may have dropped her guard at the strait. Like Hanno's, the first leg of his journey is clear enough. He skirted the Atlantic coast of Spain and the shores of the Bay of Biscay, doubled the northwest tip of Brittany and reached the Breton coast. From here he crossed the channel to Cornwall and absolved some of his obligations to his backers by reporting on the tin mining there. He watched the workers excavate ore along galleries, smelt and refine it, and hammer it into cube-shaped ingots for shipment.

Probably his next step was to circumnavigate Britain. This enabled him to report, correctly enough, that the island was shaped like a triangle, its three points being Belerium (Land's End), Cantium (Kent), and Orca (the northern tip of Scotland just below the Orkney Islands). He estimated the length of the sides of this triangle, getting the proportions right (3:6:8) but just about doubling their total extent. The only means for measuring at his disposal was by reckoning the time spent in sailing, and he must have overrated his speed; most ancient explorers did. He established the location of Britain ("it extends obliquely along Europe") and probably of Ireland, and made several visits into the interior of the former to observe the inhabitants.

So far it has been relatively easy to follow Pytheas' track. Now the trouble begins. At some point during his voyage he heard of—or perhaps even visited—an "Island of Thule" which, he reported, lay six days' sail north of Britain and only one day south of the "frozen" sea and the sun there went down for only two or three hours at night. It was surrounded by some mysterious substance which he actually saw but of which he gives an obscure and puzzling description; he may possibly be referring to the heavy sea fogs common in these regions. No known place fits his description in all respects but there are only two real possibilities: Iceland or Norway. In one part of his report Pytheas observed that some of the people in the northern regions grow oats (which he calls millet; he had probably never seen oats back home) and brew a drink of grain and honey. If he is referring to the people of Thule, then Thule must be Norway because Iceland is too far north for oats and bees. The fact that Norway is not an island poses no problem; discoverers of new regions often mistake a piece of mainland for an island.

Pytheas crossed the Channel from Britain back to the Breton shore and then proceeded to skirt the coast eastward, a journey that took him past an enormous estuary and to an island where amber was so plentiful the natives used it for fuel. This part of his travels has led to the wildest guesses of all; some commentators have taken him right around Denmark into the Baltic, a source of amber since prehistoric times. But it is more likely that Pytheas got no further than the North Sea, that his estuary was that of the Elbe and his island Heligoland, also a depot for amber.

When Pytheas finally dropped anchor in the harbor of Marseilles, he had covered between 7,000 and 7,500 miles, as much as Columbus had on his first voyage. He had completed one of the most daring feats of navigation made in any age and, from the point of view of the world's knowledge, a most important one: for centuries geographers depended for information about northern countries on his data. He opened their eyes to the fact that lands which lay so far north that everyone believed they were barren wastes were habitable. It is not strange that armchair geographers, knowing nothing of the effect of the Gulf Stream and the moist Atlantic winds on climate, found the facts he reported hard to believe.

There is some slight evidence that his backers received dividends on their investment: the tin trade, from Cornwall across the Channel to Brittany and from there across France to Marseilles, seems to have increased somewhat as a result of his undertaking. But nobody followed in his footsteps. The Carthaginians once again closed the gates of Gibraltar and shut off the Atlantic to further exploration.

Even when they were opened after the tide of Roman power swept over Spain, the North Atlantic never became a well-used waterway nor was even thoroughly investigated. Tin mines were discovered nearer home in Spain, and for communications with Britain the Romans preferred the overland route through France and across the Channel. Over three hundred years after Pytheas had reported on Ireland, a respectable geographer could still babble about the Irish custom of eating dead parents and having intercourse with mothers and sisters. It was on the Indian, not the Atlantic, Ocean that the ancient mariners next concentrated; but that story belongs to a later age (pp. 227-32).

10

The Age of Titans

AT SUNSET OF JUNE 13, 323 B.C., Alexander the Great lay dead in a room of what had once been Nebuchadnezzar's palace in Babylon. Behind the scenes his staff officers were already laying plans to pick up the reins of his power. They were no ordinary men themselves, and they had worked in harmony only while a greater had been alive to direct them. In the desperate contest that followed, two were to make maritime history: eagle-beaked, jutting-jawed Ptolemy who laid the foundations of a fleet which his son expanded into one of the greatest of the ancient world; and grizzled, one-eyed Antigonus who grasped the surpassing importance of sea power in the struggle with his rivals and whose son became a sea lord par excellence, a brilliant admiral and a daring innovator in the design and use of men-of-war.

Alexander was born into a small world; he left it a big one, setting the stage for a new era, the Hellenistic Age, which lasted three centuries after his death. There was only one great empire in his day, the Persian, and that lay off to the east and was playing only an indirect role in the history of the Mediterranean. The Greek who lived in Greece or in any of the colonies she had planted was a citizen of a city that by itself made up his nation. It was in this world of little city-states that Athens had reached her heyday as a naval and commercial power in the fifth and fourth centuries B.C.; a little frog, but bigger than all the others in the pond. Alexander changed all that. In one swoop he built up an empire that stretched from Greece to India. And when, on his death, it disintegrated, as was inevitable without his genius to keep it whole, it did not break into city-state fragments but into large chunks: one, centered on his home state of Macedon, constantly trying to exercise overlordship upon the cities of Greece and the Aegean isles; another, centered on Egypt, constantly trying to control the coasts and islands of the eastern Mediterranean; a third, centered upon Syria, constantly contesting the advances of its Egyptian neighbor. The history of the century after Alexander's death is, by and large, the story of the bitter struggles among his former officers and their successors, the rulers of these new empires.

The creation of such states brought a new dimension into Greek history: bigness. Not only did great political units replace clusters of little ones but a widespread common culture came into being. Alexander's officers were Greek and, to help them in the enormous job of ruling and policing large areas containing varied peoples and cultures, they brought in numbers of their fellow countrymen. They settled them as a trusted and favored upper class the length and breadth of their new kingdoms, and founded dozens of cities to accommodate them. As a result, a common Greek culture pervaded lands that had hardly known Greeks before: one language now took a traveler from Spain to India. Men read the same books, listened to the same plays, looked at the same sort of paintings and statues at Seleuceia in the heart of Mesopotamia, at Alexandria in Egypt, Antioch in Syria, Athens in Greece, Syracuse in Sicily. Commerce became big: caravan tracks stretched hundreds, some thousands, of miles to Arabia and India; long sea routes crisscrossed the Mediterranean and great freighters sailed over them.

Athens, even at its height, had operated on a tight budget with little left over for luxury; the new rulers could indulge in extravagance completely beyond the ken of a Greek city-state. Like the pashas of Persia, whom they supplanted in many places, they maintained elaborate courts, centers of luxurious living, which kept busy

The Age of Titans

an army of merchants and shippers and caravaneers; there were excellent profits to be made in supplying this newly created nobility with rich textiles, perfumes, gems, spices, rare woods, imported delicacies. They planted great new cities which they proudly named after themselves or members of the family, and decorated opulently with public buildings. Alexander's young cavalry officer, Seleucus, founded Seleuceia near Babylon as his capital and Antioch in Syria, named after his father, Antiochus. Egypt yielded Ptolemy the income to make the city his former commander had created, Alexandria, into an architectural glory and the intellectual center of the world; when, three centuries later, Cleopatra pressed an asp to her bosom and the dynasty came to an end, there was still an enormous amount of money left in the treasury. Even the descendants of Antigonus in Greece, where the pickings were necessarily slimmer because of the barren nature of the country, were able to found cities with imposing buildings and keep up a presentable court.

The greatest drain on the treasuries of all these kingdoms, one which ultimately bled them into financial anemia, was the military budget. Ptolemy's successors in Egypt, Antigonus' in Greece, those of Seleucus in Syria, watched one another like hawks, never daring to drop their guard; when, at the slightest sign of weakness one attacked, another ran to help the victim, in order to preserve the balance of power. Huge armies clashed; the seas saw the largest ships ever to be built and some of the greatest fleets ever to be collected in the ancient world.

Alexander started without a navy. As he swept over the Greek coastal cities of Asia Minor and the seaports of Phoenicia he picked up their squadrons and patched together a force that eventually gained the respectable total of 240 units and ended Athens' days as a sea power off Amorgos in 322 (p. 127). Like the empire that he had built up, it was dismembered at his death and the parts taken over by his successors. Seven years later the bulk of it came into Ptolemy's hands.

Ptolemy's chief rival at the moment was Antigonus the One-Eyed, founder of the dynasty that was to rule over Macedon and much of Greece until the Romans came in a century later. He worked closely with his son, Demetrius; the two present an example of harmony and affection unusual in an age that even saw fathers murdering sons and vice versa for political advantage. Antigonus, a tireless worker who rarely wasted a minute, was able to maintain an attitude of ironic tolerance toward his young partner's penchant for taking time out to play. A story is told that once, hearing Demetrius was ill, he walked to his bedroom and a girl brushed by, obviously just departing; when his son greeted him with, "I've been sick; I just got rid of a fever," "I know," replied the old man, "I met it on the way out." When, in 301 B.C., father and son fought their last battle together, Antigonus, trapped in a corner of the field, held fast to his post, repeating over and over, "Demetrius will rescue me." For once he was wrong; the odds were too great and he was cut down.

The two made a perfect team. Antigonus knew the importance of sea power, and Demetrius was not only a brilliant tactician but a gifted and bold designer of ships. In 315 B.C. they set out to build a fleet that would match what Ptolemy had taken over of Alexander's—and touched off the greatest naval arms race in ancient history.

Antigonus turned to the dockyards of Phoenicia. They were conveniently located near the cedar and pine forests of Lebanon, and their shipwrights had been at their trade for literally thousands of years. But for designs he turned to the west: Antigonus wanted a fleet, not of triremes like the Athenian, but of the newer quadriremes and quinqueremes which, invented by Dionysius of Syracuse 83 years before, were gradually making their way into the eastern navies (p. 126). Demetrius' ideas were even more grandiose: if quadriremes and quinqueremes, that is, "fours" and "fives," could be built, why not larger still?

Under his watchful eye, in 315 B.C., the Phoenician shipyards turned out some "sixes" and "sevens" for him. By 301 he had "eights," "nines," "tens," an "eleven," and even one great "thirteen"; this giant, which needed 1,800 men just to row it, was the largest type ever built as a class. A dozen years later he added a "fifteen" and a "sixteen." When he was ultimately defeated in 285, Ptolemy got the "fifteen" and the "sixteen" passed to another of his rivals. But somehow it wound up in the fleets of Demetrius' successors: when the Romans conquered Macedon in 168 they found the old ship there; it was no longer of any use in battle but they sailed it home, rowed it up the Tiber, and moored it at one of the city docks as a trophy.

The race did not stop here. Demetrius' son, Antigonus Gonatas, to match his father's "sixteen," now in enemy hands, built an even bigger ship, perhaps an "eighteen." Ptolemy's son countered this with not only a "twenty" but two gigantic "thirties." The climax was reached toward the end of the third century B.C. when Ptolemy IV built an elephantine "forty." It was over 400 feet long and 50 feet wide; the figureheads on prow and stern towered more than 70 feet above the water, and there were no less than 4,000 rowers manning its benches; the thranite oars were mighty sweeps 57 feet long. But this behemoth never saw action and may have been meant only for display; the fourth Ptolemy had a penchant for building floating showpieces (p. 174).

Just what kind of ships were these supergalleys? Seamen and scholars have wrangled over this question for centuries. The quadriremes and quinqueremes, "fours" and "fives," most are willing to agree, were vessels in which four and five men worked a single large oar, like the galleys of the Middle Ages and subsequent centuries. Very likely "sixes" and "sevens" and so on up to "tens" were based on the same principle; when Mark Antony fought the famous naval battle of Actium (p. 208) his flagship was a "ten" and yet it stood a mere ten feet above the water, which doesn't seem to allow room for more than one bank of oars. Moreover, galleys using ten-man sweeps are known from later ages. But what of the larger types, the "fifteen" and "sixteen" of Demetrius, the "twenty" and "thirty" and "forty" of the Ptolemies? There is no sure way of telling. A good guess is that they, and perhaps some of the lesser sizes as well, were oversize biremes, even triremes, that is, with two or three banks of long sweeps, each manned by a number of men (cf. Pl. 10a). Demetrius' "fifteen," for example, may have had two banks, eight men to an oar in the upper and seven to an oar in the lower. Ptolemy's "forty" was almost certainly an overblown trireme, with a total of forty men assigned to the thranite, zygite, and thalamite oars in one segment (cf. p. 94).

Greek and Roman writers are exasperatingly close-mouthed when it comes to the details of these great ships, and there are no certain pictures of any to help out (see Plate 10a which shows one of the bigger units that fought at Actium). One ancient historian mentions that quinqueremes used three hundred rowers and could hold a marine force of 120; they had, then, thirty oars on each side and were obviously provided with ample fighting decks. On the larger types the oars ran so prodigiously long that lead was sunk in the handles to help balance the outboard span. One of the most interesting innovations in these ships was in their sails. There had been up to now a sort of unwritten law of rigging: one mast and sail to a ship. Egypt's Nile and Red Sea boats, Crete's traders, Homer's rovers, Themistocles' triremes, all had carried this much and no more. But there is some slight indication that, to move the heavy supergalleys, naval architects broke with tradition and designed a rig with three sails, not superimposed—this was something that lay over a millennium and a half in the future—but hung on three separate masts. If so, one must have been the *artemon,* a bowsprit-sail set on a short raking mast forward, since this is soon to appear as a standard feature of all ships (pp. 174, 213, 218 and Pls. 10b, 11b). The other two must have been main and mizzen.

These great warships—except for Ptolemy's "forty"—were neither king's playthings nor misguided experiments. They were ships that saw hard service and proved their value in action. Antigonus Gonatas built his "eighteen" because of a defeat suffered when he had nothing to pit against the enemy's "sixteen." Ptolemy II regarded the architect of his two "thirties" so highly that he honored him with a citation carved on stone that has survived to this day. The great ships, as one would expect, brought about a rise in power all the way down the line in the navies they belonged to. A well-balanced force in Demetrius' or Ptolemy's day was led by a super-dreadnought, generally carrying the flag; included a group of battleships, anything from "sixes" to "tens"; its ships of the line were "fours" and "fives"; and triremes were reckoned among its light craft. When all types were computed together, the average power of such a force approximated that of a quinquereme.

The size as well as the power of fleets grew. In the battles between Demetrius and Ptolemy or their sons, each side could put 150 to 200 ships into the line. At one time, about 313 B.C., Demetrius and Antigonus had a navy that totaled 330 units. Fifty years later

Ptolemy II topped this with one even greater: he had 336 units with an average power of a quinquereme. It was made up of

2	"thirties"
1	"twenty"
4	"thirteens"
2	"twelves"
14	"elevens"
30	"nines"
37	"sevens"
5	"sixes"
17	"fives"
224	"fours," "threes," and smaller types
336	

His father had depended chiefly on "fives," and Demetrius' newly designed big ships had beaten him; the son learned the lesson: he cut down the number of "fives" to seventeen and built his fleet around a powerful nucleus of heavier types.

Demetrius' contribution to naval warfare did not end with the blueprints of the supergalley. He has another great innovation to his credit: naval artillery. Demetrius had always taken a keen interest in all the devices available for besieging walled towns—battering rams, storming towers, protective mantlets, but especially catapults for shooting darts and ballistas for hurling stones; his contemporaries nicknamed him Poliorcetes, "Besieger of Cities." The idea came to him of mounting catapults and ballistas on his warships, and very likely one of his reasons for designing bigger and bigger craft was to support the weight and withstand the recoil of these new weapons. On the prows of some of his vessels he set catapults capable of shooting darts at least 21 inches long. It wasn't size that mattered so much as range: as his forces approached a hostile fleet his naval artillery could shoot a preliminary barrage from perhaps four hundred yards away while the enemy would have to wait to get within bowshot to reply. Like his other inventions, it was quickly adopted elsewhere; soon petty officers called "catapultists" became a standard rating in all navies.

Artillery and bigger ships naturally had their effect on naval tactics, and sea battles were different in this age from what they had been a century earlier. They still took place near shore (p. 102); a supergalley was even harder to keep at sea than a trireme. But a fight now opened with a heavy barrage from catapults and bowmen. Lighter craft, triremes and quadriremes, still maneuvered for position and the chance for an effective blow with the ram; but larger units, all of which had massive reinforced snouts (cf. p. 105), were not afraid to meet each other prow to prow and this often resulted in close-packed mêlées in which the marines on the decks, hurling javelins or thrusting with special long spears, decided the issue. To aid in this sort of fighting, turrets were added to the ships' armament. These were movable wooden affairs that could be quickly set up at bow and stern when a vessel went into action, and their height gave sharpshooters a chance to fire down on the enemy's decks (cf. pl. 10a).

To maintain their expensive fleets the new rulers adopted the system of using trierarchs (p. 95). Athens had been able, of course, to call only on her own population; Ptolemy or Antigonus had the upper class of every city in their empires to turn to. They needed them: the sums poured into their navies were enormous. But even the pockets of the rich weren't inexhaustible, and the difficulties that arose are attested by no less authoritative a witness than a document, written on papyrus, from Ptolemy II's official files, one of the rare pieces of firsthand evidence we have for ancient maritime history. Like Wenamon's report (p. 47), it was found in the sands of Egypt and owes its preservation over the centuries to the perennial dryness of that country's climate.

It is a letter which was written in October 257 B.C. by Apollodotus, some bureaucrat in the finance ministry; his clerks must have been constantly sending out others of the same sort. The addressee was Xanthippus, a resident of Halicarnassus—a city on the southeast coast of Asia Minor which Egypt controlled at the time—who apparently was wealthy enough to have been chosen trierarch for nothing less than a "nine." But Xanthippus, it appears, just didn't have the ready cash to meet the expenses involved. So Apollodotus arranged a loan for him from public funds. He writes:

> Apollodotus to Xanthippus, greetings. In addition to the 2,000 drachmas which I have written to you about in a previous letter, I have forwarded to Antipater, who is representing you as trierarch of the "nine," 3,000 drachmas which must be made good to Apollonius, Minister of Finance.

The Age of Titans

Will you therefore kindly arrange to remit to him in accordance with the enclosed. Goodbye.

Enclosed was a memorandum with all the particulars of the trierarch's debt. It was probably difficulties like these that induced the businesslike Ptolemies to go further and get more than just the rich to share in the costs involved: they passed a "trireme tax," the proceeds of which were for the upkeep of the fleet.

In 306 B.C. the opening move took place in a seesaw struggle for control of the eastern seas that was to last a century: Demetrius, commanding his father's recently built squadrons and riding one of the new "sevens" as flagship, challenged Ptolemy's fleet off the city of Salamis on the south coast of Cyprus. Each had probably close to 150 warcraft under his command. The ships formed up face to face in two long lines at right angles to the shore. Demetrius, who always planned his tactics with meticulous care, adopted on this occasion an unbalanced line. He deliberately made his seaward wing, under his own command, very strong, with all the major units in it, and left his shoreward wing weak. And so, when, after a preliminary bombardment in which his catapults probably had the better of it, the two lines collided, they slowly pivoted about the center like a great swinging door as Demetrius' strong seaward wing pushed the enemy inshore and Ptolemy's shoreward wing pushed the weak forces lined up against it toward the open sea. This was exactly what Demetrius counted on: when the swing went full circle his ships would be between the Egyptians and the shore, thereby neatly cutting them off from land, an awkward position for any fleet but particularly for one whose rowers had just gone through hours of grueling work. Ptolemy, seeing the danger in time, broke and ran —and Demetrius wound up with forty ships captured along with their crews, eighty that had capsized and were successfully towed ashore, and the mastery of the seas for the next twenty years. In a sense he never lost it. When he was finally cornered in 285 B.C., it was on land while he was desperately trying to get back to his ships; he was captured and one of his admirals handed over the bulk of his fleet to Ptolemy.

Five years later his son, Antigonus Gonatas, tried to win the sea back. His father's gigantic "sixteen" now carried the flag for the enemy and he had nothing to match it; he was defeated and the eastern Mediterranean became an Egyptian lake. The shipyards and squadrons of the Phoenician ports of the Levant and of the Greek cities of Asia Minor were now securely in Ptolemy II's hands; he controlled the Aegean Islands north to the coast of Thrace. Antigonus had to wait until the middle of the century before he could try again. By this time he was firmly established as the ruler of Macedon, and controlled the ports of Greece with their dockyards. He built a new fleet; probably most of it was turned out by the skilled shipwrights of Corinth (p. 87). His navy was still much smaller than Ptolemy's but he was willing to gamble, and it paid off: in two clashes with the Egyptians, one near the island of Cos off the southwest coast of Asia Minor and the other on the opposite side of the Aegean near Andros, he beat them both times. No one knows how, for all details of the fighting have been lost. They were all-important victories, and it has been argued that the Louvre's famous Nike of Samothrace, that magnificent statue of a goddess alighting on the prow of a warship, was a dedication set up by Antigonus in the sanctuary on Samothrace to commemorate one of these triumphs. Yet even after this comeback on the part of Macedon, Egypt was still strong on the sea. The Ptolemies kept control of much of the eastern coast of the Mediterranean, and their squadrons moved at will in the waters north of Egypt. But both sides by now had to slacken their pace: the money and effort that had been expended just couldn't be kept up. Their supergalleys, the most expensive to maintain, like the great dinosaurs became extinct; they were dedicated as monuments or just left to rot—when in 168 B.C. the Romans found the "sixteen" in a Macedonian dockyard it was a fossil; it hadn't been to sea for seventy years. The two rivals had succeeded in canceling each other out, and the stage was set for the entrance of a new naval power.

Rhodes, located on an island off the southwest coast of Asia Minor, was a small nation compared with the mighty kingdoms that surrounded her. As an island state, her whole life was bound up with the sea and she had built up a small but highly respected navy. Now, toward the end of the third century B.C., by holding the balance of power on the water, she was able to step forward as the key naval figure in the eastern Mediterranean.

The two great rivals, Egypt and Macedon, from the very outset had been caught in a vicious circle. The Ptolemies needed a navy to defend their shores against Demetrius' or Antigonus' fleet—and to maintain one, just like the pharaohs whom they replaced (p. 4), they had to hold the Levant or the southern coasts of Asia Minor where pine and cedar forests supplied ship timber; the kings of Macedon had their native pine forests to draw on for timber and naval stores (they exported both, carefully raising the prices for all pro-Egyptian customers), but they needed the dockyards of Greece to turn out and maintain their ships—and they had to have ships or else Egypt's fleet would sail brashly across the Aegean and incite Greece to revolt. And so the struggle, largely political, went on. But Rhodes needed a navy because her economic life depended on overseas trade. She was an international port and banking center, and her merchant marine was one of the largest in the ancient world, out of all proportion to her size, like Norway's today.

Freedom of the seas was Rhodes' keynote, so that her freighters could travel where they wanted in safety. Yet the seas could hardly be called safe if a skipper had to sail with the jittery feeling that the other side of the headland he was passing hid the low black hull of a pirate craft. Rhodes bravely shouldered the burden and singlehandedly kept the eastern Mediterranean relatively free of its ancient scourge. Athens in the great days of her commerce had shied away from the job—but then Athens depended on foreign shipping (p. 120) and didn't have the investment in a merchant marine to protect that Rhodes did.

There was more involved than chasing pirates, difficult as that was, in keeping the seas free. When the city of Byzantium in 221 B.C. tried to levy a toll on the traffic through the Bosporus, it was to Rhodes that shippers who were affected sent their complaint, and a Rhodian fleet was at the trouble spot in short order. Most important of all, Rhodes had to see to it that no nation grew powerful enough to turn the Aegean or Levantine waters into a private preserve. So, when Antigonus Gonatas built a new fleet to challenge Egypt's control (p. 149), Rhodes joined him. The Ptolemies were practically her business partners—her merchant marine carried most of their vast exports of grain—but allying with their enemy gave the island a chance to restore the balance of power on the sea; from the long-term point of view—and Rhodian leaders were as farsighted statesmen as they were businessmen—this was safer than becoming a dependent, even a prosperous one, of Egypt.

Holding down pirates and upholding the balance of power on the sea demands a first-rate navy; the one the Rhodians maintained was the most efficient of its time. It was small: it averaged about forty major units, no match, for example, for Ptolemy's aggregation of over three hundred. But it was not intended for such a challenge; the statesmen would see to it that the admirals had powerful allies at their side when the time came to take on an enemy. Its units were small: there was nothing in the slips larger than a quinquereme, but the Rhodians had neither the budget nor the need for anything bigger. They particularly favored the quadrireme. The fastest type of major unit afloat, it suited perfectly their style of fighting, which depended on maneuver and on the use of the ram; some of their most spectacular victories resulted from the lightning-like moves they carried out in these craft (pp. 169-172). They even came up with a new naval weapon, the last to be invented until the very end of the ancient world. In 190 B.C. a squadron of about thirty of their ships was hopelessly trapped; but seven ran the gantlet safely because they had been fitted out experimentally with a new device, containers of blazing fire slung at the ends of two long poles which projected from the bows. If an enemy attacked, the fire pots were dropped on his deck and if he flinched he laid himself open to a stroke from the ram. But sea duty for the Rhodians nine times out of ten meant not fighting formal actions but tracking down pirates, and this called for light swift vessels. Rhodes fought the devil with fire: her fleet included a large number of a special type of craft called the *triemiolia* or "trireme-hemiolia." Long before, pirates had remodeled the two-banked galley into the *hemiolia,* the "one and a half," a craft designed for the particular purpose of chasing down merchant shipping; it allowed them to run under sail as well as oars during pursuit and yet provided room to stow the rigging away when the time came to board (p. 86). A trireme could outfight any such ship if it could catch it—but the standard model was made to go into action without any sailing gear aboard (p. 97).

Rhodian architects created the triemiolia to chase down hemiolias. It was simply a fast type of trireme revamped in the manner of the vessel it was intended to fight. It was so made that, during a chase, all banks could be manned and sail carried; when the time came to close in, it became a "two and a half": the thranite oarsmen abaft the mast quitted their benches, leaving a space into which mast and sail could be quickly lowered.

To keep this fleet with all its varied units in a constant and perfect state of repair, Rhodes maintained a vast, complex navy yard. It was the only one in the ancient world that we know had a security system: certain portions were closed, on pain of death, to all but authorized personnel.

Good ships are useless without good men; Rhodian crews were the best there were. Athens had filled the benches with citizens of the lowest class and hired rowers; in the fourth century she even hired admirals (pp. 96, 124). The Ptolemies and their Macedonian rivals used whatever they could get—island Greeks, Asia Minor Greeks, Phoenicians. But in Rhodes the navy was the senior service, and every galley in it was commanded and rowed by her citizens. They made it possible for her fleet to specialize in the use of maneuver and the ram at a time when inferior oarsmen were compelling her neighbors to give such tactics up. Moreover, they were indomitable fighters. In 306 B.C. Demetrius tried to take the city of Rhodes by storm. He moved up a fleet of 200 warships and 170 transports loaded with 40,000 men, and the very latest in heavy siege machinery; large numbers of pirates gleefully joined him. The Rhodians, though desperately outnumbered—they had about 7,000 men not counting slaves—fought him to a standstill: with courage, stubbornness, and ingenuity they repelled attack after attack; under brutally heavy fire some of their light craft dashed across the harbor and cut loose the barges carrying Demetrius' siege weapons, while others broke through his blockade of the entrance to gain the open sea and harry his lines of supply. After a year he finally gave up.

The officers who commanded these men were thoroughly trained; many had made their way up through the ranks. Archaeologists have found on the island a stone monument which the crew of a quadrireme set up in honor of Alexidamus, one of their officers; pridefully they recorded his naval career: enlisted man first on destroyers ("one and a halfs"), then on heavier units (cataphracts; p. 99); boatswain; bow officer on a "one and a half" (*proreus,* his first commissioned rank) ; bow officer on a quadrireme; they carefully noted that he had seen action in the last two assignments. Another monument sets forth the career of a certain Polycles. He was a member of the island's aristocracy and didn't have to climb the ladder like Alexidamus; he started with the command of a flotilla of destroyers (aphracts). His next assignment was command of a quinquereme and then, after a tour of duty with the army, appointment to the staff of the commander in chief of all Rhodes' naval forces. Subsequently he was trierarch of a quadrireme and led it in action. Officers like Alexidamus and Polycles literally devoted their lives to the sea. Other navies scrambled to hire them whenever they were available, and every now and then an occasion arose when a fleet of Rhodes found itself pitted against an enemy line commanded by one of her sons.

Rhodian crews respected their commanders and frequently honored them with monuments like the two described above. Excavators have dug up a number of similar citations, and because of them we know more about the complements of Rhodian men-of-war than of any other. The personnel, aside from rowers, assigned to a quadrireme, for example, included

Officers: trierarch or *epiplous* (qualified officer selected by the trierarch to substitute for him) —captain
kybernetes—executive officer
proreus—bow officer and first lieutenant
keleustes—officer in charge of rowing personnel
pentecontarchos—junior officer with administrative duties

Ratings: boatswain (*hegemon ton ergon,* literally "leader of the activities")
carpenter (*naupegos*)
helmsman (*pedaliouchos,* literally "steering-oar holder")
oiler (*elaiochreistes,* literally "oil anointer;" probably in charge of leathern gear and the like)
doctor (*iatros,* just a rating, not an officer, and

The Age of Titans

generally a foreigner; many came from the island of Cos, the home of Hippocrates)

oar-thong man (*kopodetes*, literally "oar binder"; probably in charge of straps that secured the oar to the tholepin)

Non-rated Personnel: bow deck watch (*ergazomenoi en prora* "workers in the prow," for handling sails and lines; at least 5)

stern deck watch (*ergazomenoi en prymne* "workers in the stern," for handling sails and lines; at least 5)

rowers

Fighting Personnel: artillerymen (*katapeltaphetai*, literally "catapult men"; at least 4)

bowmen (*toxotai*, at least 2)

marines (*epibatai*, at least 19)

Probably triremes and quinqueremes carried the same officers and ratings, the only real difference being in the number of rowers and of fighting men. Smaller units like the "one and a half" perhaps had to forego the luxury of a ship's doctor.

History relates in its impersonal way that Rhodes built up a fine navy and worked hard to sweep the seas clean of pirates. An inscription has been discovered on the island which tells, vividly and pathetically, what this meant in the lives of men. It is on a gravestone that once stood over the tomb of three brothers. As so many of their compatriots must have, the boys entered the navy. They had done well. One had risen to commissioned-officer rank (*proreus*). The second, though just a rower, was assigned to a flagship. The third was captain of a unit of marines; he had come up the hard way, for, in another inscription set up some years earlier, his name was cited along with a number of others for gallantry in action and he had then been only a *katapeltaphetes*, an artilleryman. All had been killed in different actions, not in major battles against enemy fleets but in the grinding daily work of the Rhodian navy, engagements with pirates. Two of these actions are merely mentioned, but the third is localized: it took place in the straits between Crete and Greece, near Cape Malea, a spot so favored by pirates that ancient

Greek mariners had a proverb that ran, "Round Malea and forget about getting home," and modern Greek sailors until relatively recently still sang, "Cape Malea, Cape Malea; help me Christ and all the Saints!"

Late in the summer of 201 B.C. a Rhodian galley nosed into the Tiber, far to the west, and rowed slowly upstream to Rome. It was carrying special envoys from the island and one of her neighbors to place before the Roman Senate a request for help. Antigonus Gonatas' grandson, Philip, had just finished building a powerful fleet. Because Egypt's navy was rotting in the slips, Rhodes, following as always its policy of maintaining the balance of power on the sea, was inviting the major power of the west, mistress of the western waters, to mix into the politics of the east. At the time it looked like a shrewd maneuver; a generation later it was discouragingly clear that the guest had moved in to stay. And Rome was a most formidable guest. At one time she had built up, off in the western Mediterranean, a fleet almost the equal of any in the east; and there were over two hundred galleys in her slips the summer that the Rhodian embassy arrived.

11 Landlubbers to Sea Lords

THE ROMANS ARE an anomaly in maritime history, a race of lubbers who became lords of the sea in spite of themselves. Only a nation of born landsmen would have dared, as they did, to pit against one of the greatest navies afloat a jerry-built fleet, manned by green crews fresh off the farms, and commanded by admirals who lost four ships to the weather for every one to enemy action. When they ultimately became the chief naval power of the Mediterranean, they felt so uncomfortable in the role that they let a mighty navy rot in the slips and for a full century exercised their control with hardly a vessel to their name.

Around 500 B.C., not long after Carthage had settled her dispute with the Greek colonists and marked off the western seas as her private preserve (p. 82), the inhabitants of an obscure village on the banks of the Tiber in central Italy began to flex their muscles—and within two and one half centuries became the masters of the peninsula from the Po Valley to the tip of the boot. They were a nation of hard-working, thrifty peasants who drew their livelihood from the land and were among the toughest fighters in the world—

on land. The waters around their newly acquired realm they left strictly alone, to Etruscans, Greeks and, of course, pirates.

Across the Mediterranean lay Carthage, literally living off the sea. She ruled a far-flung maritime empire and defended it with a navy whose traditions reached back beyond the times of King Solomon (p. 70). In her early days Rome had no bone to pick with Carthage. Hundreds of miles separated her from the nearest Carthaginian colonies in the western part of Sicily, and she cheerfully signed and renewed treaties in which she gave up trading rights in western waters—in return for a promise to keep hands off her own sphere of interest. It was an easy gesture: the Romans got nothing out of, and wanted nothing to do with, the sea.

But, as time went on, the lubbers found that, willy-nilly, they had to try the water. Their march up and down Italy had brought under their subjection the seaports of Etruria to the north and the Greek coastal cities in the south. All these lived off maritime trade—and the pirates that infested the Tyrrhenian Sea were a particularly virulent breed. So, in 311 B.C., Rome equipped two squadrons of ten triremes each to police the local waters. Twenty years later one of these fledglings decided to try its wings in formal combat, attacked the fleet of the Greek town of Taranto to the south, and got clobbered so thoroughly that the Romans hastily reverted to type: they scrapped even this miniature navy and arranged to guard the sea lanes by simply requisitioning ships from the Greek cities on the south Italian coast. Though these were subject to Rome and she was responsible for their defense, her attitude had a rough justice about it: what sea-borne trade there was lay largely in their hands; let them chase the pirates themselves.

But it soon became apparent that there was a more serious problem than piracy to worry about. A scant two miles from Italy, across the Strait of Messina, lay the island of Sicily. The eastern half was occupied by independent Greek city-states, but the western belonged to Carthage. Separated by several hundred miles, both parties had found it easy to abide by their treaties; now that Rome reached down to the Italian side of the strait, relations became strained. And when, through a complicated set of circumstances, the Carthaginians moved eastward and garrisoned the town of Messina on the Sicilian side of the strait, the two found themselves cheek by jowl. This could not be kept up for long; in 264 B.C. the First Punic War broke out. Both sides had no inkling that it was to last twenty-three years, and the Romans certainly none that the issue, almost from the first, would be fought out on the sea.

Rome's prime objective was to remove the Carthaginians from eastern Sicily. She ferried armies into the island across the strait—an enemy squadron was on hand to intercept, but no ancient blockade was ever airtight (p. 102)—and for three years campaigned with fair success. But Carthage refused to call it quits. She didn't need to: she had an impregnable position on the west coast of Sicily, a series of ports ringed with fortifications, too strong to be stormed from the land side alone and which, if beseiged from there, the home base in Africa could always supply by sea; from them, once the enemy relaxed his guard, she could always strike out again to regain what she had lost. To complete the job Rome had to push her opponent out of Sicily. But this couldn't be done by the army alone; somehow control of the water had to be wrested from Carthage's hands in order to cut off her forces in Sicily from home. In 261 B.C. Rome's statesmen and generals faced up to a dismaying reality: sooner or later they had to take the plunge and create a navy; David had to fight Goliath but not with a slingshot, with the giant's own weapons.

In the early spring of 260 B.C. the Senate—the body which at Rome usually handled foreign policy and national defense—called for the construction of one hundred quinqueremes and twenty triremes to be ready in time for the summer campaigning season; it must have sounded as fantastic to Rome as Roosevelt's call for fifty thousand airplanes in the grim spring of 1942 did to the United States. The ships had to be mostly quinqueremes. For one, this was the standard unit in the Carthaginian navy; for another, Rome had no crews and, while there was a chance of training raw recruits to handle the long sweeps of a quinquereme where one man directed the stroke and the other four just supplied muscle (p. 126), there wasn't a ghost of a chance of initiating them in that scant time into the intricacies of rowing a trireme.

The miracle was accomplished. The vessels were turned out "from the tree," as an ancient historian put it, to the last detail of rigging in sixty days. No Roman knew how to design or make ships, so the

Senate must have requisitioned naval architects and shipwrights from the subject Greek coastal cities of South Italy as well as from Syracuse, which, with a sizable navy of its own, had joined the cause. Four years earlier when the Carthaginian squadron on blockade duty in the Strait of Messina had attacked a Roman convoy, one of the galleys ran aground, and the Romans dragged it ashore. The architects used this as a model but avoided following it to the letter. Carthage favored a light fast vessel designed to maneuver and ram, which only a crack crew could handle; to put green men aboard such a craft was not only useless but practically suicide. So they adapted the design to a slower, bulkier, heavier ship which was far more foolproof and had spacious decks to carry a powerful force of marines.

But this was only half the problem. Each quinquereme was going to need 300 oarsmen (p. 146) and each trireme 170 (p. 94). It was out of the question to think of training crews for the latter, so the hard-working Greek allies were called on to supply them and the Roman commanders addressed themselves to the job of recruiting and readying the 30,000 necessary to man the bigger ships. They couldn't look to the city, for Rome, going further even than Athens (p. 96), refused to assign a citizen to the benches. They turned to the only other available source, the various Italic peoples who, over the centuries, had been conquered and made subject allies. Soon, on makeshift rowing frames set up on land, young huskies fresh from farms up and down Italy were sweating and grunting in mock oarsmanship. Then, as each galley came off the ways, they were tumbled aboard and given a taste of what the real thing was like. The whole program must have been under the direction of naval officers from the Greek allies; they very likely did as much swearing in those hectic two months as Baron von Steuben in his famous two at Valley Forge. In June, 260 B.C., the new fleet left the harbor at Ostia at the mouth of the Tiber and sailed down the southwest coast of Italy to rendezvous at Syracuse. Only Romans, with the courage that comes of ignorance, could have entertained the thought of sending it into action against the superb ships and veteran crews of Carthage.

But then a second miracle took place. While the fleet was lying in the harbor of Syracuse someone came up with an idea that was to change the whole complexion of things. Possibly it was one of

Landlubbers to Sea Lords

the Roman officers, more likely a Syracusan. The city had a tradition of naval inventiveness: its architects had designed the heavy triremes which destroyed the flower of Athens' navy (p. 105) and its onetime ruler, Dionysius, had invented the quinquereme itself (p. 125). Possibly, just possibly, the author was that renowned ancient scientist and engineer, Archimedes; he had been born at Syracuse twenty-seven years earlier and very likely was living there the day the fleet arrived. The Romans were unbeatable fighters on land; the problem

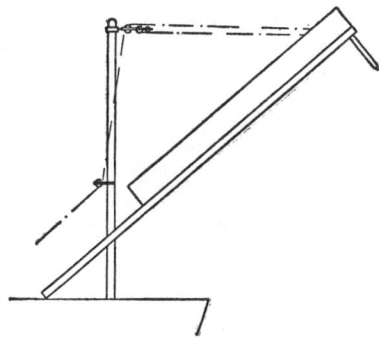

Fig. 4. Reconstruction of the *corvus*.

was to come up with something that would allow them to turn a sea fight into a land fight, some sure-fire device to enable them to grapple and board. The anonymous inventor designed what came to be known as the *corvus*, "raven," probably the sailor's slang term for it; we would call it a "crane" rather than a "raven" (Fig. 4). It was nothing more than a gangplank, thirty-six feet long and four feet wide, with a heavy spike at the outboard end and at the other a long slot which fitted around a pole set up like a mast in the bow of the ship; when raised it stood upright snugly against the pole and, when lowered, it projected far over the bow. One tackle between the farther end and the head of the pole controlled the raising and lowering, and two, made fast to the deck on either side, swiveled it from side to side. A vessel so equipped would warily keep its prow headed toward the enemy and, as soon as he closed in to ram, drop the "raven"; the spike would embed in his deck, and a boarding force could rush over the plank. Originally each Roman ship had been assigned a permanent force of forty fighting men, drawn from the lowest class of citizens, to carry on the defensive duties normally handled by marines (p. 100). Now an additional eighty first-line troops from the legions were put aboard; their job was to charge the moment the "raven" landed.

About August, 260 B.C., the test came. The Carthaginian fleet, superbly built and trained, much like the great Athenian fleets of the fifth century except that it was made up of quinqueremes instead of triremes and its flag was carried on a huge "seven," anticipating a slaughter was out to provoke an encounter as quickly as possible. It swooped down on Mylae on the north shore of Sicily and started to ravage the coast. Caius Duilius, the Roman commander, took up the challenge: his clumsy galleys, the poles and planks of the ravens standing out grotesquely on the bows, crept around to Mylae. He had about 140 ships, slightly more than the enemy.

When the Carthaginian admiral sighted the Roman fleet wallowing along he confidently let his captains surge forward to attack on their own without bothering to form a proper line of battle. They sighted the queer rigs on the Roman prows and hesitated, but only momentarily. Each ship pressed forward swiftly but smoothly, moved in for a thrust of the ram—and, with a screeching of blocks as the tackles were loosed, the gangplanks came clattering down, the spikes thudded into the decking, and the Roman crews gasped and swore as they frantically backed water to keep the enemy from running on past and wrenching the ravens loose; seconds later, legionaries had spilled all over the Carthaginians' decks. When the two sides pulled clear, no less than thirty-one ships, including the "seven" that carried the flag, were in Roman hands.

The Carthaginians, stunned but far from beaten, immediately regrouped for a second attack. This time they took no chances: they formed up to carry out a coordinated maneuver, the deadly *diecplus* (p. 101). Giving the enemy's prows with their dangerous ravens a wide berth, they raced like greyhounds past the sluggish Roman craft to take them in the quarter and stern. But Duilius was no fool and, if he had had no personal experience, he had read the books. He had started with a slight advantage in numbers and now, after Carthage's disastrous first attempt, he held at least a three to two advantage. So he was able to draw off some units and hold them as a reserve in a second line, a standard defense against the *diecplus* (p. 101). When the Carthaginians attacked his main line in flank and rear, he gave the reserves the signal: they lumbered forward and dropped their ravens on the enemy's sterns. Carthage broke and ran. She had lost in all forty-four ships and ten thousand men. It was incredible: a rank amateur had climbed into the ring with the champion and knocked him out. In Rome one can see today a column erected to commemorate what happened, either the one actually set up at the time or a copy made a few centuries later. The monument is covered with carved anchors, and bristles with adornments in the shape of ships' prows. On the base the Romans proudly recorded that Duilius

> was the first Roman to perform exploits in ships at sea. He was the first to fit out and train ships and crews and, with these, he defeated in battle on the high seas all the Carthaginian ships and their mighty naval personnel, under the eyes of Hannibal, their commander in chief. By his strength he captured one "seven" and thirty quinqueremes and triremes along with their crews, and he sank thirteen. . . . He was also the first to bring the people booty from a sea battle and the first to lead free-born Carthaginians in a victory parade.

But the Romans were not the sort merely to sit back and gloat over their accomplishment. The Senate knew that the enemy was far from being down for the count, that one reason for the success had been the novelty of their new weapon, and that a second had been Duilius' superior numbers. They could do nothing about the novelty but they could do something about the other: from this time on they stuck to a consistent policy of outbuilding Carthage.

It took five years to reach the numbers required and train the crews; some small engagements in the meantime gave the men a taste of action. The fleet was brought up to 230 units, most of them quinqueremes. As it turned out, Carthage's maximum was only about 200 and Rome by and large was able to maintain at least this edge throughout most of the rest of the war.

Now that the navy was ready the Senate determined on a bold stroke. Why not have the fleet convoy a powerful expeditionary force to Africa, land it there, storm the enemy's home base and, as it were, cut the war off at its roots? In the summer of 256 B.C. an armada was launched. Carthage tried to intercept it off the promontory of Ecnomus, about midway on the south coast of Sicily, and suffered a major defeat. She was outnumbered once again (230 to 200), her commander bungled his tactics, and because there was little or no wind the seas were smooth, ideal for the Roman ravens. The expeditionary force landed safely.

But on their home grounds the Carthaginians fought like animals at bay. The Senate, fearing that it had bitten off more than it could chew, decided to evacuate the army. So, in the spring of 255 B.C., the grand fleet once again made its appearance off the African coast. Carthage, by frantic building during the winter, had repaired her losses; she dispatched 200 ships to Cape Hermaeum to attack. As usual she was outnumbered, 250 to 200, and this time her vessels and crews, having been hastily assembled, were below their accustomed standard. To make matters worse, the commander chose a fatally weak position, with his back to the shore. His men had no room in which to maneuver and the heavy Roman fleet, moving in ponderously with the ravens at the ready, thrust his ships implacably toward the beach. It was a shattering defeat: 114 of his craft were captured and 16 sunk. Carthage was now almost without a navy. It was her turn to need a miracle.

It came. As a matter of fact, considering Rome's inexperience on the sea, the wonder is that it hadn't happened earlier. As the victorious fleet sailed back home, its ranks swelled by 114 prizes, it ran into a gale off Camarina, a town near the southeastern tip of Sicily. When the skies cleared the shore was littered with wrecks. Only 80 ships limped into port; over 250 vessels and close to 100,000 men, trapped in the rowing chambers, had been lost. It was a staggering blow. Another was soon to follow: just two years later the Romans, having with dogged energy rebuilt the fleet, saw most of it go down in a storm off the south Italian coast.

Replacing the ships was not the big problem: there were plenty of trees, shipwrights, and dockyards. But replacing the crews was another matter. Men were growing scarce and those available were hardly eager to serve under admirals who knew so little about the sea that they couldn't tell when to come in out of the weather. The Senate had to give up all thought of cutting off the war rapidly by striking at Carthage's heart in Africa. There was only one thing left to do: gradually build up the fleet again until it could blockade the enemy's ports in western Sicily and starve them out. By 250 B.C. there were enough ships, and the army and navy were sent to strangle the key Carthaginian base at Lilybaeum.

But blockading a port, the Romans quickly found out, was a branch of naval science they also had to learn from the beginning. Carthage, too, had been active during the lull, constructing ships of a new model, even lighter and faster than those she had used before and yet just as seaworthy. They were ideal for blockade running and, manned by experienced crews, could sail even when the wind was strong. Picking the right time, blustery days that kept the blockaders shorebound, whole squadrons slipped in and out carrying quantities of supplies and men. The clumsy Roman craft didn't have a chance of overtaking them, much less of dropping a raven on their decks. If Rome was to win out, she had to scrap her present navy, ravens and all, and start again from scratch. The decision was made for her when, in 249 B.C., one of her admirals lost most of his fleet in a misguided attempt to attack one of Carthage's ports from the sea and, almost simultaneously, another lost his in a gale at the very point, Camarina, where the first storm disaster had taken place; a Carthaginian squadron had been in chase but the commander prudently pulled in and let the weather do the job for him. Rome was now down to twenty ships.

Sometime earlier a crack Carthaginian quadrireme, trying to get through the cordon around Lilybaeum, had gone aground. The Romans dragged it off, refitted it, and when Carthage's best blockade runner, the fastest quinquereme afloat and manned by a picked crew, tried to slip out, they gave chase in their new ship and caught it. Roman oarsmen by this time were just as good as the best Carthage had; all they needed were the ships. This prize was to serve as the model for a new fleet. It took time—fifteen years of war had taken their toll of men, materials, and money—but the time was available, for Carthage providentially had her hands full at the moment putting down revolts in her African empire. In 242 B.C. the new navy was finally ready, two hundred quinqueremes of the latest, fastest, most seaworthy type. Near the Aegates Islands, off the western tip of Sicily, the crucial battle took place on 10 March 241 B.C. A strong wind was blowing, the sort that fifteen years ago might have torn a Roman fleet apart or at least kept it from using the ravens. But the tables were now turned: the Romans had the better ships and crews and, as always, superior numbers (200 to 170). They attacked; fifty enemy ships were sunk and seventy taken with their crews.

The war was finally over. At the end of its twenty-three long years the roles were completely reversed: Carthage, the erstwhile naval power, went into the last round with old vessels and raw crews; Rome, the nation of lubbers, ended with a navy of two hundred of the finest ships afloat, manned by veterans.

Between 218 and 201 B.C. the two powers fought another bloody war. But it was of a totally different character, one which, because of Rome's virtually uncontested control of the western Mediterranean, was waged on land; there were no great sea battles in the Second Punic War. Everyone knows the story of how Hannibal, Carthage's most famous son, led a great army, elephants and all, overland from Spain to Italy, crossing the Alps when snow already blocked the passes. He didn't do it that way because he wanted to end up in the history books but simply because the water route, the natural way of transporting an army from Spain to Italy, was closed to him. His military genius enabled him to range over the Italian Peninsula destroying Roman army after Roman army; without a fleet to win control of the seas he could neither reinforce his troops nor get supplies for them. He could ravage the farms of Italy, but merchantmen brought in all the grain Rome needed from Sicily and Sardinia, once from as far off as Egypt. Rome even learned to organize her control of the seas by setting up naval stations with permanent squadrons in Spain, Sicily, and the Adriatic. Sea power and his opponent's bulldog trait of never giving up ultimately wore Hannibal down. He shipped the remnants of his troops out of Italy back to Africa; Rome ferried a mighty army of her own there and, in 202 B.C., ended Carthage's days as a great nation.

In 201 B.C. the nation that sixty years earlier had no fleet of her own was the greatest sea power in the Mediterranean. There were two hundred galleys in her slips, all of them quinqueremes, more than double the size of any other navy afloat. A century later she was still the greatest power in the Mediterranean—but she had hardly a ship to her name. The Romans were a gifted people who, when hard necessity pushed them, were able to master the sea. But salt water was not to their taste and, as soon as they could, they gave it up.

It was in 201 B.C. that the envoys from Rhodes and her neighbor on the Asia Minor coast, Pergamum, arrived to speak to the Roman Senate (p. 156). The grandson of Antigonus Gonatas, Philip, King of Macedon, was out to win back his ancestors' position in the eastern Mediterranean. But Rhodes stood in his way. So he stirred up the pirates from that eternal breeding ground of piracy, Crete, to prey on the island's commerce, sent an agent to sabotage Rhodes' fleet (he managed to set a fire in the navy yard which destroyed thirteen triremes), and readied a navy of his own, a formidable one with more than fifty major units, most of which were at least quinqueremes and a number were heavier—"sixes," "sevens," "eights," "nines," even a "ten." To all this Philip added something new in naval tactics, the use of squadrons of the small, extremely fast, single-banked vessels called *lembi* that the Illyrians, his neighbors on the Jugoslav coast, used so successfully for piracy and plundering; like modern torpedo boats their job was to race in close to the enemy's heavy galleys and disable them by damaging whatever they could get at, particularly the oars. In two battles near Chios off the Asia Minor coast, Rhodes' home waters as it were, Philip held his own against her forces and Pergamum's combined. This was serious; it looked as if the balance of power that the island had worked so hard to maintain was on the point of being shattered. Rhodes invited the dominant power of the western waters to take a hand in the east.

A short time before the first war with Carthage, the Romans had gone through a savage struggle with one of the Greek kings of the east who, looking for a new world to conquer, invaded Italy and fought his way to within fifty miles of their capital. He was ultimately driven off, but the memory was bitter and the Romans thereafter viewed the moves of the Greek monarchs of the east with a suspicious eye. Against Philip they had a special score to settle: during the second war with Carthage, when their fortunes were at low ebb, he had jumped in to take advantage of the situation—he had his own suspicions of Rome's intentions—and to conclude a treaty with Hannibal; it looked for a while as if he was going to open up a second front, but Rome, by sending a squadron to the

Adriatic and by embroiling him with hostile neighbors, managed to keep him at home. The offer brought by Rhodes and Pergamum now provided an opportunity to square accounts, and the Senate grabbed at it. When it came to sending out the grand fleet, however, they held back. Of the two hundred galleys available, only fifty were dispatched. Why use more when there were the crack fleets of her new allies, Rhodes and Pergamum, to depend on? The Romans, after one of the most spectacular achievements in the history of naval warfare, at this point took their first step backward, a return to the old system of relying on the forces of nautically minded allies.

The move hardly affected the war she was to fight now. Her squadron of fifty, matched by twenty from Rhodes and twenty-four from Pergamum, not only bottled Philip's fleet up for the duration of the war but provided convoys for the steady ferrying of men and supplies to Greece. The enemy never had a chance on the sea, and the issue was decided on land. In 197 B.C. Philip gave in; Rome became an acknowledged participant in the affairs of the east.

Almost without taking a breather she rushed right into another war, this time with Antiochus III, king of Syria, a descendant of Alexander's cavalry officer, Seleucus. During the years that Macedon and Egypt had been dueling for the control of the eastern Mediterranean (pp. 149-50), the rulers of Syria by and large refrained from mixing in; they had troubles of their own to keep them busy in the interior of their vast empire. But Antiochus had other ideas and, when he started to build up a navy, his neighbors, Rhodes and Pergamum, grew uneasy; then, when he welcomed Hannibal, that *bête noire* of the Romans, to his court, the Senate joined in the feeling. The year 192 B.C. found the three allies once again lined up, this time to combat Antiochus.

And this time there was more for the naval arm to do than just slog along convoying supply ships and transports. Antiochus had no mean fleet and it was commanded by a skilled admiral, Polyxenidas, a Rhodian who, after learning his trade in that best of academies, the island's naval service, had for some reason been exiled. The allies had to remove this obstacle before they could safely ferry an army into Asia Minor to strike the king at home. Eight years ago, against Philip, Rome had supplied half the naval forces; this time she furnished even less: of the 160-odd ships required to beat Polyxenidas, only about seventy-five were Roman.

The first round took place in the summer of 191 B.C. off Cissus, a port on the west coast of Asia Minor just northwest of Ephesus, and it went to Rome. She had 105 major units in action, most of them quinqueremes, and Polyxenidas could match this with only seventy triremes; he had some 130 light craft of various types but apparently they weren't of much help. He locked himself up in the harbor of Ephesus and reported to the king that he needed more and heavier vessels. When he reappeared the following year it was with two fleets, both of them among the heaviest to appear in the Mediterranean in half a century. In Ephesus he had an aggregation of ninety units; over half were bigger than triremes and there were two "sevens" and three "sixes." And coming up from the ports of Phoenicia, which Antiochus controlled at this time, was another of fifty units, including three more "sevens" and four "sixes," under the command of the redoubtable Hannibal. If the two ever joined they would outweigh and outnumber the whole allied force. The crucial job of preventing this was turned over to Rhodes.

Every ship that the island had available was mustered. It wasn't much, thirty-two quadriremes and four triremes; but the officers and men were the cream of the service and the commander, Eudamus, was a skilled and astute veteran. Word reached him that Hannibal and his ships, having worked their way up the Syrian coast, were slogging westward under Asia Minor in the teeth of the prevailing northwesterlies. This gave him plenty of time to pick a point of his own choosing at which to intercept. Sometime in July or August of 190 B.C. the two drew near each other, off the town of Side on the Gulf of Adalia in southern Asia Minor.

Eudamus had a reputation for caution but this was one time when he had to take chances: if the fleets formed up facing each other in two long lines as was usual, the enemy with his superior numbers would outflank him. Hannibal, aware of that, had already drawn up his line. Eudamus took a deep breath, led his column out from shore, and suddenly, before the rest of his ships had time to set themselves fully in line behind him, darted ahead with a part of his force to engage the enemy's seaward wing, where Hannibal himself was stationed. It was a gamble designed to attract Hannibal's main attention until Eudamus could get one telling blow in somehow and even up the odds a bit. He was relying on the speed and skill of his crews and the initiative of his subordinates, and they didn't fail him. His rearmost ships, without taking time to line up formally, in a split-second maneuver swung into a *diecplus* aimed at the enemy's shoreward wing. It was executed perfectly: when they regrouped after the attack every vessel that had faced them was disabled; one Rhodian quadrireme had even single-handed knocked out a "seven." Then, in a spectacular burst of speed—among the larger units there was nothing faster than a quadrireme—they raced to seaward to help out their commander who naturally was having heavy going. Hannibal signaled the retreat; none of his ships had been sunk but over half had been put out of action. He threw over towlines to them and crept off. Eudamus took only one prize, the "seven" that had been knocked out in the first assault, but he had achieved his objective, had kept the enemy's two contingents from joining hands. It was a magnificent victory, reminiscent of the great actions fought by the Athenians in the Peloponnesian War (pp. 103-4): Antiochus, thinking to take a leaf from the Romans' book, had gone in for heavier ships, and the Rhodians had shown that light vessels and trained crews could not only beat them but give them odds to boot. Eudamus turned to join the allied fleet off Ephesus, convinced his troubles were over. He was wrong; there was one serious one left.

When the Romans took to the sea in the First Punic War they had had to put in command men who knew nothing about the water. The hair-raising losses suffered in storms forced them to work out some sort of system, and thereafter the squadrons were more or less kept in the hands of competent if not brilliant commanders. But in the war against Antiochus, the naval amateur made his appearance again and with a vengeance: even in Rome's well-filled gallery of bone-headed admirals there was none to match Lucius Aemilius Regillus, the man who in the spring of 190 B.C. had been entrusted with the fleet and now commanded the forces blockading the harbor of Ephesus. Before departing to take over his duties he had been told that the prime naval objective was to keep the Strait of the Dardanelles open so that the Roman army, marching around from Greece, could cross unmolested into Asia Minor and attack Antiochus on his home grounds. So long as Hannibal's force was licking its wounds somewhere on the south coast of Asia Minor and Polyxenidas' was securely bottled up in Ephesus, this objective was automatically attained; anyone with any sense could see this, Eudamus for example, or Polyxenidas himself, much to his dismay. Moreover the Romans already had a squadron posted at the strait. But Regillus had no sense. He was jittery: his place, he felt, was at the Dardanelles—even though it was still summer and the army, wearily tramping through Thrace, would not make its appearance until November. And he would actually have led the fleet up there, neatly uncorking Polyxenidas, had not Eudamus talked him out of it; the Rhodian had just risked his life and his nation's whole navy to win a victory against heavy odds and he wasn't going to stand by and watch all his hard-earned results go to waste. But he had to pay a price: Regillus agreed to stay put, but only on condition that twenty-three ships be detached and sent up north to reinforce the squadron there. There was nothing Eudamus could do about it; but he must have sworn some lurid Rhodian oaths since, by this move, Regillus was handing over superiority in numbers to the enemy on a silver platter.

To Polyxenidas it was like being proffered a reprieve when the noose was already around his neck. Sooner or later he would have had to send his fleet out of the harbor in a desperate move to win back the seas and block the crossing of the Roman army; now he could do it with the odds in his favor. Sometime in September he led his ships out, eighty-nine units against the allies' eighty, and drew them up in a long line off Cape Myonnesus to fight it out.

Regillus, having made the enemy a gift of the advantage in numbers, almost handed him the battle as well. He took his place at the head of the allied line—and ordered the Rhodian squadron to the rear to ride herd on stragglers. Luckily Eudamus was ready to disobey orders sooner than lose a fight. Knowing that Regillus was bound to get into trouble, he held his squadron of twenty-two quadriremes at the ready; on some of them he ran out the fire pots which had proved their effectiveness earlier in the year (p. 152). Just as he anticipated, Polyxenidas with his superior numbers began to crumple up Regillus' seaward wing. At precisely the right moment, Eudamus sent his ships racing from the rear to the rescue. The enemy vessels turned away from the fire pots, the Rhodian rams caught them in the sides, and the battle was won. Polyxenidas crept back into Ephesus and his fleet was still there when the war was decided in a great land battle the following year.

The nation which, seventy-five years before, had hardly a ship to her name now ruled the Mediterranean from the Strait of Gibraltar to the coast of Syria. She treated it like an unwanted child. She pulled her fleet out of the eastern waters and left them to Rhodes and Pergamum; in the west, where there were no maritime allies to shoulder the burden for her, she resuscitated the plan of two miniature squadrons of ten ships apiece that she had used over one hundred years earlier (p. 158). When, in 171 B.C., Rome had to wage a second war with Macedon, against Philip's son Perseus, she fitted out just fifty quinqueremes and relied chiefly on Rhodes and Pergamum, whom she had bound by treaty to furnish naval forces. Perseus, with nothing more than a catch-as-catch-can aggregation of pirate craft, was able to wreak havoc with her lines of supply. In a brief third war with Carthage in 146 B.C., fifty ships, most of them probably old, turned up again. By the end of the century her naval position seemed so secure that she shucked off even most of these.

But for Rhodes it was the end of an era. She had called in Rome to counter first the threat of Philip, then that of Antiochus. Both kings had lost their navies and there was now no one left to challenge her on the sea. Rome had even rewarded her with some territory on the Asia Minor mainland to administer. But for all that, she had lost the game. She had called in Rome for the same reason that she had built up a superb fleet, to maintain her proud independence—and that was lost, as she was very soon to find out. When it came, the blow was launched not at her navy but at her merchant marine. To understand it we must turn to the story of what was happening to trade on the sea in this age.

12 — East Meets West

IN THE BERLIN MUSEUM's voluminous collection of papyri from Egypt there used to be one scrappy piece whose battered lines of writing are the remains of a contract which was drawn up in Alexandria some time around 150 B.C. One party to the contract was a group of five merchants who were planning a trip down the Red Sea to the "incense lands," as Egyptian traders had been doing for millennia (pp. 9-13). Like most ancient shippers they were working with borrowed capital (p. 114): the party of the second part was a Greek who was putting up some of the money. The five partners too were Greek; one, as it happened, was from Sparta and a second from far-off Marseilles. Five other men endorsed to guarantee repayment; one of these was a Carthaginian, the other four soldiers stationed in Alexandria who may have had some of their spare cash invested in the venture. The funds were handled through a banker. He was a Roman.

The document is almost unique; not more than two or three others like it are in existence. But more than that, it offers a picture in miniature of the key characteristics of trade in the Hellenistic world, the wide-flung world, run by Greeks, that Alexander opened and that lasted until the first century B.C. when Rome finally swallowed it. Its commerce was international in scope and, as a consequence, its business relations were complex and its business methods highly developed; to the age-old exchange of commodities that the Mediterranean had always known it added a lucrative trade in exotic luxuries; and, during it all, Egypt managed to play a major role.

Big cargoes require roomy ships and harbors, and far-flung trade routes a knowledge of geography and navigation. The Hellenistic world met the challenge: its progress in the peaceful arts of the sea matched what it had accomplished in naval warfare (Chapter 10). The average merchantman now carried at least two hundred to three hundred tons of cargo, and many were larger. There is a description preserved of one leviathan which could hold as many as 1,600 tons—so big, in fact, that only a few ports, such as Athens' Peiraeus or Rhodes, had the facilities to handle it. In a bravura display of technical skill the shipwrights of Alexandria turned out an elephantine houseboat, a barge upon which a whole sumptuous villa was mounted, to enable King Ptolemy IV to ride the Nile in appropriate style. Bigger ships meant bigger rigging. It was probably at this time that the distinctive sail of the ancient world known as the artemon (cf. p. 146), the bowspritsail, was designed (not to add speed so much as to make the steering of the larger vessels easier), and that three-masters were first built, ships with artemon, main, and mizzen. The only superimposed sail that the ancients ever used was a triangular topsail set above the main; the earliest example does not appear until later under the Roman Empire (cf. Pl. 12), but it was very likely invented in the Hellenistic period. It is a misfortune that, like the warships (p. 145), not one picture of the merchantmen of this age has been preserved, and all the naval historian has to go on are vague clues scattered here and there in miscellaneous writings.

Good harbors were needed to handle the increased volume of trade and the bigger ships. Few Greek city-states with their limited resources could carry out such projects, but the Hellenistic rulers had adequate funds at their disposal. They improved their ports by building huge breakwaters to create capacious anchorages, setting

East Meets West

up lines of warehouses for storage, and replacing the sand beaches that had served the smaller ships of an earlier day with stone quays. Of the seven wonders of the ancient world two, the colossus of Rhodes and the lighthouse at Alexandria, adorned harbors of this age.

Skippers had at their disposal new improved charts and up-to-date "coast pilots," the result of spectacular progress in scientific geography. Eratosthenes, the great mathematician-astronomer-geographer, calculated the circumference of the earth and arrived at a figure that came within two hundred miles of the true one; he pointed out that all the oceans were one, and concluded that a ship could eventually reach India by sailing westward from Spain—thereby influencing the thoughts of an imaginative Genoese lad who came across an echo of his words some seventeen centuries later. Maps of the known world were constructed with parallels of latitude and meridians of longitude; in the best-known areas, for example, the parallel that ran from Gibraltar through Rhodes, they were remarkably accurate. And the only ancient navigational instrument known to us belongs to these times (p. 189).

In the third century B.C. Egypt played the leading role in commerce that Athens had in the one previous. Like her predecessor she had the products to export, controlled the major trade routes, and maintained a powerful navy to police them. She had one great additional advantage: her rulers at the time, the first three Ptolemies, were among the shrewdest and most efficient businessmen known to history.

What they were after was simple: export as much and import as little as possible, and keep the profits for themselves. They achieved it by a remarkable system of taxation, monopolies, and tariffs. The basic commodity of the ancient world was grain. Egypt had always produced and exported huge quantities. The Ptolemies reorganized her agriculture to yield the absolute maximum, taxed it so that the peasant was left with just enough of his harvest to live on, put the rest in the royal silos at Alexandria, and, exporting it all over the eastern Mediterranean, pocketed the proceeds. This didn't cut into the sales of other producers, such as Sicily and south Russia, but simply made available larger quantities of grain; it was the basis of the ancients' diet and there was always a seller's market in it. When the king of Syracuse, for example, launched a huge grain carrier (the 1,600-tonner mentioned above) and then discovered that it was too large to enter the harbors he shipped to, he willingly gave it to Ptolemy III. Next in importance to grain in the international market were olive oil and wine. Neither of these was produced in any quantity in Egypt: the people traditionally washed and cooked with vegetable- and seed-oil, and drank beer. The Ptolemies saw to it that they continued to do so by levying a tariff of 50 per cent on imported olive oil and $33\frac{1}{3}$ per cent on imported wines, and turned brewing and the manufacture of oil into government monopolies. The ancient world's writing paper was either papyrus or parchment; papyrus was cheaper, practically all of it came from Egypt, and its manufacture and sale belonged to the crown. So too did the textile industry which, using locally grown flax, produced for export not only fine fabrics but very likely much of the linen that went into sailcloth. It was from such sources as these that the income came which enabled the first Ptolemies to build their capital into a magnificent showplace and an intellectual center, and the later to indulge their taste for such extravagances as floating villas. When ancient writers tried to describe the family's wealth they couldn't find terms lavish enough—and no wonder.

Egypt's trade was not completely a one-way affair. There were certain things she had to import, but even here the Ptolemies were in luck, for territories under their control produced most of what was needed. Timber for the navy came from the pine forests of southern Asia Minor and the cedars of Lebanon. Pitch had to be bought; although one possible source, Macedon, was out of the question for political reasons, the kings of Pergamum who controlled the rich producing area around Troy were friendly. Cyprus was an Egyptian possession, and its prolific mines supplied all the copper needed. Tin and iron had to be imported, the first very likely from Carthage (cf. p. 72), the second from the southeast shore of the Black Sea and possibly from central Italy. There was a brisk traffic in delicacies for the gourmet tastes of the wealthy Greeks of Egypt: honey from Athens, cheese from the Aegean Islands, nuts from the south shore of the Black Sea, figs from Asia Minor. This class of course wouldn't condescend to drink the peasants' beer, and insisted on the fine wines of Syria and of western Asia Minor and its offshore islands. They paid the heavy tariff with no more reluctance than the American who today buys French champagne. What they imported, however, was strictly for their own tables; if they tried to sell any it was subject to confiscation.

To make sure that nothing was smuggled in or out, the Ptolemies rigidly regulated their harbors. Ships had to have permission to enter, were assigned berths, had their cargoes checked item by item against cargo manifests, took on a return load under equally careful supervision, and left only after receiving clearance from the harbor master. An example of a cargo manifest has actually been preserved. Apollonius, Minister of Finance, Commerce and Industry under King Ptolemy II around 250 B.C., had as secretary a certain Zenon who was the sort that never threw away any papers. By great good luck part of his voluminous files were discovered, preserved from decay by Egypt's perennially dry climate (cf. p. 46). One of the documents recovered happens to be the manifest of two small coasting vessels that had loaded up at some Syrian port to discharge at Alexandria. They were carrying a cargo of expensive delicacies clearly intended for the tables of the rich, perhaps even for Apollonius himself, for the items included

table wine	63 jars [probably holding 7 gals. each]
	2 half-jars
dessert wine	10 half-jars
olive oil	2 jars, 1 half-jar
vinegar	2 jars
honey	7 half-jars
dried figs	10 jars
nuts	1 jar, 3 baskets [= 2½ bushels]
seeds	1 basket
cheese	1 jar
wild boar meat	10 jars
venison	2 jars
goat meat	2 jars
rough sponges	1 basket
soft sponges	1 basket

The Mediterranean had from very early times maintained some commercial relations with India and Arabia and Ethiopia (pp. 5-9), but the great period of such trade dates from this time. Around the middle of the fourth century B.C. Theophrastus, the famous Athenian botanist, knew pepper, which came from India, only as a medicinal drug; three centuries later a rich Athenian had so much he could give away four quarts. The new wealthy class—the great kings, the commanders of their armies or powerful bureaucrats in their administrations, the prosperous merchants and bankers and shippers—wanted and could afford exotic luxuries. During the third century B.C. much of the traffic in them passed through the hands of the Ptolemies and their agents.

From Yemen and the Hadramaut in south Arabia came perfumes and the myrrh and frankincense that smoked daily on thousands of altars all over the Mediterranean world; from Somaliland and Ethiopia, incense and ivory. Most of such imports traveled by caravan through Arabia and either discharged at Gaza and Alexandria or continued farther north to the Phoenician ports; Egypt controlled all these terminal points. Some went by ship up the Red Sea and thence to Alexandria, either through the canal at the head of the Red Sea or, unloading at the ports on its west coast, by caravan across Egypt's eastern desert to the Nile and then downriver. This commerce was as old as the pharaohs (pp. 9-13), but the Ptolemies gave it their characteristic efficient organization. They improved the caravan tracks across the eastern desert, set up new harbors on the west coast of the Red Sea, and stationed a flotilla to hold down the pirates who haunted that body of water then and are still a problem there today. Until it reached the Mediterranean ports the traffic was almost wholly in the hands of Arab sailors and caravaneers, in particular the Nabataeans whose capital at Petra, located near a nexus of caravan routes, embarked on its prosperous commercial career at this time. Only at the terminals did it pass to Egyptians or Syrians or Phoenicians. This created no conflict. None of the merchants of the ports were interested in camel driving, and they were perfectly willing to let Arab mariners struggle with the shoals, foul winds, and sizzling temperatures of the Red Sea.

From India came such luxuries as pearls, gems, tortoise shell, perhaps even silk shipped there from China. But the big trade was in the plants, bark, and wood from which cosmetics and spices were made—spikenard, nard, cinnamon, ginger, and above all pepper, which swiftly became a standard entry in ancient recipes; in a world of hot temperatures and no refrigeration, a strong seasoning unquestionably came in handy. There were a number of ways of getting these exports to the Mediterranean. One, the overland caravan route, ran through northwest India and Afghanistan and Iran to Seleuceia, the new capital the Seleucids had founded northeast of Babylon, near modern Baghdad. From here it followed the tracks along the Tigris and Euphrates rivers to northern Mesopotamia, where it split in three directions, either south to end up at the Phoenician ports of Tyre and Sidon, or west to Antioch, or on through lower Asia Minor, reaching the sea at Ephesus. A second route, in use for millennia (p. 8), combined sea and land: ships loaded at India's northwest ports, coasted westward, and turned up the Persian Gulf to discharge at its head; from there camels took the merchandise to Seleuceia where it merged with what came by way of the overland route. A third was all by water but it involved a wearisome voyage through pirate-infested seas, and the Ptolemies weren't overly enthusiastic about it so long as they had their share in the alternative caravan routes. It skirted the west coast of India, crossed the entrance of the Persian Gulf, and proceeded along the south shore of Arabia to the mouth of the Red Sea. From there it followed the track of Arabian and African goods to Alexandria. Indian and Arab sailors carried the cargoes as far as the Red Sea but only Arabs from that point on; they considered this body of water their private preserve and let no outsiders in. The Ptolemies had a stranglehold on this phase of commerce too: all Indian, Arabian, and African goods that entered Alexandria had to be sold to them and, if it was raw material, was processed in government-owned workshops. In some of these, the incense factories for example, workers were stripped naked on leaving to make sure they departed with nothing more valuable than their skins. The Ptolemies left little to chance.

The large-scale and varied activity of Alexandria's waterfront, from the stevedoring of cheap bulky cargoes of grain to the delicate handling of expensive shipments of spices and incense, demanded the best in harbor facilities; the Ptolemies created there the finest port of the Mediterranean. Breakwaters strengthened and extended the arms of a natural lagoon and the whole expanse was split into two harbors, an eastern and a western, by a huge mole, three-quarters of a mile long. It led at its seaward end to the island of Pharos on which the architect Sostratus, at the command of Ptolemy I or II, built the famous lighthouse. This was a massive square tower on top of which eight columns, arranged in an octagon, framed a blazing fire; their roof supported a huge statue, probably of Ptolemy I, which brought the whole structure up to the impressive height of four hundred feet. It quickly came to symbolize the city, as high monuments have a way of doing, and tourists brought back souvenirs adorned with its picture as enthusiastically as today's visitors to Paris collect gimcracks showing the Eiffel Tower. As time passed, its influence spread: it was hailed as one of the seven wonders, Roman architects modeled their major lighthouses on it, and it very likely had some effect on the form of Arab minarets. It stood nearer the eastern division of the harbor, which was the more important: here the waterfront was ringed by the fine gardens that surrounded the royal residences, museum, and library, as well as by rows of warehouses and dockyards. The western harbor was for smaller craft, and channels leading out from it enabled them to sail through from the Mediterranean to the Nile.

Three hundred and twenty-five miles north of Alexandria lay another great port which, in the first half of the Hellenistic period, moved into a position of wealth and commercial importance, partly by riding Egypt's coattails. Rhodes had a fine geographical position near the center of the eastern Mediterranean's trade routes, a large merchant marine, a powerful navy to protect it, and a business-minded aristocracy with ample capital at its disposal. Most of the thousands of bushels of grain that the Ptolemies shipped out yearly, as well as much of their other exports, left Egypt in Rhodian bottoms and proceeded to Rhodes for transshipment to the ultimate destinations. But Rhodes' commercial relations were limited neither to Egypt nor to freight charters. She had two other sources of profit: banking and the wine trade. The island was one vast vineyard which produced lavish quantities of cheap wine. This was shipped out in large, distinctively shaped jars, and archaeologists have found remains of literally hundreds of thousands of these containers in ancient sites from the shores of the Black Sea to the coasts of Spain. They turn up in quantity, as one would expect, in Egypt and the Aegean isles. But many have been found in south Russia; Rhodian ships must have been busy in that area, ferrying in wine in exchange for return cargoes of grain to be distributed to the Greek world (cf. p. 113). Wherever Rhodian cargoes went, Rhodian bankers followed; when, for example, an Arab sheikh of what is today Algeria decided to try to enter the international market with some of his surplus grain, he worked through a Rhodian banker. Nothing shows more clearly how crucial a role the island played in the international economic scene than what happened when, in 226 B.C., a disastrous earthquake hit her. All the great powers and some of the smaller rushed in handsome grants of aid. Ptolemy IV, in particular, sent thirty thousand tons of grain, the second largest single shipment recorded in antiquity—Rhodes was, after all, one of his best customers. The island collected an annual return of one million drachmas from the 2 per cent tax on all merchandise that went in and out of her harbor (cf. p. 111), five times what Athens had netted from the same source two hundred years earlier. It is no surprise that the first organized code of maritime law, one that contained some of the seeds from which our present law of the sea has grown, was laid down and codified by the Rhodians.

Three characteristics in particular marked the island's way of doing business: efficiency, fair dealing—and Rhodes for the Rhodians. Athens had been forced to depend heavily on foreigners (p. 120); she had had the capital to invest, but few citizens interested in the shipping trade. Rhodes had both. The foreigners to be found there were chiefly Phoenicians and Greeks from Asia Minor and Egypt, men whose presence business required. None were granted full citizenship. The citizens made the profits and with them maintained their superb navy, constructed a port that was a model of efficiency, and adorned their city with imposing public buildings and expensive works of art, among them (until the earthquake toppled it) the famous colossus that was one of the seven wonders of the world, a huge statue of the sun god set on the seaward end of an arm of the harbor.

Rhodes and Alexandria were in a class by themselves. Together they handled a vast trade in grain which no other port could match, and to this they were able to add a share of the lucrative transit trade in caravan goods. This was the icing on their cake of commerce: it gave extra work to sailors and longshoremen, opened new sources of profit for bankers and brokers, and, through the standard fee of 2 per cent on harbor traffic, helped fill the public treasury. But the two were merely the greatest among a dozen rich and active Mediterranean entrepôts. Ephesus shipped out fine Asia Minor wines, Sidon expensive glassware, Tyre her traditional purple-dyed fabrics, and all three at the same time served as terminals for the caravans from India and Arabia. Others, too, had their share of this traffic, Gaza, Beirut, Seleuceia the port of Antioch. Athens fell behind in this age because, although she still did a brisk business in exporting olive oil and importing grain, the transit trade largely bypassed her: to reach her, ships from most of the caravan ports had to detour to the north and buck the Etesian winds (p. 115) in the process. Far off in the western sector of the Mediterranean, Carthage was still going strong on transit trade, the forwarding of British tin and Spanish minerals to customers all over the Mediterranean (p. 72).

By 150 B.C. or a little later Rhodes' trade had been given a bruising blow, Egypt was almost shut out of the traffic in caravan goods, and Carthage lay in ashes. A new character had come upon the stage, and her entrance changed the commercial *mise en scène* as much as the political: Rome became not only the east's acknowledged master, but its best customer as well.

It wasn't Egyptian grain or Greek olive oil or Asia Minor wines the newcomer bought; she exported such products herself, and the trade in these commodities in the eastern Mediterranean went on much as before. The powerful senatorial families who ran Rome and her conquered territories at this time were now rich men, living on vast estates and able to afford whatever luxuries were available. They wanted two things above all else: slaves to run their plantations, and art and exotic wares to add grace to their way of life. The east was ready to supply both, and the business-minded Greeks of south Italy (cf. pp. 79, 158) were ready to step in and act as middlemen. The flow of goods from India and Arabia, which had been steadily growing since the Hellenistic period opened, now swelled to a flood and channeled itself toward Italy. Rome's unceasing wars, first with Carthage and then with the Greek powers of the east (Chapter 11), had thrown thousands of prisoners on the slave markets; the movement of this commodity, too, now turned toward the west and when, with the end of hostilities, the supply started to run low, pirates stepped in to replenish it. And Athens got a new lease on commercial life by mass-producing works of art for the Roman market, both originals as well as copies of old masters; some of the ancient statuary in museums today was turned out in her workshops at this time. Luxuries and art and slaves for Rome were the outstanding ingredients of trade in the second half of the Hellenistic age. But neither Rhodes nor Alexandria played the leading roles they had earlier.

Rhodes was a proud nation run by an exclusive group of aristocrats who found it hard to flatter the new ruling power and followed as independent a line as possible. In 167 B.C. the Romans brought her sharply to heel by hitting her where she was most vulnerable.

In the middle of the Aegean lies the tiny island of Delos. Despite its size, it was from earliest times important as the site of a sanctuary of Apollo where a great yearly festival took place. During the first part of the Hellenistic age the island was independent and in a small way started to develop some sidelines to its annual pilgrim trade. Rhodes in particular used it as a distribution point for grain shipments to nearby islands and as a branch banking center. Delos was the instrument the Romans used to teach Rhodes a lesson. In 167 they handed it over to their faithful ally, Athens—with the stipulation that it was to be a free port, that no harbor or customs dues were to be collected there.

Within a year harbor receipts at Rhodes plummeted from 1,000,000 drachmas to 150,000. The island did not go bankrupt. It still had its merchant marine and there was still money to be made hauling Egyptian and south Russian grain, and selling wine. But her harbor revenue was now limited to the big ships carrying bulky cargoes of grain and wine, which found it convenient to use her capacious port; the trade in slaves and caravan goods went to the free port of Delos. Funds were no longer available to maintain the fleet and its vital anti-pirate patrols, a turn of events that quickly proved disastrous for international commerce; probably the Rhodians got some belated satisfaction when the Romans eventually turned out to be the chief sufferers (p. 201).

By about 130 B.C. Delos hit her stride. The harbor was far from large, and poorly protected, much inferior to Rhodes' or to any number of others nearby, but that hardly mattered. Slave ships were built to put in anywhere, and small freighters could carry a fortune in spices and perfumes. French archaeologists have completely excavated the island and they have discovered that its long lines of warehouses were connected only with the quays, not with the town behind—striking evidence that Delos' trade was strictly transient: the merchandise moved in, unloaded, reloaded, and moved out. The slave market could handle thousands daily, and business was so good that the locals had a saying: "Merchant, sail in and unload! Everything's as good as sold."

There was more than merely the free port to bring the trade in luxuries and slaves to Delos. Rhodes prided itself on fair dealing, was ruthless with pirates, and maintained a standoffish attitude toward foreigners. Delos was frankly devoted to making money. Sharp south Italian dealers, wily near-Eastern traders, and raffish pirate slavers found its realistic commercial atmosphere and its society, where money gave entrée to the best circles, far more to their taste than that of the stiff-necked city which had created an effective sea police and laid down the world's first maritime code. It was the difference between doing business in Tangiers, say, as against London.

Like filings to a magnet there flocked to the island Greeks from Asia Minor and Alexandria, Phoenicians, Syrians, Jews, even far-distant Arabs—Nabataeans from Petra, Minaeans and Sabaeans from Yemen and the Hadramaut, the land of Saba (or Sheba as the Bible calls it). To meet them came Rome's middlemen, the south Italians, who soon formed the largest group on Delos. All brought their gods with them, as foreigners always do, and archaeologists have uncovered shrines or statues of Asia Minor's Cybele, Syria's Hadad and Atargatis, Phoenicia's Melqart; Apollo was sharing his sacred island with some curious colleagues. Inscriptions have been found in Latin and Greek and Semitic characters; the port must have heard a babble of tongues. The various groups formed associations—"Merchants and Shipowners of Tyre," "Italian Oil Dealers," "Merchants, Shipowners and Warehousemen of Beirut"—primarily for religious and social reasons but, just as many a deal today is consummated at the bar of a golf club, they served business purposes as well. They actually became the government after a time: when Rome made the island a free port she gave it to Athens to administer; three decades or so later a coalition of these associations governed the island.

From the great terminals at the end of the caravan routes merchants brought to Delos their precious wares and from everywhere, but particularly from Syria and Asia Minor, slavers their pathetic cargoes. The lion's share was turned over to the South Italians who paid for it partly in Italian wine and olive oil but mostly in cash, and forwarded it to Puteoli, Pozzuoli today, the port of Naples. In the background were local shippers, wholesalers, shopkeepers, and the like, who were needed to supply with all the necessities of life a motley population of twenty thousand to thirty thousand souls packed in an area a little over one square mile in extent. It was only in this traffic in goods for home consumption that Rhodes now played any part: she sold the island grain and wine. Egypt narrowly avoided being squeezed out completely.

Ever since the end of the third century B.C. Egypt had been in a decline. The complex administrative machinery so painstakingly built up by the first Ptolemies began to run down. Macedon broke their command of the sea (p. 150), and Rhodes and Pergamum now shared the waters they once had ruled. More important, Egypt lost many of her extraterritorial possessions. The worst blow came when, in 198 B.C., the Seleucids took away Syria and Phoenicia through which so much of the caravan traffic passed. She was reduced to what came by the Indian Ocean and the Red Sea, and competition from the alternative caravan routes, strenuously encouraged by her rivals, bit deeply into this. Help was needed; it came in an unexpected way.

The sea voyage between India and Egypt is actually relatively easy because of the phenomenon of India's monsoons. From May to September the winds blow steadily from the southwest. A skipper can leave the mouth of the Red Sea, stand off the south coast of Arabia, and then strike boldly across open water, and the southwest monsoon, coming steadily over the starboard quarter, nearly astern, will carry him directly to India. By delaying his return until any time between November and March, when the monsoon shifts to exactly the reverse direction, the northeast, he can make the voyage back just as easily. The Indians, who used sturdy seagoing craft, must have made full use of these winds, but the Arabs only in part, since their boats were too light. Arab shipwrights used to fasten the planks of a hull by stitching them to each other with coconut fiber, instead of pinning them firmly to ribs; they did it at first probably because iron for nails was scarce, but, with the seaman's usual conservatism, they clung to the tradition long after, up to the fifteenth century as a matter of fact, even though it meant as much bailing as sailing for the crews in any sort of weather. Such craft could travel westward before the northeast monsoon without any trouble since it is fairly moderate, but the blustery southwest monsoon kicks up a considerable sea and Arab skippers must have stuck close to shore during the eastward voyage or squeezed both legs into the season of the northeast monsoon, as they did in the Middle Ages and still do today. In any event, both Indians and Arabs cooperated in keeping what they knew about the behavior of these winds strictly to themselves, since neither was minded to divulge trade secrets to possible competitors. The Arabs, moreover, went on the assumption that any strangers in the area were fair game for attack.

The merchants of Egypt were familiar with the long coastal route to India but it did them little good: the Indians and Arabs along with Egypt's rivals, the Seleucids, controlled the whole of the shore line involved, and even the most adventuresome skipper wasn't going to risk a voyage where there was no place to take refuge either from the weather or from attack. What was needed was a way to reach India that would bypass these obstacles. The answer came sometime around 120 B.C. A half-drowned sailor was brought to the Court of King Ptolemy VII. After being nursed back to health and taught Greek he gave out the story that he was an Indian, sole survivor of his crew, and offered to prove it by showing anyone the king picked the way back to his home. He was lucky: Eudoxus, the most daring and energetic explorer of the day, happened to be in Alexandria at the time (he was a native of Cyzicus, a rich commercial city on the Sea of Marmora). He made two round trips to India.

On his return from the second he ran straight before the monsoon instead of keeping it on his quarter, and landed well south on the east coast of Africa where, in the best explorer tradition, he made friends with the natives by giving them strange delicacies (bread, wine, and dried figs apparently did the trick). On both trips he brought back a load of spices, only to see them confiscated by Ptolemy's customs officials. To avoid such humiliation a third time he made the decision, drastic but characteristic, to sail to India by going around Africa and thereby bypass Ptolemy's inquisitive agents. He got together a well-equipped and well-planned expedition (there were even dancing boys and girls aboard, whether for the harems of Indian rajahs or to help while away the long days at sea, we can't be sure), and made it as far as the Atlantic coast of Morocco where a mutiny turned him back. Undiscouraged he fitted out a second expedition just as carefully—like Necho's Phoenicians (p. 131) he included in his plans stops en route to sow and reap crops—and it vanished without a trace. Bad luck dogged him even after his death. It must have been he who brought back to the Greeks the secret of the monsoons, but later generations gave the credit to a pilot named Hippalus. Nothing else is known about this figure. It's a shrewd guess—but only a guess—that he was Eudoxus' navigator.

In any event, the explorer's voyages put Egypt back in the running. She now had a quick route, relatively safe from attack—warships and pirate craft were too light to venture far from the shore (p. 102)—which could successfully compete with the caravan tracks. Alexandrian warehousemen set up on Delos, Greek merchants in India, and Indian shippers in Alexandria.

The second half of the Hellenistic age was the heyday of the south Italian businessman. Delos was not the only place where he was found; he followed the Roman armies into Greece, Thrace, Asia Minor, and Syria. Nor did he stick to the coast. He was a banker and investor as well as a merchant, and was willing to put his money into anything that promised a profit. He bought and ran farms, invested in mortgages, lent money to businessmen, to cities, even to kings. It is no surprise to find in the contract mentioned at the beginning of this chapter that the funds were handled by a banker with the good Roman name of Gnaeus.

In 88 B.C., during a bitter war between Rome and Mithridates VI, one of the powerful kings of Asia Minor, Delos was sacked. It had just about staggered to its feet from this blow when, in 69 B.C., a band of pirates overran and utterly devastated it. The island never recovered. It had served its purpose. When the dealers in caravan goods were first sensing the new drift in the current of their trade, toward Italy, they needed a convenient clearing house; moreover Delos was perfectly located for the traffic in slaves from Thrace, Syria, and Asia Minor. But when the current of trade established itself and the supply of slaves began to peter out, the island lost its reason for being. Italians and foreigners moved out, lock, stock, and barrel, set themselves up at Pozzuoli, and made it into a second Delos. The abandoned site lingered on as a ghost town to become eventually an ideal subject for the excavator's spade.

In the west the South Italians had a bonanza: they fell heir, jointly with the merchants of Marseilles, to the rich traffic that had once passed through Carthage. But this was not all. There was another phase of their activity in this area that remained all but unknown to history until very recently when archaeology's newest branch, underwater exploration, uncovered it.

13 Sea Digging

SHORTLY BEFORE EASTER in the year 1900 a group of Greek sponge divers, returning from their season off Tunisia, ran into a storm and took refuge in a sheltered cove on Anticythera, a little island off the south coast of Greece. Just to pass the time, some of the crew slipped over the side. When, a few minutes later, one reappeared lugging the bronze arm of a Greek statue, underwater archaeology was born.

Its babyhood was spectacular. The divers had had the astounding good fortune to stumble upon the wreck of a vessel which had been carrying works of art from Athens to Italy (cf. p. 183) some time in the first century B.C. when it went down. The Greek government undertook to salvage the cargo. The only personnel available for the work were sponge fishermen who, though they found excavating statues buried on the bottom a far cry from cutting away sponges, through herculean efforts managed to carry it off successfully. What they rescued was priceless: some fine bronzes, two of which are among the Athens Museum's prize pieces, a row of magnificent glass bowls, very likely imports to Athens from Alexandria or Syria, even a nautical instrument, a form of astrolabe.

A few years later came another rare piece of luck, again involving sponge divers. A group which had been working off Mahdia on the coast of Tunis circulated the story that they had seen a row of cannon on the sea floor. It came to the local director of antiquities, Alfred Merlin, and piqued his interest. He sent some divers down and quickly found out that the so-called cannon were a row of prefabricated temple columns lying on the deck of a ship that had sunk probably in the early part of the first century B.C. Merlin decided to carry out a full-fledged underwater excavation. He rounded up a squad of sponge fishermen, got the French navy to lend a hand by supplying a salvage ship, and in 1907 began the first of a series of grueling campaigns. It was a fight against time and wind and weather—the navy kept recalling its ship, rough seas often prevented any diving, storms occasionally destroyed his markers and the wreck had to be painfully discovered all over again—and, despite seven years of work, the job was never fully completed. But what he found well paid for his efforts. The vessel, in addition to the prefabricated parts, turned out to have been carrying works of art—it, too, was probably on the Athens-Italy run when it went down—and his divers rescued enough to fill half a dozen rooms of the Bardo Museum in Tunis with sculpture.

The two discoveries naturally raised the highest hopes for the future. World War I interrupted things for a while, but prospects again brightened when fishermen, working in the strait between the Greek mainland and the northern end of the island of Euboea, brought up a superb bronze statue of Zeus, now one of the treasures of the Athens Museum. The wreck itself, however, was never discovered, and no further reports of finds were forthcoming.

It was not until decades later that anything like the thorough investigation Merlin had carried out at Mahdia was again attempted. The fishermen of Albenga, a town on the Italian Riviera, had known since 1925 of the presence of a wreck with a cargo of clay jars off their shores. In 1950 one of Italy's famous salvage experts was persuaded to try his hand at it. He put one of his superbly equipped salvage ships at the disposal of archaeology and in twelve days his men managed to bring up 700 jars and some scraps of the hull and its fittings. Those few days were all the salvage vessel could be spared for, and the rest of the cargo, over two thousand more jars according to the best estimate, had to be left on the bottom.

Sea digging such as took place at Albenga and Mahdia had little future. The one had depended on the philanthropy of a salvage company, the other on sponge fishermen and a helping hand from the French navy. Underwater archaeology had to find other resources if it was to get anywhere. A French naval officer, Commandant Jacques-Ives Cousteau, supplied the answer.

An apparatus that did away with the need for pumps and crews, expensive diving suits and helmets, had been known in one form or another since as early as the 1860's. In 1943 the commandant perfected a simplified version, now known as the Cousteau-Gagnon apparatus, which transformed diving from a strictly professional field into one that was open to amateurs. It consisted of one to three bottles of compressed air connected with a mouthpiece and held by a harness which the diver strapped on his back. A big goggle fitting over eyes and nose, and a pair of rubber fins that slipped over the feet, items for sale in any sporting-goods shop, completed the outfit.

The use of the new device—called free diving to distinguish it from that in which the diver is coupled by an airhose to the surface—found its most enthusiastic practitioners among the French. They concentrated their efforts at first along their own Riviera, and very quickly startling reports began to come in of the discovery of not one or two, but of numbers of Greek and Roman wrecks. Soon they, as well as others infected by their enthusiasm, moved farther afield; and wrecks began to turn up along the Italian Riviera, in the straits between Sardinia and Corsica, off Greece and the Aegean Islands. However, unlike the first discoveries, none of these, it turned out, were carrying works of art. Like the one off Albenga, they had been loaded for the most part with the items that bulked so large in the commerce of the Greeks and Romans, wine and oil.

Shippers package cargoes today in wooden tubs or barrels, paper cartons, metal drums or the like. In the ancient world the standard shipping container was the amphora, a heavy clay jar that generally held between five and ten gallons. Long before any ancient wrecks were discovered a good deal was known about these containers because quantities of them turned up in many an archaeological excavation on land; the ones used by the Rhodians are a notable case in point (p. 180). The key element in underwater archaeology today is these jars. The wrecks that the free divers were discovering were not at all like the mental image we commonly have of a romantic hulk half buried in sand; most often all that was left of them were the containers which held their cargoes, a mound of amphorae jutting up from the sea floor or an expanse of them strewn over it (Pl. 9a). When such objects, crusted with marine growth, are brought to a museum curator he can hardly be blamed for not displaying them among his treasured pieces any more than a gallery of modern art will put on a showing of packing cases. But the naval historian is delighted to get them. These ugly ducklings of archaeology are the living proof of the breadth and volume of ancient commerce.

The first scientific investigation of a wreck with the use of the new apparatus took place in February 1952. A few miles outside the harbor of Marseilles lies a cluster of tiny islands which are little more than barren outcroppings of rock. Off one of these, the Grand Congloué, a diver had spotted in 1949 a group of amphorae lying on the sea floor. The word subsequently reached Cousteau, and the idea came to him of excavating it just as an archaeologist would a site on land. The wreck was ideally located. It was about 130 feet below the surface, deep enough to escape the attentions of souvenir-hunting French amateurs and yet above the point where the water gets too cold for free divers to work in. More important, it lay right alongside one slope of the Grand Congloué so that Cousteau was able to set up diving installations on the island itself and do away with the delay and expense of ferrying divers in and out daily. With Cousteau providing the technical know-how and Fernand Benoit, director of antiquities for the region and curator of the museum at Marseilles, looking out for the archaeological end, the work got under way.

Progress was painfully slow. The divers were limited to twenty minutes on the bottom, including the time it took for them to get up and down; only two dives a day were permitted, and there were usually not more than two or three men on hand at any time. Often the weather stopped all work. Not only muck and marine growth covered the wreck but huge boulders had crashed down into it from the slope above, and the divers had to remove all this before they could get at the vessel itself. Moreover, since they were pioneers, they had to invent the art of underwater archaeology as they went along. They perfected important tools: a basket raised by a derrick to bring up heavy objects, a powerful underwater vacuum cleaner to suck away sand or mud or marine growth, underwater lights to illumine the work. They perfected techniques of mapping with precision what they had found on the bottom, and of photographing underwater to record it before it was disturbed.

The ship proved to be a big merchantman, about one hundred feet long, that had been carrying a capacity cargo of wine and perhaps oil. The hold was filled with tubby amphorae of a shape common in Greek archaeological sites in the eastern Mediterranean. The deck was covered (cf. Pl. 9b) with jars of a tall slender shape found in Italy and generally assigned to the second century B.C. These had been stowed, standing upright, on every square inch of space available; almost two thousand have been recovered and brought to the Marseilles Museum and many more are still in place. They had been smeared on the inside with resin to prevent seepage and sealed so carefully that a number still had their plugs in place, a cork topped by a cement stopper. Some bore on the stopper the name of the wineseller who had filled them, and some on the lip the name of the shipper who had exported them. In the hold, along with the jars there, was a shipment of cheap dishware, of a type frequently found in South Italy. A number of miscellaneous objects were recovered: dishes and bowls that probably came from the ship's galley, bronze fittings, an anchor, some fragments of the hull—all in all, enough to fill a bank of display cases in the Marseilles Museum with a unique display.

Cousteau supervised the actual digging, but it was Benoit's task to reconstruct the story of the vessel. All he had to go on was the contents of the cargo and what was generally known of the movements of ancient commerce. The end of the story was the easiest: the vessel clearly had shoved off from some South Italian port, most likely in the area of Naples, some time in the second century B.C. with a deckload of the fine wine grown in that area and a hold full of Greek wine or oil, perhaps 15,000 to 20,000 gallons in all. It was headed for Marseilles where the bulk of the cargo would be distributed to the interior. Almost within sight of the destination, while threading the needle of the narrow channel between the Grand Congloué and the mainland, the ship went down. Just how is anybody's guess; but there's little doubt that the top-heavy deckload was a hazard. The beginning of the story is not so certain.

The vessel may have started the voyage that was to be its last in eastern waters, where it picked up the Greek jars, and then made for Italy. Or these may have reached Italy on some other boat and the whole cargo, the load in the hold as well as on deck, been taken on there.

It had been known in a general way that Italy exported wine and oil to France in the later part of the Hellenistic age, but until the sea diggers started work no one realized that vessels and shipments so large were involved. Neither the Grand Congloué ship nor the one found off Albenga were little tramps that worked the coast picking up general cargo as they went along; they were big freighters carrying a full load from one major point to another. Moreover, from French amateurs, diving at random along the Riviera, reports started to come in thick and fast of additional finds: a jar or two in one place, a scattering of them in a second, an imposing mound in a third. When it was all collated, the results were astounding: between Marseilles and the Italian border alone there were seventeen wrecks pinpointed with certainty and the likelihood that there were many more. They ranged in date from the sixth century B.C. (a vessel carrying Etruscan jars) to the fourth A.D., although most belonged to the second and first B.C. Where their size could be estimated they turned out to be big, one hundred feet long or better. Here was proof positive that the coastal area from Italy to Marseilles was a waterway for international trade as early as 600 B.C. and that shortly after 200 B.C. it was the scene of traffic on a large scale, the equal of anything that was going on in eastern waters among the Greek states.

Wine and oil were not the only items that traveled along this coast. Though they are, to be sure, two of the most important commodities handled by shippers all during ancient times, they also happen to be the ones the sea diggers find most easily. A clay jar is practically everlasting whether buried in earth or in water, and a load of them, lying on the bottom like a stack of huge frankfurters, is an eye-catching sight (Pl. 9a). Ships carrying other cargoes must have been wrecked along the coast but they left either no trace—grain, for example, packed as it was in sacks would disappear completely—or such slight ones that divers have not yet learned to recognize them.

Before the days of underwater archaeology discouragingly little was known of the size and capacity of ancient seagoing merchantmen and practically nothing of their construction; all there was to go on was a handful of paintings and sculptures and a batch of stray remarks in ancient writers, and neither source had much detail to offer. The sea diggers are gradually filling in some of the information needed. They have produced the first concrete evidence of the size of these vessels—the wrecks of the Grand Congloué and Albenga are about 100 feet long and a third, off Anthéor, is just slightly less; that off Mahdia is over 130 feet long and about 40 in beam, and another in the Strait of Bonifacio is about 100 x 25. And, in the museums at Marseilles and Cannes and Albenga the visitor can examine actual pieces of the hull and bits of the hardware and gear of vessels over two thousand years old.

Albenga is particularly interesting. Besides examples of the sort of equipment divers usually recover—bronze rings probably once sewn to the sail as fair-leads for the brails (cf. Pl. 12), anchor stocks, pieces of lead sheet, and the like—there is on display a fragment of a rib and a chunk of the planking which reveal the care and craft of the shipwright who constructed this vessel. He used ribs of oak, four inches square, set them 8 ¾ inches apart, and covered them with a skin of fir planking, one inch thick. The specifications seem rather light considering the vessel's size, but his method of joining more than made up for this; it is more cabinetwork than ship carpentry. He pinned planks to ribs by wooden pegs as ship builders have done in all ages, but to make sure his pegs fitted tightly he drove copper nails through the middle of each to make it expand and sit snugly in its hole. Moreover, to keep a plank from working loose where there were no pegs to hold it fast, he locked each to its neighbor above and below with mortise and tenon joints at the midpoint of the spaces between the ribs. As a result of all this, the hull must have been extraordinarily strong and tight. Like the builders of later ages, to keep marine borers and growth from spoiling his handiwork he sheathed at least the underwater surface with lead sheeting and pinned it to the wood with stumpy copper nails.

As it happens, the construction of the Albenga ship is not unique. It is paralleled in a pair of boats which came to light as the result

more of a feat of hydraulic engineering than of sea digging. The Roman emperor Caligula kept two enormous pleasure barges—he may have got the idea from Ptolemy IV's floating villa (p. 174)—on Lake Nemi, some twenty miles south of Rome. In the 1930's, at

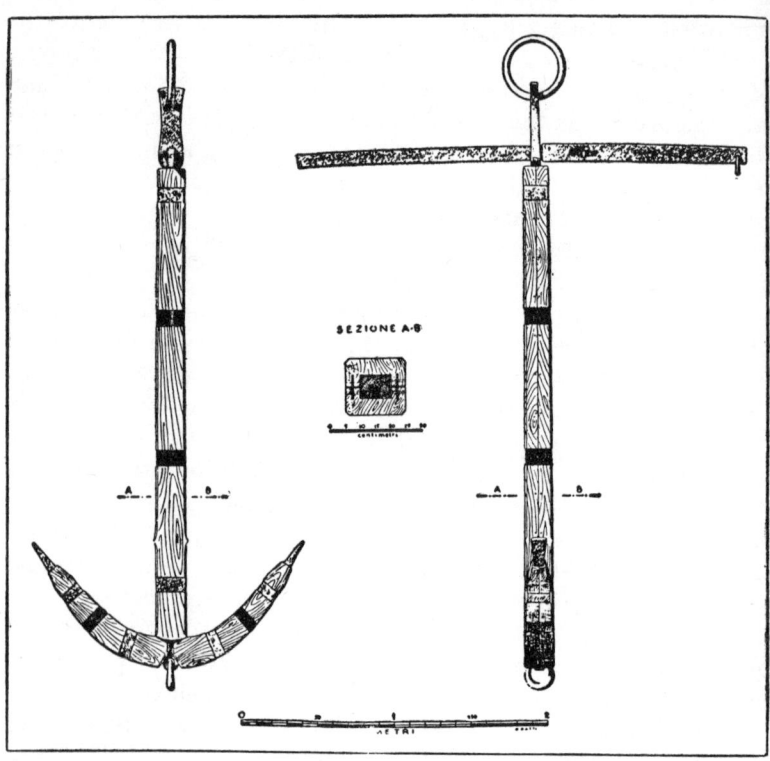

Fig. 5. Anchor with removable stock from one of Caligula's barges.

the cost of a vast amount of money and trouble, the Italian government pumped out the lake until the barges were visible, raised them, and put them in a museum specially built for the purpose on the shore, where they stayed until the Nazis wantonly burned them when they evacuated the area in 1944. The superstructures were gone but the hulls were in very good shape; one measured overall 240 feet in length and 69 in beam and the other was just a shade smaller (234 feet by 66 feet). What is particularly interesting is that the hulls were put together practically the same way as that of the Albenga boat: the planks were fastened to each other by mortise and tenon joints and pinned to the ribs with pegs through which copper nails were driven; and the whole outer surface was sheathed in lead laid over a skin of woolen fabric impregnated with tar.

Since every ancient vessel of any size carried several anchors—five were counted in the site off Mahdia—the sea diggers, once they locate a wreck, usually come up with at least one and, consequently, there are a good many specimens on display in the museums; the room of maritime history at Marseilles, for example, has a fine selection. The piece most often recovered is the stock because it was made either all of lead or of lead wrapped about a core of wood; the shank and arms, being of wood, have, with few exceptions, been destroyed by the action of the water. The stocks found are often very heavy: seven hundred and eight hundred pounds is not unusual, and one giant, fished up off Cartagena in Spain, is over seven feet long and weighs better than fifteen hundred pounds—another indication of the large size of the vessels involved. Not all are alike. Some were socketed permanently to a shank but others were removable; that is, they could be slipped off the shank so that the whole anchor could be made to lie flat on the deck and out of the way when not in use (Fig. 5). Apparently this convenient type was forgotten even before the end of the Roman Empire and stayed forgotten until the Dutch rediscovered it in the eighteenth century and the British navy adopted it in the middle of the nineteenth. Sometimes anchors were made all of iron or of iron sheathed in wood (Fig. 5) and a number of these have been fished up in various places.

The great hope, of course, is that the sea diggers will eventually do what the Italian engineers did for Caligula's barges: raise a whole hull and give the world its first look at an ancient merchantman. Such an achievement is not very likely at the moment. The expense would be enormous; but, even more serious, the care of the wood—it deteriorates as soon as it leaves the water—poses a problem that no one has yet solved. But this is a minor disappointment. Underwater archaeology is still very, very young and a long career lies ahead. It has much to add to many a chapter in the story of ancient commerce and naval architecture.

14 The Pirates of Cilicia

IT CANNOT HAVE BEEN long after merchantmen first cleaved the waters of the Mediterranean before pirates started to dog their tracks. "Strangers, who are you?" asks the Cyclops of Odysseus and his men, "Do you wander about as traders or risking your necks as pirates?" In the age Homer was describing, piracy was a profession that energetic and adventuresome men entered as a respectable way of making a living.

The profession lost some of its respectability as the centuries passed but none of its attractions. It was so widespread that it actually affected the course of early Greek civilization: people moved their settlements away from the sea where they were a target for raids to points more inland, and surrounded them with protective walls. The Athenians at one time had to set up a naval base on the Adriatic solely to protect their shipping from freebooters. Loss to pirates was one of the risks that bankers, shippers, and shipowners always reckoned in when they drew up contracts or fixed prices. The pirate even gained a place for himself in literature. A standard scene in Greek comedy was the reunion of a long-lost child with its parents from whom pirates had snatched

The Pirates of Cilicia

it as an infant to sell into slavery. Eventually the pirate wound up as wildly romantic as the Arab sheikhs of the drugstore novels who gallop off into desert sunsets with fair captives across their saddlebows. Every reader of an ancient Greek novel knew that hero and heroine, once aboard ship, would somewhere along the way be carted off by a band of brigands, of whom some were bound to fall in love with the girl and one might even turn out to have the traditional heart of gold.

Roving cutthroats who operated for their own profit weren't the only pirate menace. Any number of states considered piracy a legitimate form of maritime enterprise, and their flotillas were to be found ranging up and down the trade routes. When in 230 B.C. the Romans sent an embassy to Queen Teuta, who ruled the Illyrians of the Jugoslav coast, to complain about attacks on their shipping, she pointed out with wide-eyed innocence that Illyrian sovereigns never interfered with what their subjects did on the seas. (Eighteen centuries later Queen Elizabeth I put on more or less the same act about Hawkins and Drake.) Moreover, it was as hard in those days as later to distinguish between pirates and privateers. In an age that had no international law, about the only way a government could force an alien into compliance with a given obligation was by indiscriminate reprisal, and even the most respectable Greek states didn't think twice about sending off their captains to attack the unsuspecting and innocent fellow citizens of a recalcitrant foreigner. Some captains, especially when their pay was in arrears, would interpret their orders liberally and attack any likely looking prize they came upon. As far as the victim was concerned it made little difference whether a gang of freebooters boarded him for their own profit or the crew of an Athenian naval unit because of some alleged offense on the part of one of his compatriots: he lost his vessel and cargo. Every now and then a state would use pirates as a temporary addition to its navy, thus throwing large-scale opportunities their way. Demetrius enlisted whole bands when he laid siege to Rhodes (p. 153), and Philip V quietly engaged the pirates of Crete to concentrate on Rhodian shipping (p. 167). Nineteen centuries later the Dutch and English were making the same sort of deals with Barbary corsairs.

The ancient pirate, like his later brethren, chased and boarded merchantmen. But his stock in trade was not that; it was slave running. An attack on the high seas was a hit-or-miss sort of thing: a pirate chief could never tell from the look of a merchantman plodding along whether it was carrying a load of invaluable spices or of cheap noisome goathides. But a swift swoop on any coastal town was bound to yield, even if the place was too poor for plunder, a catch of human beings who could be held for ransom or sold for the going price on the nearest slave block. "Pirates came into our land at night," runs the inscription on a monument which the people of Amorgos set up shortly after 300 B.C., "and carried off young girls and women and other souls, slave and free, to the number of thirty or more. They cut loose the boats in our harbor [no doubt to prevent pursuit] and, seizing Dorieus' boat, escaped on it with their captives and booty." Amorgos was a very small island, and the loss of even thirty people must have been a blow; luckily two brave and persuasive captives talked the pirate chief into holding them as hostages—the monument had been erected in their honor—and sending the rest back. An inscription that the people of nearby Naxos set up at about the same time records a large-scale operation in which pirates seized no less than 280 people; they were all ransomed eventually, but it must have cut deeply into many a Naxian's savings. In attacks of this sort, if the alarm was given in time the populace scampered to safety or rounded up forces to drive the raiders off. It was not often that they captured any, for pirates, knowing what was in store for them, played it safe. There is a case on record of a Turkish corsair of the sixteenth century who, when caught, was roasted alive for three hours; it's very likely that ancient townspeople showed as little mercy to those who fell in their hands. When Caesar rounded up a gang (p. 203) he sentenced them to crucifixion, as nasty and lingering a death as any.

Although no coastal town anywhere along the Mediterranean and no merchantman anywhere on it was safe from attack, there were certain areas which were particularly dangerous. The "Tyrrhenians" got a reputation for buccaneering very early in the game; the name was probably a catch-all for the various groups that operated in the Tyrrhenian Sea west of Italy, Etruscans, Italians, Sardinians, Greeks from South Italy. Dionysius I of Syracuse, that

The Pirates of Cilicia

able and inventive general and admiral (p. 125), managed to hold them down, but when he died they bounced back as strong as ever. The Illyrians of the Jugoslav coast were a particularly virulent breed, the only group who succeeded in making a contribution that outlived them: they designed a boat so light and fast—the Liburnian—that the Romans paid them the compliment of adopting it as a standard naval unit (p. 213). The Illyrians had a field day in the Adriatic until Rome, between the two Punic wars, finally took some action; but since, in her usual fashion, she didn't follow up by establishing a permanent patrol in the area they were quickly back in business. They worked in large packs—at their height they had a fleet of 220 ships—and frequently hired out to the neighboring kings of Macedon, especially after the latter had lost their own naval power (p. 167). They met their end when they made the mistake of joining King Perseus in open war against Rome (p. 172). Farther to the east, the Cretans were notorious pirates as early as Homer's day (cf. p. 43). It was they who made the trip past Cape Malea, which every vessel plying between Greece and Italy had to round, touch and go for even well-armed ships, and for years they were the chief targets of Rhodes' patrols. But neither the Tyrrhenians nor the Illyrians nor the Cretans matched for size, organization, and destructiveness the group that played out the last, lurid act in Mediterranean freebooting, the pirates of Cilicia.

Cilicia, on the southern coast of Asia Minor, is an area whose inland portion is a stretch of rugged mountains and whose shore line a serrated succession of precipitous headlands. This is a combination ideal for pirates: the trackless interior protects them from any attack by land forces against their back, and the coast offers a choice of lofty lookouts and well-hidden strongholds. Some time after the middle of the second century B.C., when Rome had defeated the Seleucid Empire which bordered on Cilicia, and delivered her telling blow against Rhodes (p. 183) who used to police the waters round about, this region became a spawning ground for a pirate movement that, within a half-century, managed to bring chaos into every corner of the Mediterranean.

The pirates of Cilicia made their headquarters in a town called Coracesium, a miniature Gibraltar perched on a rock that dropped a sheer five hundred or six hundred feet to the sea and was connected to the mainland by only a narrow isthmus. As word of their successes got about there flocked here not only the riffraff of every nation in the area but even men of means and family eager to add the spice of danger to their lives. Eventually they had enough crews and ships to reorganize themselves on naval lines: they formed flotillas commanded by commodores, even fleets under admirals; to Liburnians and hemiolias (p. 152), the standard craft of the profession, they added ships of the line, even triremes. When Mithridates VI of Asia Minor began his bloody and long-drawn-out revolt against Rome in 89 B.C., the Cilician pirates joined him and thereby put at his disposal the best fleet available at the time in the Mediterranean. They had an efficient system of intelligence: agents would fraternize with the crews of merchantmen along the quays or in the waterfront saloons, discover their destinations, and relay the information to headquarters. But attacks on shipping were just a sideline. Their specialty was slave running, and they raided the coasts with such ruthless efficiency that they actually depopulated certain areas. Numbers of cities were glad to get off by paying them protection money, and some entered into formal treaties permitting them access to their ports and markets. These brigands now supplied the bulk of the slaves sold at the great market on Delos, satisfying even the ever increasing demands of Roman plantation owners (p. 182). Eventually they opened a market of their own at Side, a convenient thirty-odd miles by water from their headquarters, which became second only to Delos.

By the early part of the first century B.C. the pirates of Cilicia literally controlled the seas. The Rhodians had been forced to cut back their navy, the Seleucids had lost theirs to Rome, and Rome had given hers up. Very likely, when the pirates were first getting under way, rich Roman plantation owners who found their services so useful had gone about discouraging any talk of taking action against them. By now no aggregation of a few squadrons or even a standard-sized fleet was going to do the job: the pirates commanded over a thousand ships; their arsenals were stocked with weapons and supplies; and, in concert with other miscellaneous packs, they were operating all over the Mediterranean—one group even helped a Spanish rebel to capture from Rome some of the Balearics, far off in the west.

The Pirates of Cilicia

Shortly before 70 B.C. their activity reached a crescendo. Landings were made on the shores of Italy itself and noble Roman ladies, not remote provincials, were now carried off for ransom. One gang kidnaped the granddaughter of an admiral who had once led an anti-pirate campaign, and another hauled off two high-ranking Roman officials with their staffs. The Appian Way, Rome's chief highway, was no longer safe to travel on. A squadron broke into the harbor of Ostia and smashed a consul's flotilla at anchor. The Roman plantation owner was the ultimate purchaser of most of the captives the pirates put on the block, but that didn't deter them from taking particular enjoyment in biting the hand that fed them. For Roman citizens they had specially worked up an ancient version of walking the plank. When a captive, in the hope that it might help, declared that he was a Roman, the pirates would go through a carefully rehearsed act. First they pretended to be thoroughly scared and humbly asked for pardon, then they solicitously dressed the victim in his toga (the mark of the Roman citizen), assuring him that it was to keep them from making the same mistake a second time, and then, when well out to sea, they threw over the ship's ladder and prodded him down with best wishes for a pleasant stroll home. On one occasion the jokes went the other way. A gang seized Julius Caesar when, as a young man, he was sailing from Rome to Rhodes to study law there, and made the mistake of not recognizing that their captive was something out of the ordinary although he gave them plenty of clues. When they set a ransom of twenty talents on his head Caesar genially pointed out that he was worth at least fifty. They accepted the revised figure with alacrity and willingly sent off some companions who had been taken with him to collect the cash. While they were away Caesar treated these cutthroats as if they were a personal bodyguard: he would order them to keep quiet whenever he was ready for his siesta, commandeer an audience whenever he wanted to practise his oratory, and dress them down whenever he felt they failed to appreciate the finer points of his style and delivery. The pirates were amused no end by all this and made the slip of staying amused when Caesar good-humoredly promised that he would come back after his release and hang them all. The moment the ransom was paid he made his way to Miletus nearby, raised a fleet, returned, and did just what he had said he would: he had as many as he could catch crucified. As a special favor for their rather decent treatment of him during his captivity, he allowed their throats to be slit before nailing them to the cross.

In 69 B.C. things came to a head. A pirate fleet sacked Delos for a second time, ending once for all the island's commercial career (p. 188). The seas became practically closed to shipping. It was this that finally goaded Rome into action: the city fed on imported grain and the pirates had now hit it in its most sensitive spot, the belly. What ensued was one of the most remarkable operations in naval history.

Actually there had been some paving of the way. Since 77 B.C. Roman armies had been slowly slogging through the mountains of the hinterland behind the pirates' coastal strongholds. But this was only setting the stage: the *coup de grâce* had to be delivered on the sea. The man who planned and executed it was, as every school boy who has been put through Cicero's speeches knows, Caesar's famous rival, Pompey the Great.

In 67 B.C. when the pirate menace had become a national crisis, the people of Rome handed Pompey a blank check to cope with it. The whole shore line of the Mediterranean up to a point fifty miles inland, with all the resources therein, was turned over to him; he had the authority to requisition ships or men or money or whatever else he needed from any governor of any Roman province or from any king bound by allegiance to Rome. Pompey must have anticipated something like this, for the plan he put into action was too carefully thought out to have been made up on the spur of the moment. It was a masterpiece of strategy and it went off like clockwork.

He had to have ships. He got them, as Romans had ever since the Second Punic War, by commandeering the forces of such allies as Rhodes, the Phoenician cities, Marseilles, and so on. But the key to Pompey's success was not his ships—Roman admirals had gone after the Cilician pirates with powerful forces before and failed—but the scale and thoroughness of his planning: his strategy left nothing to chance and it embraced the whole of the Mediterranean. He divided the shore line into thirteen sectors each with its own commander and fleet. The essence of his plan was cooperation: each fleet was to attack the pirate nests in its sector simultaneously while Pompey, at the head of a mobile force of sixty vessels, swept from Gibraltar eastward, driving all before him either into the jaws of the forces on the shores or straight ahead into an ultimate cul-de-sac off Cilicia.

Within forty days Pompey had cleaned up the west and was ready for those who had fled headlong before him to the home base. As he approached, first individual ships then whole packs started to surrender. When he drew his siege lines around Coracesium the last hard core gave up. It was a spectacular operation, brilliantly conceived and magnificently executed. In three months Pompey had accomplished what no power had been able to do for centuries. Except for a spasmodic outburst now or then, the age-old plague of the Mediterranean was ended for a long time to come. No doubt the job of keeping it that way got off with flying colors when Pompey, instead of butchering his captives and thereby building up a debt of hate, in a sociological experiment that seems startingly modern carefully selected those he judged capable of reforming and resettled them in towns in the interior where they could start a new life away from the temptations of the sea.

Actually, Pompey did more than exterminate piracy. While he was about it he laid the foundation for a revival of the Roman navy, and provided the pattern for its organization. The squadrons he had activated were, in the next half-century, to grow into the fleets that fought in Rome's bloody civil wars and, when these had ended, to form the nucleus of the magnificent force that turned the Mediterranean into a Roman lake.

15 Rome Rules the Waves

On 11 January 49 B.C. Julius Caesar crossed the Rubicon, and the fires of civil war blazed forth all over the Mediterranean. Not until two stormy decades had gone by were they stamped out, after tens of thousands of men had been killed and a thousand ships sent to the bottom. And the nation that had once abandoned its navy saw the last round of its bitter internal strife fought out on the sea in a battle which pitted against each other two of the largest fleets ever assembled in ancient history.

When the curtain rose on the conflict in 49 B.C. Caesar held the west and Pompey the east with the ships and seamen that meant control of the water as well. Sea power, however, in those days had its limitations (cf. p. 102), and Caesar, gambling shrewdly on them, was able to ferry an army across the Adriatic through Pompey's blockade lines to Greece where he ultimately won complete victory. He now inherited some two hundred ships, all his opponent had left, but the daggers of Brutus and Cassius prevented his ever using them. And, although his grandnephew Octavian—or Augustus as he was later called—in a series of daring moves gathered into his hands the power his great-uncle once held, the fleet slipped through his fingers. Through the quirks of Roman politics and the irony of fate most of it fell into the grasp of none other than Pompey's son, Sextus. He knew how to use it: he was as skillful a seaman as he was a political gambler.

By 42 B.C., a scant two years after Caesar's death, Sextus commanded 130 ships and was ready to play his own hand. Almost immediately he got a windfall: Augustus and Mark Antony had joined forces to crush Brutus and Cassius who, in what was by now a tradition, had commandeered the ships of the east; after their defeat, the remnants of their fleet joined Sextus. Augustus was faced with the job of consolidating his rule in Italy with barely a vessel to his name while a wily and able opponent held the waters round about with a force of over two hundred. He sorely needed a navy and someone to head it; he created the one and found the other.

In 38 B.C., by exacting huge contributions and digging deep into his own pockets, Augustus managed to muster a fleet of 370 ships, including units up to "sixes," the heaviest aggregation seen in over a century. He gave the command to his right-hand man Agrippa. Agrippa had already shown himself a skillful general; now he was to reveal equal gifts as an admiral, not only on the deck but at the planning table as well. He had a special base built just north of Naples, where he spent a winter putting the raw recruits Augustus handed him through a rigorous training. But there was still more to be done. Agrippa knew that he couldn't hope to win by ramming: his men, despite the winter's work, were still beginners as against Sextus' crack crews, and, with their heavy ships, didn't stand a chance of getting in a blow at the enemy's light fast craft. There remained only boarding, but boarding Sextus' slippery units posed a problem almost as difficult. Agrippa solved it by inventing a new weapon. His vessels were big enough to carry catapults. He mounted the arrow-shooting type (p. 147) but, instead of a shaft with the normal pointed head, he used one tipped with a grapnel and made fast at the other end to a length of line. It was a most ingenious device: not only did it have a much greater range than a hand-thrown grapnel, but it was far harder for the enemy to handle; to cut it away his axes had to bite through a stout pole instead of a slender rope. In September of 36 B.C., after several preliminary clashes, the two grand fleets, totaling, it was reported, over six hundred ships, squared off near Naulochus on the north coast of Sicily. Both sides fought savagely; the battle was close, but the catapult-grapnel carried the day.

After destroying Caesar's assassins in 42 B.C., Augustus and Antony had divided the world between them, the one taking Italy and the west, the other the east. A showdown between the two was inevitable. Augustus had had to delay it until Sextus was out of the way. Now he was ready. The fight came in 31 B.C., and the final round was fought on the second of September. The site was Actium, just north of the western end of the Gulf of Corinth and not far from the spot where, fifteen centuries later, another historic naval engagement was to take place, the Battle of Lepanto. Antony commanded, it was said, over five hundred ships. Like Augustus', it was a heavy fleet, reminiscent of the mighty aggregations that Demetrius and Ptolemy had led three hundred years earlier. Every size from trireme to "nine" was represented, and a great "ten" carried the flag. Agrippa had four hundred units equipped, as at Naulochus, with his new catapult-grapnels. Both sides had added to their vessels a sort of armor belt of squared timbers shod with iron as a protection against ramming. The engagement itself was anticlimactic. Months before, Agrippa had seized bases from which his ships could intercept the grain freighters from Egypt that were supplying his enemies, and Antony found it harder and harder to feed the enormous masses of men in his army and crews. When his rowers took their places on the benches on September 2nd they were underfed, sick, and discouraged. Nor did it help matters that, just before they shoved off, the unusual order came down to keep the sails on board (cf. p. 97); it may have been part of some subtle tactical plan, but to the men it smelled of flight. When the lines locked in conflict, Antony didn't even wait for the finish: Cleopatra's squadron of sixty ships hoisted sail to make a run for it and he ingloriously followed with forty more. A year later the lovers committed suicide, and for the first time in history the Mediterranean, from the Strait of Gibraltar to the Dardanelles, was in the control of one man. Augustus had ushered in the great era of the Roman Empire on the sea; it was to last for the next two hundred and fifty years.

Rome Rules the Waves

Mastery of the Mediterranean was Augustus' first step. His next was just as important: to hold what he had won he created a complex, finely organized navy. And for two centuries thereafter his successors maintained and improved upon what he had founded.

Following the trail blazed by Pompey in his whirlwind campaign against the pirates, Augustus divided the sea into sectors and apportioned them among two major and a number of minor fleets. On Misenum, the cape that stands at the seaward end of the northern arc of Naples' great bay, he erected a headquarters for his principal fleet: though its immediate job was the patrol of the waters westward, it had a general responsibility for all the waters both east and west. Here he maintained a force of some ten thousand men and fifty-odd ships of the larger types—mostly triremes, some quadriremes and quinqueremes, and a "six" as flagship—plus an appropriate number of smaller craft. Substations north along the Italian coast and on the islands of Corsica and Sardinia opposite served as convenient ports for patrols. The officer in charge, Prefect of the Misene Fleet as he was termed, became one of the more important government officials in the Roman state. His area of command was so widespread and complex that the bulk of his work was administrative, and most of those chosen were political career men who, attaining the post after a lifetime of public service, were far more at home in an office than on the deck of a ship. Pliny the Elder, who was Prefect of the Misene Fleet in A.D. 79, the year Mount Vesuvius buried Pompeii under a rain of volcanic ash, was typical. He had previously served in the army as an officer, studied law, spent some years in practice, and put in a term as governor of the province of Spain. Though a conscientious administrator, his ruling passion was not his various offices—certainly not the navy—but the collecting of material for his famous encyclopedia. When Vesuvius began its fateful eruption he ordered the ships out, primarily to get him near enough for a good look at the unique spectacle and, as an afterthought, to pick up survivors. Whatever rescues there were took place without him because, in his eagerness, he pressed in too close and lost his life.

A second major fleet, also made up chiefly of triremes, was located at Ravenna far up the Adriatic. Its task was to patrol the Jugoslav coast opposite, whose pirates had given so much trouble in earlier days (p. 201). It was less important than the fleet at Misenum and its prefect subordinate in rank. When required, its units cooperated with those of the other.

The basic importance of these two squadrons was their very existence: so long as they stood by in watchful readiness no potential rival had a chance to build up and launch a force that could match them. When the need arose, they ferried army units from place to place, and at all times performed such useful functions as transporting important personnel and carrying dispatches. In addition to all this were two duties only remotely related to the sea. To satisfy the Roman appetite for public spectacles Augustus and his successors varied the regular fare of gladiatorial combats and horse races by occasionally staging mock sea battles. They had artificial lakes dug out, surrounded them with seats—sometimes they just flooded regular amphitheaters—and staged on them full-scale sea battles: the crews were condemned criminals and the fighting was to the death. It was the job of the sailors of the fleet to see to it that lake, ships, supplies, and the like were all in proper order. A second responsibility assigned them was the handling of the huge awnings that were spread over the seating expanse of arenas to shield the spectators from the sun; sailors were a natural choice for this work since they were the most knowledgeable in the technique of dealing with canvas and ropes. Special detachments from Misenum and Ravenna were at times stationed at Rome just for these extracurricular chores.

Augustus was fully aware that policing the Mediterranean meant more than holding a powerful naval force at the ready. It also meant running down sporadic pirates, patrolling harbor traffic, and ensuring quick communications between ports, duties for which the two major fleets were too far away and their units too heavy. So he began the building up of small provincial squadrons, located at strategic points like Alexandria (Pl. 11a) and Seleuceia, and equipped wholly with light fast craft. His successors followed his lead and, by the end of the first century A.D., such groups were stationed not only in the Mediterranean but wherever Rome had shipping to protect: in the Black Sea, on the Danube, near the mouth of the Rhine, by the English Channel.

The sailors and marines who manned the fleets were not Romans. They were Greeks, Phoenicians, Syrians, Egyptians, Slavs—members of those races who for centuries had gone down to seas or rivers in ships. They entered the service generally between the ages of eighteen and twenty-three, signed up for a hitch that was no less than twenty-six years in length and, if they lasted, were rewarded at discharge with Roman citizenship. When Augustus was desperately trying to build up a naval force to combat Sextus he enlisted slaves—but he made certain to free them before sitting them on the benches; there were no slaves then or thereafter in the Roman navy. On shipboard things were run as they had been in the Hellenistic navies, for most of the officers were Greeks who naturally tended to follow the traditions they had been brought up in, and the Romans for their part had little to add. Generally officers came up from the ranks: a man could work through the various grades to captain of a warship *(trierarchus)* or even leader of a squadron *(navarchus)*. This last position was usually the end of the road inasmuch as the top ranks, certainly the prefectures of the fleets, were open most of the time only to Roman citizens.

We know the sailors of the Roman navy more intimately than those of its predecessors. For one, archaeologists have excavated their graveyards around Misenum and Ravenna and read the inscriptions on their tombstones; from these we learn the countries they came from, their average span of service, a bit about their careers, and so on. For another, a good many came from Egypt; like servicemen in all times and places they wrote home frequently, and excavators have recovered a few of their letters from Egypt's dry sands (cf. p. 46). These are unique documents, for they provide what is so rare in ancient history, the warm light of personal experience.

The Roman army was the service with the long, honorable tradition. Since the navy was a newcomer and drew mostly upon foreigners for its personnel, it was a reluctant second choice for most boys. "God willing," wrote a young recruit who, around the beginning of the second century A.D., was a marine on a destroyer attached to the provincial fleet stationed at Alexandria, "I hope to be transferred to the army; but nothing will be done around here without money, and letters of recommendation will be no good unless a man helps himself." The boy was especially bitter because his father was a soldier who had served out his time and received an honorable discharge. In any event the story has a happy ending, for a later letter reveals that he finally got what he wanted.

But other letters show that some boys were well satisfied with the navy. There is a particularly engaging one from a young boot, Apion, who, sometime in the second century A.D., had left his little village in Egypt, been shipped to Italy, and there received word that he was assigned to the fleet at Misenum. He writes to his father full of enthusiasm:

DEAR FATHER,

First of all, I hope you are well and will always be well, and my sister and her daughter and my brother. I thank the God Serapis that when I was in danger on the sea he quickly came to the rescue. When I arrived at Misenum I received from the government three gold pieces for my traveling expenses. I'm fine. Please write me, Father, first to tell me that you are well, second that my sister and brother are well, and third so that I can kiss your hand because you gave me a good education and because of it I hope to get quick promotion if the gods are willing. Love to Capiton and my brother and sister and Serenilla and my friends. I've given Euctemon a picture of myself to bring to you. My name is Antonius Maximus, my ship the *Athenonice*. Goodbye.

P.S. Serenus, Agathodaemon's son, sends regards, and so does Turbo, Gallonius' son.

Apion was fortunate: he had met a number of boys from his home town; he had been given duty on a ship in the finest fleet; he saw—perhaps a bit overoptimistically—a chance of getting ahead. Like any young recruit in any age, he hungers for news from home and sends the family a picture of himself, undoubtedly showing him in his new uniform. In these pre-camera days it had to be a miniature, and in these pre-postal service days he must find someone heading for his home town to deliver it. Now that Apion is in the Roman navy he drops his Egyptian name for a good Roman one. We don't know whether his rosy vision of quick promotion ever came to pass but we do know that he prospered in other ways. A letter he wrote a number of years later is also preserved: Apion now uses only his Roman name; he had married a girl he met around the base, and he has three children, a boy and two girls.

The story revealed by this and similar letters is typical. All over the Mediterranean youngsters left their little villages, went overseas to Misenum or Ravenna, and there they settled down, married, raised families, and were buried. The process of recruiting had to be kept up continually, for the children of these men did not often follow in their footsteps. If they could, they went into the army or some other more attractive way of life.

Augustus and the emperors who came after him were proud of the navy that kept the seas safe for them. They stamped pictures of its ships on the coins they minted or had them carved on the monuments they set up—and thereby provided for posterity a fairly good idea of what Roman men-of-war looked like (Pl. 10; cf. Pls. 11a, 13c). The most striking thing about these representations is that, from the ram on the prow to the ornament on the stern, they reveal nothing, aside possibly from some details, that was not known in earlier days: the triremes, quadriremes, quinqueremes, and occasional "sixes" in the slips of Misenum and Ravenna were little different from those that fought in the great Hellenistic fleets; in a navy that had been built about a nucleus of ships from the eastern Mediterranean and that, throughout its history, was commanded by Greek officers, it could hardly be otherwise. Some of the galleys pictured carry the artemon (Pl. 10) but this, though appearing now for the first time, was quite possibly invented in the Hellenistic age (p. 174). The stempost ends in a big volute (Pl. 10a) and aft there is a curved wickerwork shelter for the captain or important passengers (Pls. 10b, 13c); these may have been Roman additions. Possibly the heavier units were protected against ramming by belts of timber shod with iron as those at Actium had been.

One new type of warship does appear in the Roman navy, the Liburnian (Pls. 10b, 11a). It was a destroyer, a light, fast, highly maneuverable vessel, ideal for pursuit of pirates or for quick communications. A pirate tribe from the Jugoslav coast had invented it, and the Romans found it useful enough to adopt as a standard unit, particularly for the provincial fleets which used such craft almost exclusively (Pl. 11a). Originally it was most probably single-banked, but its borrowers developed a heavier version driven by two banks of oarsmen. It must have served the purposes that the triemiolia had for the Rhodians (p. 152). Though the latter was available for adoption, Roman admirals preferred the Liburnian. Its two banks were easier to handle than the three of the other and possibly its rig was too; its mast and sail, for example, perhaps could be lowered under way for a fight without disturbing the rowers. The Liburnian became so popular in the Roman navy that the term eventually came to mean warship in general.

A Roman man-of-war was given a name but it was not inscribed on the hull as today. Instead an illustrative carving was set on the bows, for example, a relief of a god if the ship was called after one (Pl. 10a). As it happens, many were, with an understandable preference for deities of the sea like Neptune, Nereis, Triton, or for such sailors' favorites as Isis and Castor and Pollux. A number of ships bore geographical names, and here there was a tendency, natural enough, to go in for rivers; at one time or another all the great rivers of the ancient world, the Tigris, Euphrates, Nile, and Danube, were represented in the fleets. But quite a few were named after abstract qualities, and the fact that it was a peacetime navy seems reflected in the choice: names such as *Triumphus* or *Victoria* are rare; the christeners preferred *Concordia, Iustitia, Libertas, Pax, Pietas,* and the like.

The Roman navy, as mentioned earlier, was not maintained to fight enemy fleets; one of its key duties was to guard the trade routes. During the two hundred years after the birth of Christ these were traversed by the mightiest merchant marine the Mediterranean had ever seen or was to see for over a dozen centuries. The various types of craft that made it up are the best known of the ancient world, for even more representations of them are extant than of the contemporary men-of-war (Pls. 9b, 11b, 12-14). Sailors liked to have portrayed on their tombs the ship they had worked on, shippers had a weakness for having theirs decorated with pictures of the vessel they owned coming safely into harbor, and Roman emperors would issue coins stamped with a boat or a harbor scene to commemorate acts of theirs that had benefited commerce. After a gap of five centuries we can again see what merchantmen looked like, observe the form and fittings of their hulls, make out the details of their rigging, even watch them in action.

Some of the features of the ships so pictured appear for the first time, but this doesn't prove that they were innovations, and certainly not that the Romans had a hand in them. Though Rome now ruled the Mediterranean world, the people who handled its commerce were still Greeks and Phoenicians and Syrians and others who had made their living this way for centuries. The ships they used were, in all likelihood, basically the same as their fathers had; seamen by and large are a conservative lot. Whatever looks new may have been invented any time before, and most of it probably goes back to Hellenistic times when marine architects were called upon to meet the needs of a great expansion of trade (p. 174).

One thing is clear: there were many more big merchantmen afloat now than ever before. The freighters that carried official government cargoes were commonly 340 tons' burden, and those of Rome's crack grain fleet (pp. 235-36) ran to 1,200 tons; seventeen centuries were to pass before merchant fleets of such tonnage again sailed the seas. Circumstances occasionally called for even greater ships. The best examples are the leviathans that were specially built to haul from Egypt the enormous obelisks the Romans had a penchant for setting up as monuments in their capital. The shaft now in front of St. Peter's stands about 130 feet high and weighs, together with its pedestal, just under five hundred tons; the Emperor Caligula had it brought over about A.D. 40 and the vessel he constructed to carry it was ballasted with eight hundred tons of lentils—a total load of 1,300 tons. When Pope Sixtus V's architect, Domenico Fontana, in 1585 moved the obelisk from its orginal location in Nero's circus to where it now stands, he used 800 men, 140 horses, and 40 rollers, and the whole contemporary world broke into applause at the feat. But Caligula's seamen and engineers had taken the monument from Heliopolis near Cairo, barged it down the Nile, loaded it on its ship, sailed it successfully across the Mediterranean, transferred it again to a barge to get it up the Tiber, and re-erected it at the point where Fontana found it.

Mediterranean merchantmen had always carried a handful of oars for emergency or auxiliary work. In the pictures of this age merchant galleys now make their appearance, freighters specifically designed to be driven by sail and rowers together (Pl. 9b). They unquestionably go back to earlier times; the horse transports that formed part of the Athenian fleets (p. 102) were in effect the same sort of ship. Most were small, for plying between nearby coastal points, but many were of fair size, particularly useful for longer voyages where foul winds were to be encountered or when speed was essential. There must have been a good many such engaged in the transport from Africa and Asia of the wild animals that were in continual demand at Rome for the gladiatorial games; the trip was hard on the beasts and had to be made as rapidly as possible. Those that were light and fast enough could, when the occasion called, be pressed into service with the navy.

Back in the second millennium B.C. Minoan shipwrights had designed a hull for their sailing vessels that was well rounded and had stem and stern posts which curved upward in graceful arcs (p. 25; Pl. 1c, e). And, since the ancient mariner was as resistant to change as his later brethren, it remained the commonest type in the Mediterranean throughout ancient times (Pls. 11b, 12-14). A variant was also in existence, one in which the prow curves inward, as on a fighting galley, and ends in a projecting forefoot (Pls. 9b, 11b, 13a, 15a). It is at least as old as the other, for it occurs on some representations of skiffs found in Minoan sites. Now it appears, and very frequently, not only on skiffs and similar small craft but on large-sized merchantmen as well. The forefoot often extends far enough to look for all the world like a ram, yet to explain it as such makes no sense, since a ram has no place either on a heavy freighter, powered only by sail, or on a tiny rowboat. Possibly the design was intended for areas where there were few quays and a skipper would often have to drive his ship right up on the beach; a projecting forefoot would act as a buffer and protect the stem and keel from damage. The shape clearly was useful, for a version of it was still to be seen a dozen centuries later in the waters about Java.

From contemporary writings, especially Pliny the Elder's voluminous encyclopedia (p. 209), and from the pictures, a good deal is known about how merchantmen were built and handled. For safety as well as for increased cargo capacity they were made fairly beamy: a length to beam ratio of four to one was common and some, like the one found off Mahdia (pp. 190, 195), ran even wider. Freighters of any appreciable size had a cabin aft (Pls. 12, 13a), but it was big enough to house only the skipper and mates. Passengers lived and slept on deck, no hardship in the mild Mediterranean climate and unquestionably pleasanter than a stuffy berth below; when they wanted privacy they set up little tent-like shelters. Water was carried in tanks in the hold, and the food available included porridge and meat, cooked on a fire in a carefully protected hearth. Behind the cabin rose the sternpost, which was almost always carried up high, brought downward in a graceful curve, and finished off with the figure of a goose-head, a sharp contrast to the stem, which was left blunt and squarish (Pls. 12, 13a). Sometimes the latter bore a relief illustrating the vessel's name; the one in Plate 12 portrays Liber, the Roman god of wine, and very likely the *L* on the sail is his initial. On larger ships a gallery girdled the stern and occasionally another was put around the prow to protect the hands when working sail there (Pls. 12, 13, 14a). Shipwrights used pine or fir or cedar, depending on what was available, for the planks of the hull; for the keel they preferred pine and, for the false keel, oak to withstand the wear and tear of hauling out. The builders of Caligula's barges limited themselves to species of pine and fir and oak which were available in Italy. Inside, practically any wood was used: oak, pine, plane, ash, elm, while for oars and spars the favorite was fir because of its light weight, although pine was acceptable. Yards were sometimes made of two saplings fished together just as the Egyptians had done centuries earlier (p. 16). Sailmakers worked chiefly with linen, and riggers with ropes of flax, hemp, twisted papyrus or, on occasion, strips of leather. Sand was the commonest form of ballast, but anything conveniently heavy could be used: rocks, old building blocks, even discarded inscribed stone slabs; divers found a number of these in the wreck off Mahdia (p. 190). A hull whose planks were joined to each other like those of Caligula's barges or of the wreck near Albenga (p. 195) would need little caulking; on ships not so carefully constructed caulkers filled the seams with tow, then worked in pitch and then smeared the whole hull with pitch. Often they sheathed the underwater surface with sheet lead, placing a layer of tarred fabric between it and the wood; on Caligula's barges the whole outside of the hull was covered first with a woolen fabric impregnated with tar and then with sheet lead. Ship's paint was encaustic, that is, wax heated until it was soft enough to be mixed with coloring matter and applied with a brush. A number of colors were available: purple, blue, white, yellow, green, and a shade that matched sea water which reconnaissance vessels and pirate ships used as a sort of camouflage. One colored mosaic of a good-sized freighter shows that the Mediterranean penchant for gaily colored vessels has ancient roots: the hull is done in bands of red and dark blue, the stern gallery, trim, and steering oars in yellow, and the stern ornament is gilded.

The pictures of this age are absolutely invaluable when it comes to rigging: they portray not only the types in vogue but individual features as well. The standard rig is still the squaresail. Most ships carry an artemon (p. 146) also, and larger ones show, above the main, a topsail, the only superimposed sail found in the ancient world; it was a triangular piece of canvas that had its base spread along the upper surface of the yard and its apex hauled up to the truck of the mast (Pls. 12, 14a). The biggest freighters were rigged with all these sails and a mizzen as well (Pl. 11b). A relief carved on a stone plaque that was found in the port of Rome illustrates in detail the complicated tackle that a seagoing sailing vessel carried (Pl. 12). Projecting over the bows is the artemon mast. An extremely heavy forestay running from mast truck to the bow and an elaborate cluster of shrouds, with tackles for adjustment, steady the mast. The mainsail, broader than it is high, is made up of square or rectangular patches sewn together and protected along the edges by bolt ropes; figured on it is a picture of the she-wolf suckling Romulus and Remus, the legendary founders of Rome. A dozen brails (p. 38) for shortening sail run from the foot through fair-leads to the head and then, probably rove through blocks on the yard, are brought down to the deck. Above the main is the topsail, split in the middle to allow the forestay to pass through. The huge steering oar hangs in a rope strap and, socketed to the handle at right angles to the blade, is a long tiller which the helmsman pulls toward him or pushes away to twist the blade in the water and thereby direct the course. Two vessels are shown. In the left-hand side of the plaque, one has just entered port: sail is beginning to be shortened; the ship's boat, which had been in tow at the end of a long line, is being brought up to the vessel's

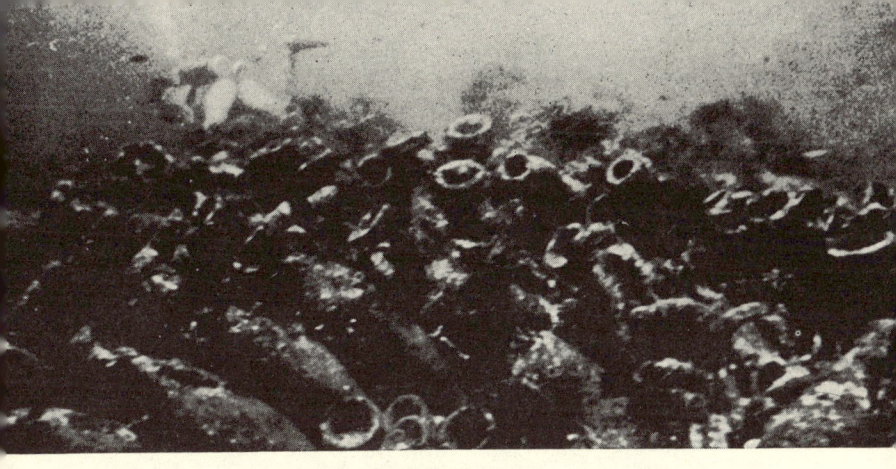

PLATE 9
The Standard Ancient Shipping Container: The Clay Jar

a. Amphorae from a wreck, dating around the end of the first century B.C. or the beginning of the first A.D., on the sea floor near the Ile du Levant off Hyères on the French Riviera.

b. A Roman merchantman traveling under sails and oars with a full deckload of amphorae. Second or third century A.D.

PLATE 10

Roman Warships

a. One of the heavy ships that fought in the Battle of Actium, 32 B.C. The vessel has two banks of oars, each oar manned by multiple rowers.

b. Two-banked Liburnians under oars and a trireme under oars and the artemon. Ca. A.D. 106.

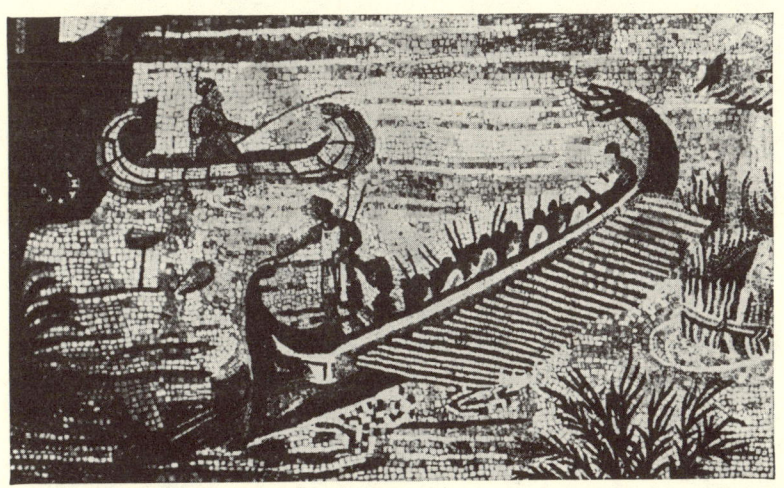

PLATE 11
Roman Warships and Merchantmen

a. Two-banked galley on the Nile, most likely a Liburnian attached to the fleet stationed at Alexandria. First century B.C. or first A.D.

b. Mosaic on the floor outside the office maintained at Ostia by the Shippers of Sullecthum ([Navic]ulari Syllecti[ni]), a town on the Tunisian coast. Second to third century A.D.

PLATE 12

Merchantmen in the Harbor at Portus, C2 A.D. 200

PLATE 13

Merchantmen and Warships of the Roman Empire

a. Three merchantmen at the entrance to the harbor of Portus. Third century A.D.

b. Detail of the above showing the sprit.

c. Roman warships, probably Liburnians, racing across the waters of a harbor. First century A.D.

PLATE 14
Merchantmen of the Roman Empire
a. Model of a large merchantman.

b. Small freighter, probably the type used to carry grain from Portus or Ostia to the docks on the Tiber. The vessel may have been sprit-rigged. Second or third century A.D.

PLATE 15
Small Craft of the Roman Empire

a. A shipwright at work. The inscription means, "Longidienus pushes ahead on his work."

b. Skiff in the act of warping a vessel into harbor; note the towing line running from the stern upward and off to the left. With the mast set so far up in the bows the boat must have carried some form of fore-and-aft rig, probably a sprit.

c. Boat rigged with a short-luffed lug.

d. Vessel traveling "wing and wing" under two spritsails.

PLATE 16

The Byzantine Age

a. Model of a dromon of the tenth century A.D.

b. Ship of the fleet of Emperor Michael II (A.D. 820–829) destroying an enemy with "Greek fire."

side; the landing plank has been made fast to the artemon halyard and a hand is standing by ready for the order to lower away; and the captain with his family cluster about an altar set up on the poop to offer sacrifice in thanks for a safe return. In the right-hand side, a sister ship has already made fast to the quay and is in the process of discharging; the topmen have gone aloft to secure the sails. The cargo was packed in clay jars—most likely it was wine—and a stevedore is shown walking off the quay bent under the weight of one balanced on his shoulder.

It has always been assumed that the square rig was the only type the ancient mariner used. But very recently a number of tombstones that had been hiding in dark corners of European museums were brought into the light and these reveal that he not only knew the fore-and-aft rig but at least two versions of it. One is the short-luffed lug (Pl. 15c), a sail so close to the lateen that there is good reason to think the ancients knew this one too, even though no examples have been found as yet. The other is the sprit (Pls. 15d; cf. 14b, 15b), a rig so much at home in northern waters that finding it in the Mediterranean came as a considerable surprise; it was always thought to be a Dutch invention that went no farther back in time than the fifteenth century. The sprit-rigged craft that appear on these tombstones are for the most part small, fishing smacks or the like, but there is a carving, done sometime in the third century A.D., on the side of a sarcophagus, a stone coffin, that shows one which is much bigger (Pl. 13a, b). Three ships are portrayed, neatly illustrating different types afloat at the time. The two on the outside are square-rigged; the one on the left has the traditional round hull, while that on the right has the bow with projecting forefoot. The one in the center is round-hulled and the same size as the others, but it carries a sprit-rig. The mast is stepped far up in the bows and the sail made fast to it by the luff, very loosely, as was the Dutch practice occasionally centuries later. The sprit, a long spar running diagonally across the windward side of the sail, supports the peak, and a double-ended vang made fast to its upper end permits trimming of the peak; no vertical brails are visible since they have no place in such a rig. The square-rig of the vessels on either side, with the mast stepped amidships and the prominent vertical brails, forms a sharp contrast.

Thus the skipper of a merchantman in this age had under his command a well-built, tight, well-rigged vessel. He had charts to plot courses on and "coast pilots" to guide him when he neared land. He carried a lead line to test depths, and the lead had a cup for tallow so that he could bring up samples of the bottom. He sent messages to other ships or the shore with semaphore flags. He had a ship's boat for emergencies and for use in harbor; if his vessel was large enough he could hoist it aboard; but usually, as large sailing ships did until just a few centuries ago, he towed it with a hand stationed aboard at all times (Pl. 12) — it provided the best chance of making a rescue if any of the crew fell overboard. The one thing he did not have was a compass; but in the Mediterranean, where distances over open water are never too great and where visibility is exceptionally good, this lack was not as serious as it might have been elsewhere. The reason the ancient mariner limited himself to a sailing season that ran from April to November (p. 39) was less the fact that winter brought storms — in later times Venetian galleys, for example, operated all year round — than that it brought frequent cloudy weather which, obscuring sun and stars and landmarks, made voyaging without some device to give direction hazardous.

The merchantmen of this age carried less canvas than they could have and they carried it low; this made them slow but at the same time safe. When the breeze was favorable they could average between four and six knots, when foul little more than two since their square rig could get no closer than seven points off the wind; those that were sprit-rigged, of course, could do considerably better. The carving on the sarcophagus mentioned above (Pl. 13a) shows particularly well the ancient skipper's skill in sailing against the wind. It is remarkable for being the earliest detailed representation in existence of a crisis at sea. The coffin held the remains of a boy — or man — who had drowned, and the coffin maker decorated it with the dramatic story of how he met his end. The scene is the mouth of the harbor of Rome. Here, on a windy day when the waves were running high, the boy had fallen out of a tiny skiff in which he had been rowing, perhaps in the very sight of his parents standing at the end of a mole. Two vessels race to the rescue from inside the port, one slightly ahead of the other. At the criti-

cal moment the one in the lead finds itself in imminent peril of
colliding with a ship heading into the harbor. It is this moment
that the artist chose to portray, and he left enough clues for us to
work out precisely what happened. The two rescue ships, facing
right, are traveling with the wind on the port quarter. The one
entering is on a starboard tack. Clearly there is a strong wind
blowing, for the square-riggers have shortened sail by taking up
on the brails, and the sprit-rigger by tricing up the tack of the
mainsail. The latter, though in the lead, suddenly finding itself in

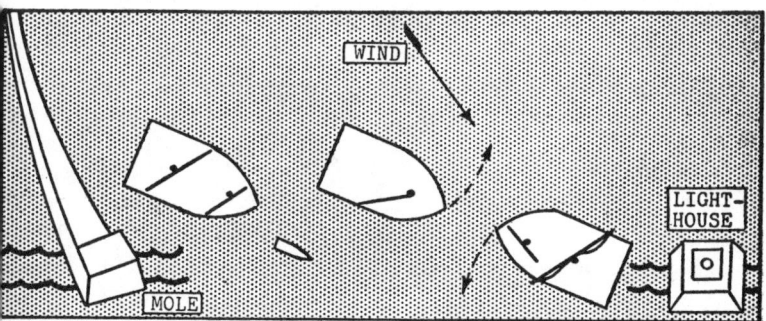

Fig. 6. Reconstruction of the sailing maneuvers pictured in Plate 13a.

danger has had to give up all thought of rescue. The one behind
has taken over that task, and one of the crew is leaning anxiously
over the bow ready to reach out a hand to the boy in the water.
Apparently he isn't aware of help from this quarter: his attention
is riveted despairingly on the ship nearest him which, confronted
by its own peril, can no longer bother with him. The two vessels
in the collision zone are maneuvering swiftly to avoid disaster.
Both have excellent skippers; they are doing precisely what is called
for. On the square-rigger the skipper has backed the mainsail. This
will slow his forward motion. The artemon is still drawing, which
will throw his bow to port and carry him past on the outside of the
other ship (Fig. 6). Very likely he wants the artemon trimmed, but
he is getting somewhat less than perfect cooperation: his hand forward has given up in fright, rushed amidships, and settled down to
pray. On the other vessel the skipper is working to swing his bow
to port and pass on the inside. This will bring him from a broad to

a close reach, and his hands accordingly are busy trimming sail: the one aft has grabbed the leech to get the sail inboard in a hurry. Another minute will tell the story. We know the rescue attempt was unsuccessful; let us hope that at least the collision was avoided.

The nation that had entered the First Punic War with a squadron of twenty vessels had come a long long way. The triremes and Liburnians of its fleets ringed the Mediterranean and the multifarious craft of its merchant marine thronged its waters. The one guarded, and the other carried, a far-flung and intensely active commerce—but that is a story that needs a chapter for itself.

16 All Routes Lead to Rome

"I BUILT MYSELF five ships, loaded them with wine—which was worth its weight in gold at the time—and sent them to Rome. Every single one of them was wrecked, that's the god's honest truth; Neptune gulped down a cool thirty million in one day. I built myself some more, got another cargo of wine, added bacon, beans, a load of slaves . . . the little woman sold all her jewels to raise the cash. I netted a cool ten million on that one voyage." The speaker is Trimalchio, Petronius' famous character, the ex-slave who became a multimillionaire. Petronius is, of course, exaggerating for literary effect but not too much. There was a fortune to be made in maritime commerce in Roman times. Marcus Porcius, a wealthy wine shipper who worked out of Pompeii, made enough money to contribute half the cost of building for his town a public theater large enough to seat fifteen hundred people. Sextius Fadius Musa, who exported wine out of what is now Burgundy, set up a rich trust fund, the annual proceeds of which were to go for a big blowout to be celebrated on his birthday forever; archaeologists have found hundreds of wine jars stamped with his name in France and Italy, testifying to his wide-flung activities. Businessmen like these were to be found from Spain to Syria, thousands of them. Augustus had launched and his successors maintained two centuries of peace; in this favorable climate commerce grew like a weed, outstripping in extent, volume, and velocity anything that had gone on before. It was more than just the total of what the Hellenistic world had carried on earlier in the east and of what Carthage had in the west. Its greatest component was something which, growing steadily since the middle of the second century B.C., now reached full maturity: filling the needs of the one million souls who lived in the city of Rome.

The Roman man in the street ate bread baked with wheat grown in North Africa or Egypt, and fish that had been caught and dried near Gibraltar. He cooked with north African oil in pots and pans of copper mined in Spain, ate off dishes fired in French kilns, drank wine from Spain or France and, if he spilled any of his dinner on his toga, had it cleaned with fuller's earth from the Aegean Islands. The Roman of wealth dressed in garments of wool from Miletus or linen from Egypt; his wife wore silks from China, adorned herself with diamonds and pearls from India, and made up with cosmetics from South Arabia. He seasoned his food with Indian pepper and sweetened it with Athenian honey, had it served in dishes of Spanish silver on tables of African citrus wood, and washed it down with Sicilian wine poured from decanters of Syrian glass. He lived in a house whose walls were covered with colored marble veneer quarried in Asia Minor; his furniture was of Indian ebony or teak inlaid with African ivory, and his rooms were filled with statues imported from Greece. Staples and luxuries, from as near as France and as far as China, poured into the capital, enough of the one to feed a million people, and of the other to satisfy the extravagances of the political, social, and economic rulers of the western world.

Until the middle of the first century A.D., the bulk of this trade was channeled through Pozzuoli. It had a fine natural harbor capable of handling large ships, while the only port near Rome, Ostia at the mouth of the Tiber, had nothing better to offer than an open roadstead which was constantly being silted up by the mud the river carried down every year. This meant that all cargoes had to be transferred to smaller craft to be carried up the coast, a procedure involving trouble, delay, and expense. The Emperor

All Routes Lead to Rome

Claudius finally decided to do something about the matter and in A.D. 42 began to build in the marshy plains north of the Tiber's mouth a big, completely man-made harbor to which he gave the matter-of-fact name of Portus "the port." Two enormous curving moles, each 1,900 feet long and 180 wide, formed the arms, and they enclosed an anchorage of 130 acres. In the space between the seaward ends Claudius had a concrete island constructed; to serve as its foundation he ordered sunk in place the great ship that his predecessor had built a few years earlier to carry the Vatican obelisk to Rome (p. 215). The island, by narrowing the entrance to two slender channels, kept the waters inside calm in all weather. On it a lighthouse was set up which rose in four diminishing stages, three square topped by a round (see Pl. 12, which probably in the main represents Portus, and Pl. 13a, which shows one of the entrance channels); it was modeled on the one at Alexandria and, like it, soon became famous enough to serve as a pattern for beacons elsewhere. A canal connected the new port with the Tiber. An incoming vessel either discharged its cargo onto barges which were drawn by oxen, trudging along a towpath, through the canal and up the Tiber to the great docks of the city, or transferred it to smaller craft which went around by sea the two miles to the mouth of the Tiber and then upriver (Pl. 14b). But even the new harbor wasn't enough to handle Rome's ever increasing traffic; consequently, between A.D. 101 and 104, the Emperor Trajan dug out a hexagonal inner basin behind Claudius' port to add seventy-eight acres of additional anchorage, lined it on all sides with warehouses, and widened the canal that led to the Tiber.

As a result of all this, Ostia boomed. Streets in the business section were lined with lofts and offices; in the residential area apartment houses rose up to take care of the burgeoning population. Members of the various trades and business enterprises in the time of the Roman Empire liked to band together in social clubs; the list of those at Ostia is practically an index to the activities of a busy port in any time or place. There were half a dozen for the different categories of boatmen: riverboatmen and bargemen to carry cargoes up the Tiber; ferrymen to transport passengers; tugboatmen to man the stout skiffs that warped vessels into or out of the harbor (Pl. 15b). There were clubs of shipwrights, caulkers, riggers, "sandmen" (to handle the sand commonly used as ballast), divers (to salvage goods dropped overboard), stevedores, warehousemen, watchmen. And, of course, dealers in grain, wine, oil, hides, and so on. Agents from the towns, big or small, that did business with Rome set up residence at Ostia. The colonnade behind the theater was ringed with their offices; by walking just a few steps along it a buyer could order ivory from the representatives of Sabratha in North Africa, oil from those of Carthage (refounded by Julius Caesar and now a flourishing export center), grain from those of Narbonne (cf. Pl. 11b).

The vast flow of goods to Rome was the most notable phase of the commerce of the age but not the only one. Italy sold abroad pottery and metalware and quantities of wine (cf. p. 194) up to the end of the first century A.D. when her best customers, the provinces, began not only to produce for themselves but to export to their former supplier. In the second century she partially made up for this loss: marble had then become the popular material for public buildings and she shipped out large amounts from the famous quarries at Carrara; off Saint-Tropez on the French Riviera sea diggers in 1951 fished up thirteen prefabricated column drums and bases and other architectural members, in all two hundred tons of Carrara marble, part of a shipment that was probably destined for a big temple in Narbonne some 160 miles farther west. All of Rome's provinces traded with one another as well as with the capital. Spain sent garum, its famous expensive fish sauce, to France and its dried fish to Greece; colored marbles from Asia Minor went into buildings in North Africa; statuary from Athens' workshops adorned the houses of the well-to-do throughout the west; Egypt shipped its papyri in all directions. In the east, ports of long standing such as Ephesus and Miletus, which had been slowly dying in the confusion and confiscations of Rome's civil wars, came to life; in the west, along the coasts of North Africa and Spain, the construction of moles, quays, and warehouses gave once primitive harbors a new look. The Emperor Nero undertook no less a project than cutting a canal across the Isthmus of Corinth (cf. p. 80). It was one of his bravura gestures of generosity toward Greece, of help almost solely to her commerce because the major sea routes for the most part now bypassed her; as it happened, political troubles made him give up the work and the isthmus remained uncut until 1893.

Thus the commerce of the Roman Empire embraced hundreds of places and products, all of what had gone on in earlier ages plus all that was brought into being by the new world Rome created. Yet, within this far-flung and complex network two lines of trade stand out conspicuously above all others, one for the distances it spanned and the exotic nature of the products it dealt with, the other for the vast bulk of its shipments and the mighty organization it required: Rome's trade in the Indian Ocean, and the Alexandria-Rome grain service.

"The beautiful large ships of the Yavanas come bearing gold and making the water white with foam, and return laden with pepper." So wrote an Indian poet sometime in the second century A.D. "Drink," another suggested to his king, "the cool and fragrant wines brought by the Yavanas in their vessels." "Yavanas" were, strictly speaking, men from any part of the west but, on the tongue of an Indian of the time, it almost always meant the Greeks and Egyptians who ran the trade between the Mediterranean and India. Their ships lined the quays of Indian ports and their sailors haunted the waterfront dives. In the residential areas behind, their agents established little foreign quarters for themselves, anticipating by a millennium and a half the employees of Britain's East India Company.

Official embassies passed back and forth between East and West. India sent several during the reign of Augustus, one from Ceylon visited the Emperor Claudius, and they kept coming as late as the reign of Constantine the Great. Chinese records contain a long and rather flattering account of how people lived in Rome's eastern provinces based in part on the report of an ambassador who had gone to Mesopotamia in A.D. 97. (It has the surprising observation that the people there "are honest in their transactions and there are no double prices," something not often said about Near Eastern tradesmen.) One group of westerners made their way to the very borders of China, for the same account notes that in "the ninth year of the Yen-hsi period, during the Emperor Huan-ti's reign [A.D. 166] . . . the King of Ta-ts'-in, An-tun, sent an embassy which, from the frontier of Jih-nan [Annam], offered ivory, rhinoceros horns and tortoise shell. From that time dates the intercourse with this country." Ta-ts'-in is the Chinese name for the Roman Empire, and An-tun is Antoninus, the family name of Marcus Aurelius. The account goes on to comment about the very ordinary gifts the embassy brought for the emperor; there were, for example, no jewels. Most likely it wasn't an official body at all but a group of shippers who, to get one jump ahead of their competitors, were trying to buy their silk directly from China instead of through middlemen.

What came from India and Arabia in the days of the Ptolemies (p. 185) was a trickle compared with the flow that took place after Augustus brought peace to the Mediterranean world. As before, the ultimate consumer of most of it was the city of Rome. Pepper and other spices arrived in such quantities that the Emperor Vespasian sectioned off part of a colonnade in the heart of the city, the *horrea piperaria,* "pepper sheds," for the exclusive use of spice merchants; when Alaric the Goth in A.D. 408 agreed not to sack Rome, part of the price paid was three thousand pounds of pepper. Silks and jewelry poured in so profusely that there was concern about the drain on the city's financial resources. "The ladies and their baubles are transferring our money to foreigners," grumbled Emperor Tiberius, and Pliny the Elder worried about how imports from Arabia, India, and China cost Rome 550,000,000 sesterces annually.

In Augustus' day 120 ships set out each year for India from Myos Hormos, "Mussel Harbor," on the Red Sea, six times as many as under the last Ptolemies, and there were two other ports in the same area that sent out fleets as well. Troops of archers were carried as guards against pirate attack, and a detachment of the Roman navy patrolled the Red Sea. The vessels sailed, as under the later Ptolemies, with the southwest monsoon almost astern to the mouth of the Indus River near Karachi (p. 185). A few decades later, a little after the middle of the first century A.D., skippers weren't afraid to bring the wind on the starboard quarter and, though it added five hundred miles on the open sea, to head for the southwest coast, the heart of the pepper country. Starting from Egypt in July, they made the fourteen hundred miles down the

Red Sea in thirty days, and the two thousand miles from there to the Malabar coast in another forty; about the beginning of December they caught the northwest monsoon back. To help matters along, the Emperor Trajan once again had the old canal between the Nile and the Red Sea (p. 10) dredged out.

The Rome-India run was the most remote trade route of the age, yet it is the one we know best. An anonymous merchant who operated a ship on it shortly after the middle of the first century B.C. compiled a *Periplus Maris Erythraei*, "Guidebook of the Erythraean Sea", that is, of the Indian Ocean, the Red Sea, and the Persian Gulf. There must have been similar manuals covering every sea lane in the Roman Empire, but this is the only one that has survived. It was written both for skippers and for shippers: it was a "coast pilot" for the east shore of Africa as far south as Zanzibar and the coasts of Arabia and India, and at the same time a merchant's guide to what could be bought and sold at each point along the way. It has no more literary merit than a United States Navy publication, and it is a scant twenty-five pages long, but it is a mine of priceless information.

The author deals first with the African coast. On this leg, he reports, the important items a trader can pick up are tortoise shell, ivory, and incense, and they are to be had in exchange for cheap clothes, metals, and trinkets. He frequently warns against unfriendly natives; it's wise, he notes at one point, to take "a little wine and wheat, not for trade but to get the goodwill of the savages."

But the heart of the handbook is the trip to India, and for that the author returns to the starting bases of Myos Hormos and Berenice. First he describes the passage down the Red Sea and along the south shore of Arabia. The harbors are mostly poor and the coastal voyage along the south of Arabia is particularly dangerous. At one port on the Arabian shore of the Red Sea the trader still runs into reminders of the extent of Rome's power: an official backed by a garrison of soldiers levies a toll of not less than one-quarter of all merchandise brought in. At a town near the mouth of the sea is the first occurrence of that ubiquitous concomitant of trade in the East, bakshish: here "the Sheikh and his Chief are given horses, pack-mules, gold vessels, polished silver vessels, expensive garments, and copper vessels." The product par excellence of the area was, of course, myrrh, and the natives were chiefly interested in various types of textiles. After a very brief look at the Persian Gulf—it was held by Rome's enemy, Parthia, and entering its ports was no doubt risky—the author gets to India.

He reaches it at the mouth of the Indus. Here was a market where fabrics and vessels of glass or gold or silver could be exchanged for certain Indian spices and perfumes, semiprecious stones, muslin, and silk yarn. The place was obviously a terminus for transit trade because few of these products were local: the stones came from Afghanistan and Iran, and the silk all the way from China. Farther down the coast at Broach, two hundred miles north of Bombay, all these items were available plus other kinds of cotton cloth and some pepper; among the things the natives would take in return was "wine, Italian preferred." The bakshish here ran very high: "for the rajah there are brought . . . very expensive silver vessels, singing boys, beautiful maidens for the harem, fine wines, expensive fine-woven garments and the best ointments." Navigation along this coast from the Indus to Broach was tricky and the author describes the hazards with vivid detail. One of the worst was getting into the ports, particularly difficult because of rocks, sand bars, and the steep rise and fall of the tides. His bald businessman's style even takes on color as he tells of one harbor where "at the new moon the force of the sea as it surges in, especially when the flood tide comes at night, is so powerful that if, taking advantage of slack tide, you have already started to enter, from the mouth of the river you first hear something that sounds like an army far off and, very soon after, the sea itself spills in over the shoals with a roar." Here the local rajah helped out by furnishing native fishermen as pilots. It was in part to avoid this stretch of coast that skippers who traded farther south brought the wind well on the starboard quarter as soon as they left the Red Sea and held to a course over the open water.

Finally the author reaches the Malabar coast which, as the source of pepper and gems, was far and away the most important trading area. Here, in a port on the site of what is today Cranganore, the really big freighters were found, those that had made the voyage straight across the ocean. They came because of the enormous quantities of pepper and malabathrum [a form of cinnamon]. The place imports first and foremost a great amount of coin; also topaz, a little fine-woven clothing, figured linens, antimony, coral, crude glass, copper, tin, lead, a little wine . . . , realgar and orpiment [red and yellow pigment respectively], and enough wheat for the ships' crews since the local merchants don't deal in it [they obviously handled only rice]. The place exports pepper, produced in quantity in only one place nearby, a district called Cottonara. It also exports good amounts of fine pearls, ivory, silk cloth, spikenard from the Ganges, malabathrum from the places inland, transparent stones of all kinds, diamonds, sapphires, and tortoise-shell.

One of the most interesting bits of information in this passage is that the products here were paid for primarily with "a great amount of coin." Tiberius had grumbled about this, Pliny the Elder had given statistics—and archaeologists have found the concrete proof: a considerable number of Roman coins have been discovered in the southern tip of India, all silver and gold, no copper. Because the natives at the time had no coinage, these must have been treated as bullion: the medium of exchange was not the face value of the coins but a miscellaneous batch totaling a given weight. Those that have turned up date from the reign of Augustus to Nero, but this doesn't mean that trade ended abruptly at that time. Nero and his successors issued debased money which the Indians refused to accept; merchants thenceforth had to pay either in the older coins or in goods.

The trade route did not stop at the southern tip of India but continued up the east coast. A recent archaeological excavation has uncovered near Pondicherry the remains of a western trading station that was active from the middle of the first century A.D. to at least the end of the second. The author of the guidebook is familiar with this coast but only as far as the mouth of the Ganges. At this point his information peters out. He knows about Malay only vaguely and, making a mistake common in descriptions of remote places (cf. p. 139), calls it an island. And beyond Malay he reports a land where "there is a great inland city called Thina, from which raw silk and silk yarn and silk cloth are brought overland. . . . But this land of Thina is not easy to get to; very few men come from there and seldom."

This is where this unique manual ends—but not where the ancient mariners stopped. By the end of the second century A.D. they had pushed as far as Annam and possibly beyond. The man who led the way was a courageous Greek about whom nothing else is known except that he was called Alexander. He discovered that there were monsoons in the Bay of Bengal east of India as well as in the seas to its west and, taking advantage of this knowledge, made two voyages of exploration. The first carried him only across the bay as far as Burma but, on the second, he sailed down the Burmese coast, passed through the Strait of Malacca into the South China Sea, and got as far as Hanoi or perhaps even Canton. Soon the merchants who followed his lead were sailing directly across the mouth of the Bay of Bengal and trading with Malaya, Sumatra, and Java, and some, like the so-called "ambassadors of An-tun," were in contact with China. Here their eastward push finally came to a halt. They had carved out a trade route that, reckoned from Rome, spanned almost a third of the globe, and they had reached a region that westerners were not to see again until the beginning of the sixteenth century. For at least a hundred years more they kept coming: Chinese records mention a certain Lun—was he a Greek named Leon?—who reached Cochin-China (South Vietnam as it is currently called) by sea in A.D. 226, and a party that brought gifts to the emperor in 284.

This, then, is the general picture of one of Rome's great commercial achievements, her incredibly far-flung trade with Africa, Arabia, India, and the Far East. A hasty glimpse at it gives the impression of tremendous complexity: the author of the handbook that provides so much of the available information drops the names of dozens of ports and of a bewildering variety of objects of trade. But a closer look reveals a simple pattern behind it all. There were, basically, four key products Rome drew from these lands and they came from four distinct areas: incense from Arabia, ivory from Africa, pepper from India, and silk from China (for the most part through India). The first was and always had been a necessity, something ancient religion could not do without; but the others were sheer luxuries, things a wealthy Roman insisted on having to improve the taste of his food or the looks of his furniture and wife, though he had to pay for them in hard cash. Rome's second great accomplishment in commerce is precisely the opposite in every respect: instead of rare and exotic luxuries intended for the rich, it involved a bulky and cheap commodity essential for the daily existence of a million people—grain. And most of it didn't cost her a cent.

The city of Rome posed a problem in supply that was unique. Starting out as a mere village, it had grown by Augustus' time into a sprawling metropolis of one million souls, much too big to look to the surrounding country for its food. As a matter of fact, long before it reached this size, it had begun to draw its grain from overseas and the government found itself obliged, like the Greek cities (p. 121), to assume the responsibility for seeing to it that supplies were adequate. The vagaries of politics compelled it to expand the role it played. Around the end of the second century B.C. large quantities of grain were flowing in as taxes in kind from some of the provinces Rome now ruled. To curry favor, politicians started the practice first of selling grain to the citizens at below the market price and later of distributing it to them free. Once something like this gets going it can rarely be stopped: during the first three centuries after Christ an average of 200,000 people were receiving such handouts. To complicate matters further, the city by this time was getting most of its wine and oil from abroad. Between what was needed for the dole and for the open market, every emperor from Augustus to the last to sit on the throne found the *annona,* as the supply of food for the city was called, one of his most pressing problems. It grew worse in the third century A.D. when handouts, first of oil and then of wine and pork, were added to the traditional one of grain. The *praefectus annonae,* "Minister of Supply," became one of the most harried officials in the government. It wasn't the cost of the commodities involved that caused him trouble: most of Rome's grain came to her free of charge as taxes in kind from Sicily and North Africa and Egypt, and she drew enough taxes in money from all her provinces to pay for whatever else she required. His problem was getting transportation, getting the cargoes moved from overseas to the capital.

One of the rare statistics preserved from the ancient world is the figure for the amount of grain shipped yearly from Egypt to Rome

—150,000 tons. And this satisfied merely a third of the city's requirements; the rest came from Sicily and North Africa. On the outskirts of modern Rome, near the point on the Tiber where the ancient docks used to be, is a fair-sized hill called today Monte Testaccio, "Mount Potsherd." It is composed, from foot to summit, of broken pieces of pottery, remains of the containers in which over the years millions of gallons of oil and wine had been shipped from North Africa and Spain. Now, the run from Sicily was a matter of two days, from North Africa of three, and from Spain of little more than a week. But Egypt was something else again.

Egypt lies to the southeast of Rome. The winds that prevail over the waters between, during the summer months when the ancient mariners sailed, are northwesterly. This meant that freighters raced downhill from Ostia or Pozzuoli to Alexandria with the wind on their heels in ten days to two weeks. Everything added up to a quick voyage: the direction of the wind made possible a direct trip, the winds themselves were strong and steady, and the vessels most often traveled in ballast since Rome had a lopsided balance of trade, taking in far more than she shipped out. But the skippers paid heavily for all this on the return: it was uphill work against foul winds every mile of the way. The northwesterlies dictated a course that was a third again as long as the voyage out. The ships, now fully laden, had to head for the south coast of Asia Minor on a port tack, there turn west and, on a starboard tack, coast along to Rhodes. From here they worked south of Crete and then, with continuous tacking, beat their way to Syracuse in Sicily, with perhaps a stop at Malta en route. Here they could wait, if they had the time, for a southerly to carry them through the Strait of Messina and north; otherwise they headed into the northwesterlies once again and slogged it out the rest of the way. The voyage took at least fifty days and on occasions as much as seventy. A vessel could count on only a single round trip or, at most, a trip and a half during the sailing season.

Whatever the winds, the grain Egypt consigned to Rome, all 150,000 tons of it, had to reach the docks on the Tiber or the city went hungry. When Vespasian got control of the east in A.D. 69 and was planning to take over Rome, his first step was to seize Egypt: by cutting off its grain he could starve the capital into submission.

All Routes Lead to Rome

Once when supplies in the city were running low, the Emperor Claudius offered special rewards to skippers who were willing to sail during winter, even those whose ships held no more than seventy tons. Hardly an economical way of doing things, but he had no choice.

There was only one way to meet the problem: see to it that enough big ships were available and shuttle them between Rome and Alexandria. Augustus took the first step—he probably started with a group of Alexandrian shipowners who had hauled grain for the Ptolemies—and his successors followed his lead in this as in so many other things. The result was the crack fleet of Rome-Alexandria grain "clippers."

By luck we happen to know what the ships on this run looked like. One day sometime in the second century A.D., one of them ran into a particularly bad stretch of weather, was blown far off course, and wound up, of all places, in Athens' port, the Peiraeus. This was a far cry from the place it had been formerly: Athens was now a sleepy university town and its once great harbor handled little more than local traffic. The arrival of a ship from the famous grain fleet created a sensation; the *Queen Mary* or any of our Atlantic superliners wouldn't cause more had they suddenly appeared at a dock in Mobile or New Orleans. The whole town turned out to see it—including, fortunately for posterity, Lucian, one of the most famous and prolific writers of the age. He and a group of friends walked the five miles from Athens to the Peiraeus to get a look at what was causing all the excitement. He was astonished. He wrote:

What a size the ship was! [cf. Pl. 12] 180 feet in length, the ship's carpenter told me, the beam more than a quarter of that, and 44 feet from the deck to the lowest point in the hold. And the height of the mast, and what a yard it carried, and what a forestay they had to use to hold it up! And the way the stern rose up in a gradual curve ending in a gilded goose-head, matched at the other end by the forward, more flattened, sweep of the prow with its figures of Isis, the goddess the ship was named after, on each side! Everything was incredible: the rest of the decoration, the paintings, the red topsail, even more, the anchors with their capstans and winches, and the cabins aft. The crew was like an army. They told me she carried enough grain to feed every mouth in

Athens for a year. And it all depends for its safety on one little old man who turns those great steering oars with a tiller that's no more than a stick! They pointed him out to me; woolly-haired little fellow, half-bald; Heron was his name, I think."

A length of 180 feet, beam of more than 45, a hold 44 feet deep —it was a mighty ship, probably able to carry between 1,200 and 1,300 tons of grain. It was as big as our *Constitution*, the famous frigate now in Boston Harbor. It held three times as much cargo as any merchantman that plied between Europe and America before 1820; it was not until 1845 that the North Atlantic saw a ship its size. If all employed on the run were the size of the *Isis*, Rome needed a fleet of about eighty-five to ferry the 150,000 tons she took yearly from Egypt. If any were smaller she needed correspondingly more.

There were no such things as special passenger ships in the ancient world. The traveler generally boarded whatever trading vessel turned up and made his way, hopping from port to port, to his destination. One exception was the voyage from Rome to Alexandria and back: the great grain ships provided an excellent passenger service. "If you are going from Rome to Palestine," Emperor Caligula told the young Jewish princeling Agrippa, "don't bother with galleys and the coastal routes but take one of our direct Italy-Alexandria merchantmen." Even the Roman emperors used them. When Vespasian wanted to return from Egypt to Rome in the spring of A.D. 70, he had at his disposal any galley in the navy, but he preferred to take passage on a grain clipper. The big vessels, keeping to the open sea, didn't waste time in daily stops along the way, and—a point that very likely was uppermost in Vespasian's mind as he contemplated the two-month voyage ahead—they offered accommodations that were luxury itself compared with cramped quarters on the poop of a cockleshell man-of-war. There was plenty of room aboard: when Josephus, the Jewish historian, crossed in A.D. 64 he had no less than six hundred fellow passengers.

A traveler from Italy would board at Pozzuoli or, after Claudius and Trajan had finished their work, at The Port in the spring when the part of the fleet that had lain over there set sail, generally in ballast, for Alexandria; the ships would arrive in a few weeks and thus have practically the whole summer before them for a round trip from Egypt. The rest of the fleet, which had wintered in Alexandria, had a much harder schedule. They left there, fully loaded with grain and passengers, just as soon as the sailing season opened, and made port in late May or June. They were easy to spot as they neared the harbor, and their arrival was a great event. An eyewitness recounts:

Today the ships from Alexandria suddenly came into view, at least those which are usually sent ahead to announce the coming of the fleet, the "despatch-boats" as they are called. It is a welcome sight to the country. The whole mob at Pozzuoli stands on the docks; they can recognize the ships from Alexandria even in a crowd of vessels by their sails. For, though all ships carry topsails on the open water, these are the only ones allowed to keep them up. . . . When they have passed Capri all other vessels have orders to make do with the mainsail, so the topsails on those from Alexandria stand out conspicuously.

Once arrived at Pozzuoli or The Port, the ships had to hope for a quick turn-around since they had a full circuit, to Alexandria and back again to Rome, to fit in before the sailing season ended. This, however, couldn't always be counted on. Much was involved: the vessel had to be checked into port, it had to shift its load to barges or small freighters, and then it had to wait around until it got clearance from the authorities to leave. All this could take more than a month. There is a letter preserved which a hand on one of the grain ships wrote to his brother in Egypt sometime in the second or third century A.D.; the latter read it, threw it away, and it lay intact in Egypt's protecting sands until it was dug up at the end of the last century. It speaks for itself:

DEAR APOLLINARIUS,

Many greetings. I pray continuously for your health; I am well. I'm writing to let you know that I reached land on June 30 and that we unloaded on July 12. I went up to Rome on the 19th and the place welcomed us as the god wished. We are daily expecting our sailing orders; up to today not one of the grain fleet has been released. Best regards to your wife, and Serenus, and all your friends. Goodbye.

Your brother IRENAEUS
August 2

Irenaeus' ship clearly would not be getting back to Alexandria until late in August, and squeezing in another trip to Rome before the sailing season closed down was going to be nip and tuck. But the pressure was such that skippers had little choice: they had to shove off even though they ran the risk of being forced to winter at some harbor along the way. As a matter of fact, this is precisely what happened during what is probably the best-known voyage in ancient history, St. Paul's trip to Rome in A.D. 62.

At Myra, a port on the south coast of Asia Minor, the Roman centurion who was escorting the group of prisoners that included Paul "found a ship of Alexandria sailing into Italy, and he put us therein. And when we had sailed slowly many days, and scarce were come over against Cnidus, the wind not suffering us, we sailed under Crete." Although it may have seemed so to the passengers, this was nothing unusual: their skipper would have been surprised had he picked up a fair wind on this leg. But Paul was soon to face far worse. The ship he had boarded was one of those that had already completed a round trip that year and was now trying to cram in a second run to Rome; the passenger list was consequently light—there were only 276 aboard, counting the crew. By the time his vessel made Crete it was dangerously late in the season, and both skipper and owner elected to play it safe and put in at some small haven for the winter. As luck would have it, a favorable breeze sprang up and the decision was reached to take advantage of it to try for a harbor with better facilities a little farther along the coast. Soon after they put out to sea an east-north-east gale struck them. Centuries before Paul's time the same wind had blown Colaeus to fame and fortune (p. 80), and sailors today still keep a weather eye out for the Gregale, as they call it. For fourteen days the vessel rode helplessly before it under bare poles; the crew kept the seams from opening by passing girding ropes around the planks, they cut away part of the rigging, and at the very end jettisoned the cargo of grain to lighten ship. Colaeus had been driven all the way to Spain, but Paul was luckier: at midnight of the fourteenth day the seamen suddenly sensed that land was near. The leadsman was ordered to take soundings. He reported first twenty fathoms then, very soon after, fifteen; the water was shoaling dangerously fast. The skipper had four anchors heaved astern to hold on until day broke. As soon as there was some light, he saw that there was only one thing to do: try to run the ship ashore. He ordered the

All Routes Lead to Rome

artemon raised, the anchors cut away, and the helmsman to head for the beach. The gamble worked: everyone aboard was rescued, although the vessel broke in two. The land turned out to be Malta, and Paul spent three months there until another grain clipper, one that had started from Alexandria a little ahead of his ship but had prudently put in at the island for the winter, took him on the last leg of the journey when the sailing season reopened the following spring.

The Apostle's voyage graphically points up the hazards that faced the ships on the Rome-Alexandria grain run. The creation and maintenance of this fleet was Rome's single greatest maritime achievement, at once a great passenger and a great freight service. The vessels, like practically all other merchantmen, were owned, commanded, and manned by Greeks or Phoenicians or Syrians, but it was the Romans who called the fleet into being and it was their genius that lay behind its organization and administration. For size of vessels and volume of cargo, it had no peer until the British East Indiamen of the early nineteenth century. Year in and year out the great ships kept sailing until, in A.D. 330, Constantine the Great finished building another city to serve as the capital of the empire, Constantinople, on the site of the ancient Greek town of Byzantium (p. 78). He took over the fleet to bring the grain of Egypt to his new foundation and left those who remained at Rome to be fed by the quick shuttle service from North Africa and Sicily.

17 — An End and a Beginning

IN A.D. 269 a horde of Goths ripped up and down the Aegean, spreading havoc among the islands. Goths on the warpath were nothing new: the movement of barbarian peoples that was to tear huge rents in the fabric of the Roman Empire was well under way by this time. What was new was to find them on the sea. After two centuries of easy living, carrying out peacetime maneuvers and ferrying troops, Rome's great navy had, like so much else in the empire, gone soft. By A.D. 230 the plague of piracy had erupted again; between 253 and 267 mobs of Goths were using the waterways, the Black Sea and the Aegean, to get to the scene of their maraudings; by 285, when Diocletian was crowned emperor, the provincial squadrons had vanished from the Mediterranean and the big Italian fleets had shrunk to mere skeletons; and in 324, when Constantine the Great fought it out on the sea with one of his rivals, both sides had to commandeer ships from the maritime cities of the east. A full cycle had been traversed: Rome was again virtually without a navy.

In A.D. 395 the Roman Empire broke into two parts, an eastern and a western; whatever warships were left moved to the east—and

An End and a Beginning

the Vandals had a field day in the western Mediterranean. They were a Germanic tribe that had spilled over into North Africa. From there, practically without breaking stride, they took to the sea, captured Sardinia and Corsica and other strategic islands, and in 455 even succeeded in sacking Rome. There was no one to stop them; matters were worse than in the worst days of the pirates of Cilicia (pp. 201-3). But when their leader, Gaiseric, died in 477, their plunderings came to a halt. Gradually another fleet arose to restore and maintain some order on the water. The credit goes to those most able of the ancient mariners, the Greeks of the eastern Mediterranean; it was the last contribution they were to make, and it was a notable one.

The western part of the Roman Empire little by little fell into the hands of invaders from Germany. But the eastern was made of sterner stuff: the Byzantine Empire, as the nation that took root here is called, did not come to an end until 1453 when the Turks finally took Constantinople, its capital. One of the chief reasons for this long life was sea power. Shortly after A.D. 500 the empire launched a navy that managed to fill the gap left by Rome's collapse on the sea. In the seventh century a dangerous enemy unexpectedly appeared on the scene: in 636 the Arabs embarked on their meteoric career by conquering Syria; a few years later they added Egypt and, by the end of the century, all of North Africa. To meet the new menace, the empire built up its navy into a powerful force, big enough to be divided, like its predecessor, into a home fleet and a number of provincial detachments. Until the eleventh century it was the strongest in the eastern Mediterranean, although it had to fight some bitter battles against the squadrons of Islam to hold the distinction. The new navy was no warmed-over version of what the Romans had used: the ships were of different design and, from A.D. 678 on, they mounted a new and terrible type of weapon. Its introduction came at a dramatic and timely moment.

In 673 the Arabs began an all-out attack by water against Constantinople. Every summer for the next five years their ships sailed from an advanced base on the island of Cyzicus in the Sea of Marmora to harry and blockade the Byzantine capital. A sack seemed just a matter of time—and would have been were it not for one man. Callinicus, an engineer, had fled to Constantinople from his native town when the Arabs flooded into Syria. At one and the same time he paid off both those who had driven him out and those who had taken him in: he saved the city by coming up, in the nick of time, with a new way of using an old weapon, fire.

The Greeks and the Romans had for centuries tried fire in one form or another. On the sea, back in the second century B.C., the Rhodians had won some spectacular victories by hanging blazing fire pots in front of their galleys (pp. 152, 171). The key ingredient in almost all the formulas for "Greek fire"—as the various inflammable mixtures came to be called in later times—was what the ancients referred to as naphtha, crude oil which, throughout the oil-rich areas of the Near East, could be scooped up at dozens of points where it seeped out of the ground. Although it was inflammable enough in its simple state, the usual practice was to lace it with sulphur or pitch or quicklime. Then came a revolutionary discovery: if saltpeter were included, a mixture resulted which was capable of spontaneous combustion. Callinicus has been given the credit for having been the first to hit upon this. If he wasn't, he must have at least developed a formula vastly more effective than any hitherto known: it not only saved the Byzantines at the time, but provided them with their chief weapon for the future; merely by keeping it a secret from the Arabs they were able to hold a clean advantage on the sea for centuries.

Callinicus' phenomenal success turned fighting with fire into one of the major modes of warfare of the age, and a whole arsenal of new weapons came into being. Ships were now fitted with two types of incendiary artillery. One was the catapult now loaded, not only with arrows and stones, but with clay jars filled with the latest, most improved version of Callinicus' self-igniting mixture; on impact they shattered and the contents, splattered about, burst everywhere into flame. The other was probably the most advanced military device before the cannon: an incendiary rocket and the mechanism to launch it. A bronze tube was mounted on deck and into it was slipped a reed that had been filled with Greek fire and stoppered. The tube was aimed and a fuse was lit; it ignited the reed, which burst into flame; the gases released shot it out of the tube, and a shaft of fire streaked through the air toward the target. But it was fighting at close quarters rather than at a distance that

An End and a Beginning

called into play the Byzantines' most deadly weapon, the one that became standard equipment on all their warships. This was a great long tube, of wood lined with bronze, that was set on the foredeck with its mouth trained outward. Its other end was coupled to an air pump. It was loaded with Greek fire; this was ignited, the pump was worked—and a shaft of flame belched forth from the mouth (Pl. 16b). It was the world's first flame-thrower, and a terrifyingly effective one. There was even a miniature model, small enough to hold in the hand, which marines used: they kept it hidden behind their shield and, at the appropriate moment, fired it at the enemy.

The naval arms of the age were new and so were the ships that carried them. The Romans had gone in for two-banked vessels to some extent, but the backbone of their navy was the trireme (pp. 209, 213). The ship of the line of the Byzantine fleets was the *dromon,* "runner" (Pl. 16a). It was designed, as its name shows, particularly for speed and it was always two-banked; triremes, quadriremes, and so on were now things of the past. It carried one hundred oars, twenty-five in each level on each side. They were all worked through ports in the hull; the outrigger (p. 92) had gone out with the third bank. Though there were larger and smaller classes of dromons, all ran more or less about the same length, 130 feet or so, enough to provide room for twenty-five oarsmen and for fighting decks fore and aft. It was their beam that varied. Some were wide enough to seat two rowers, and the largest class three, at each of the upper oars, with correspondingly greater space for marines and armament. These beamier types struck a balance between power and speed: to a basically fast design they added the force that comes from propulsion by multirower oars.

The dromon was a blunt ship with angular rather than smoothly flowing lines. Near the prow and stern the ribs rose almost vertically from the keel; elsewhere they branched out horizontally from it, then turned abruptly upward. To reduce weight and increase speed, the amidships section was left open; three long catwalks, one down the center and two along the gunwales, linked up the decking in the fore and after areas. The decks rose a few feet above the line of the gunwale and, along the low waist between, a light wooden frame was erected on which shields were hung, very much as on Viking ships, to protect the rowers. The ships carried two masts, sometimes three, and, in the later centuries at least, these were fitted with lateen sails. Since this rig is light and easy to handle, the sails were carried during battle and not left ashore as had been the practice previously (p. 97).

The prow of a dromon, like all earlier warships, jutted forward to end in a ram. But more important were the new fire weapons and the armament connected with boarding and fighting at close quarters. In the bows was a forecastle from which marines could sweep an enemy's deck with missiles. The largest dromons added a second castle amidships with long overhangs projecting laterally over the gunwales; on each a heavy weight was suspended and, when an enemy came so close that these were poised over his rowers, the lashings that held them were loosed or cut away. Every ship carried a flame-thrower in the bows; larger units mounted rocket-launchers and catapults; and the largest had all this plus an extra pair of flame-throwers, one amidships and one at the stern. Since the enemy also used fire in some form, vulnerable parts of the vessel were protected with stretched hides which, in battle, because water was ineffectual against Greek fire, were saturated with vinegar.

The dromon was the ship of the line not only of the imperial navy but, with some modifications, of its principal rival as well. The Arabs who overran Syria and Egypt were a people far more at home on the desert than on the water, and the keels of their first squadrons were laid down in the dockyards of Alexandria by Greeks and Egyptians who shortly before had been building ships for the Byzantine fleet. For centuries afterward the new rulers drew on their conquered subjects not only for shipwrights but also for crews. In the first and second centuries A.D. Egyptian youngsters had rowed the vessels of Rome's Misene fleet (p. 211); in the seventh and eighth and even later, they manned the benches of the Caliph's Egyptian squadron, while Arab marines fought from its decks.

The imperial navy was a worthy replacement for Rome's. It had to be: without a first-rate fighting force the Byzantines would have lost their commerce to Arab raiders and their capital to the Arab grand fleet. In the field of merchant shipping, however, though they carried on for a while an active and widespread commerce,

An End and a Beginning

they produced nothing to match the achievements of their predecessors. Rome's greatest efforts had been called forth by her trade in the Indian Ocean and by the challenge of the run from Alexandria to the Tiber; the one played only a short-lived part, and the other none, in the commerce of her successors.

In the second century B.C. the Ptolemies had broken the age-old monopoly of the Indians and Arabs in the trade with India (pp. 185-7). By the beginning of the sixth century A.D., Persian shippers and sailors had taken most of it over from the Greeks and Egyptians. The *coup de grâce* came in 641: in that year the Arabs captured Egypt, and Byzantine merchants were once for all cut off from direct contact with the Red Sea and Indian Ocean. From that time on, Persians and Arabs shared the commerce in these waters until Vasco da Gama sailed his squadron into the harbor of Calicut on May 20, 1498.

The Arab conquest of Egypt meant, too, that the Nile's harvest now went down the Red Sea to Mecca and Medina instead of across the Mediterranean to Europe. But it was not this which brought about the end of Rome's great fleet of grain carriers; that had taken place hundreds of years before. Soon after Constantine had founded his new capital, the huge cargoes of Egyptian grain that used to go to the Tiber were diverted northward to the Bosporus. Getting it to the new destination was far simpler than to the old; there was no need for a fleet of superfreighters. The run was so much shorter and easier that vessels could make two or even three round trips a season. The only difficulty was navigating the Dardanelles (cf. p. 76) and the Emperor Justinian, in the early part of the sixth century, solved this by building a big granary on the island of Tenedos near the mouth of the strait. It was 280 feet long, 90 wide, and quite tall, large enough to hold the combined cargoes of all the vessels on the run. When the wind in the strait was foul, ships unloaded here and hustled back to Egypt, leaving it to small craft to carry the grain the rest of the way as soon as a favorable breeze came along. The debacle of 641 brought even this service to an end. From then on the capital depended on the supplies it could shuttle in from the Balkans and South Russia.

All this does not mean that the Byzantine Empire abandoned maritime commerce once Egypt was lost to it. For over a hundred years thereafter its traders were still to be found in every major port from Italy to the Black Sea, and its fleet not only guaranteed safe passage for their freighters but, in certain areas, ensured a monopoly by keeping those of competitors away. Persians and Arabs brought the products of the East to the Mediterranean, but it was the Byzantine merchant who forwarded them to the West. As time went on, however, he became soft, preferring the office and warehouse to the deck. The empire's merchant marine gradually dwindled away; Constantinople remained a great commercial center, but what it imported and exported traveled now in Arab or Syrian or Italian bottoms. By A.D. 1100 the Byzantines had completely relinquished their old role: the energetic traders of Pisa and Genoa and Venice now held the commerce of the Mediterranean in their grasp, and Italian fleets were in control of its waters.

A century or so later came the great contributions of the Middle Ages to the arts of the sailor: helmsmen now steered by the compass instead of by the stars or sun or wind, and with an efficient stern rudder instead of the old steering oars. Moreover, the time was drawing near when the ram and the flame-thrower were to make way for naval cannon. The day of the ancient mariner was truly ended.

Table of Dates

Dates before 500 B.C.
are all approximate.

B.C.		See page
3500–3400	Invention of sails (?)	2
2900	Earliest pictures of sails	2
2650	Pharaoh Snefru imports timber from Lebanon	4
	Earliest contacts between Egypt and Crete	21
2550	Pharaoh Sahure ferries troops	14
2500	Trade between Mesopotamia and India	8
2375	Pharaoh Pepi ferries troops	27
2000	Pharaoh Mentuhotep III sends a ship down the Red Sea	10
	Pharaoh Senusret cuts a canal between the Nile and the Red Sea	10
2000–1500	Heyday of Minoan maritime activity	21
1500–1100	Mainland Greece foremost in the Aegean	24, 31
1500	Queen Hatshepsut's expedition to Punt	11
1490–1436	Thutmose III	16, 27
	Rekhmire	18
1413–1377	Amenhotep III	17, 29
	Kenamon	17
1380–1362	Ikhnaton	24, 28
	The Tell el-Amarna letters	29
1300–1000	Age of the Sea Raiders	31, 43
1190	Ramses III defeats the "Northerners of the Isles"	31
1184	Traditional date of the fall of Troy	34
1100	Wenamon's voyage	47
	Dorian Greeks migrate into the Greek peninsula	66
	Voyage of the *Argo*	60

Table of Dates

Date	Event	Page
970	Phoenicians supply timber to Solomon	69
	Phoenician trade with India	70
1000–700	Phoenicians colonize the west	71
800–550	Age of Greek colonization	72
800	Invention of the ram and penteconter	84
700	Invention of two-banked galleys	86
550	Invention of the trireme	92
600	Necho's expedition circumnavigates Africa	129
500	Hanno's voyage	133
490–479	Wars between the Persians and Greeks	89
480	Battles of Artemisium and Salamis	90
480–322	Athens controls the Aegean	103, 127
431–404	The Peloponnesian War	102
429	Battle of Patras	103
415–413	Syracusan expedition	105
406	Battle of Arginusae	101
405	Battle of Aegospotami	106
398	Invention of the quinquereme	125
384–322	Demosthenes	116
336–323	Alexander the Great	127
322	Battle of Amorgos and destruction of the Athenian navy	127
310 (?)	Pytheas' voyage	137
323–31	The Hellenistic Age	141
305–283	Ptolemy I (Soter)	141
	Antigonus the One-Eyed	141
	Demetrius Poliorcetes	144
285–246	Ptolemy II (Philadelphus)	150
279–239	Antigonus Gonatas	149
264–241	First Punic War	159
260	Battle of Mylae	162
256	Battle of Ecnomus	164
255	Battle of Cape Hermaeum	164
241	Battle of the Aegates Islands	165
246–221	Ptolemy III (Evergetes)	176
221–203	Ptolemy IV (Philopator)	145, 181
221–179	Philip V	156, 167, 240
218–201	Second Punic War	166
201	Rhodian embassy to Rome	156, 167

Table of Dates

200–197	Rome defeats Philip V	167
192–190	Rome defeats Antiochus III (the Great)	168
191	Battle of Cissus	169
190	Battle of Side	169
	Battle of Myonnesus	171
171–167	Rome defeats Perseus	172
167	Delos becomes a free port	183
146	Destruction of Carthage	172
120 (?)	Eudoxus sails to India	186
89–85	Rome's first war with Mithridates VI (Eupator)	188, 202
88	First sack of Delos	188
69	Second sack of Delos	188
67	Pompey destroys the pirates of Cilicia	204
48	Caesar defeats Pompey	206
44	Assassination of Caesar	206
42	Defeat of Brutus and Cassius	207
36	Battle of Naulochus	208
31	Battle of Actium	208
27 B.C.– A.D. 180	Heyday of the Roman Empire	
27 B.C.– A.D. 14	Augustus	208-209
14–37	Tiberius	228
37–41	Caligula (Gaius)	215, 236
41–54	Claudius	225, 235
54–68	Nero	226
62	St. Paul's voyage to Rome	238
69–79	Vespasian	228, 234, 236
79–81	Titus	
81–96	Domitian	
96–98	Nerva	
98–117	Trajan	225
117–138	Hadrian	
138–161	Antoninus Pius	
161–180	Marcus Aurelius	228
253–269	Goths in the Aegean	240
285–305	Diocletian	240
311–337	Constantine	240
330	Founding of Constantinople	239, 245
395	Division of the Roman Empire	240
455	Vandals sack Rome	241

527–565	Justinian	245
636	Arabs conquer Syria	241
641	Arabs conquer Egypt	241, 245
673–678	Arabs besiege Constantinople; defenders use Greek fire	241

Selected Bibliography

The bibliographies listed below for the various chapters are each divided into two parts. The first part gives the source of more important passages quoted, and of documents treated at length, in the text. The second provides a list of works selected with two ends in view: first, to furnish the reader with some idea of the evidence upon which the statements in the text are based; second, to enable him to pursue the subjects in greater detail. Writings in foreign languages are included only where nothing adequate exists in English.

Chapters 1 and 2

References

P. 4, "Bringing of . . . cedar logs . . ." J. B. Pritchard, *Ancient Near Eastern Texts* (Princeton, 1950), 227.

P. 5, "No one really sails . . ." Pritchard, *op. cit.*, 441.

P. 9, letter of Ea-nasir. A. L. Oppenheim (see Bibliography below), 10-11.

P. 10, inscription of Henu. J. H. Breasted, *Ancient Records of Egypt* (Chicago, 1906), Vol. 1, § 430.

P. 11, story of the shipwrecked sailor. A. Erman, *The Literature of the Ancient Egyptians* (London, 1927), 29-35.

P. 13, Hatshepsut's expedition to Punt. Breasted, *op. cit.*, Vol. 2, §§ 246-295.

P. 20, "Minos is the first . . ." Thucydides 1.4.

Bibliography

A convenient summary of Egyptian and Mesopotamian trade can be found in James Hornell's "Sea-Trade in Early Times," *Antiquity* 15 (1941),

233-256. The business records of the traders of Mesopotamia are described by A. L. Oppenheim in "The Seafaring Merchants of Ur," *Journal of the American Oriental Society* 74 (1954), 6-17. T. Säve-Söderbergh's *The Navy of the Eighteenth Egyptian Dynasty* (Uppsala, 1946) contains an excellent exposition of Hatshepsut's expedition to Punt and of Thutmose's use of sea power in his campaigns. Sahure's and Hatshepsut's ships are discussed in detail in R. O. Faulkner's "Egyptian Seagoing Ships," *Journal of Egyptian Archaeology* 26 (1940), 3-9. Faulkner has also given a detailed description of the ships pictured in Kenamon's tomb in "A Syrian Trading Venture to Egypt," *Journal of Egyptian Archaeology* 33 (1947), 40-46.

The archaeological evidence for trade in the eastern Mediterranean in the third millennium B.C. can be found in *Relative Chronologies in Old World Archaeology*, edited by Robert W. Ehrich (Chicago, 1954), and for the second millennium in H. J. Kantor's *The Aegean and Orient in the Second Millennium B.C.* (Bloomington, Indiana, 1947). Early trade in the west is discussed in T. J. Dunbabin's "Minos and Daedalos in Sicily," *Papers of the British School at Rome* 16 (1948), 1-18. The chapters on trade and international relations in G. Glotz' *Aegean Civilization* (New York, 1925), 185-226, although somewhat out of date now, still provide an entertaining and useful survey of Cretan and Mycenaean trade and present what is known of the ships used. Michael Ventris has presented a brief, simplified account of his decipherment of the Mycenaean script in "King Nestor's Four-Handled Cups," *Archaeology* 7 (1954), 15-21, and George Mylonas a résumé for the general reader of the light they throw on the history of Greece in the second millennium in "Mycenaean Greek and Minoan-Mycenaean Relations," *Archaeology* 9 (1956), 273-279.

Chapters 3-5

References

P. 28, "Every port town . . ." Pritchard, *Ancient Near Eastern Texts*, 241.
P. 29, letters of Rib-Addi. S. Mercer, *The Tell El-Amarna Tablets* (Toronto 1939), Nos. 85, 98, 101, 105, 111, 113, 114.
P. 30, letter of the King of Cyprus. Mercer, *op. cit.*, No. 38.
P. 31, Ramses' defeat of the Northerners. Breasted, *Ancient Records of Egypt*, Vol. 4, §§ 75, 77; Pritchard, *op. cit.*, 262-263.
P. 39, Odysseus' boatbuilding. *Odyssey* 5. 244-261.
P. 43, Odysseus' tale. *Ibid.*, 14. 245-359.
P. 45, Menelaus' experiences. *Ibid.*, 4. 81-85.
P. 46, Odysseus' sack of a town. *Ibid.*, 9. 40-42.

P. 46, "In ancient times . . ." Thucydides 1. 5, 7.
P. 47, Wenamon's narrative. Pritchard, *op. cit.*, 25-29.
P. 64, "precipitous cliffs . . ." *Odyssey* 12. 59-60.

Bibliography

The story of Egypt's navy is told by T. Säve-Söderbergh in *The Navy of the Eighteenth Egyptian Dynasty* (Uppsala, 1946). A. R. Burn's *Minoans, Philistines and Greeks* (London, 1930) has imaginative and well written chapters on the sea-raiding peoples (108-172), piracy (173-188), Jason's voyage (189-197), and the Trojan War (198-222). A brief summary of the piracy of the age can be found in H. A. Ormerod's *Piracy in the Ancient World* (Liverpool, 1924), 80-94. All that Homer has to say about ships is nicely summarized in T. D. Seymour's *Life in the Homeric Age* (London, 1907), Chapter XI.

Chapter 6

References

P. 68, "unload their wares . . ." Herodotus 4. 196.
P. 69, "Now therefore command . . ." I Kings 5. 6-11.
P. 70, "And King Solomon . . ." I Kings 9. 26-28.

Bibliography

For an up-to-date general work on the Phoenicians, see G. Contenau's *La civilisation phénicienne* (Paris, second edition, 1949), and for a recent account of their activities in the west see G. Bosch Gimpera's "Phéniciens et Grecs dans l'Extrême-Occident," *La Nouvelle Clio* 3 (1951), 269-296. There is an interesting chapter (5) on the Phoenicians in Julian Huxley's *From an Antique Land* (New York, 1954); see in particular pages 73-76 for his description of the dyeing industry.

For the earliest contacts between Greeks and Phoenicians, see H. L. Lorimer's *Homer and the Monuments* (London, 1950), Chapter II, where the archaeological evidence is exhaustively treated. There is a convenient résumé of Greek colonizing activity in *The Cambridge Ancient History*, Volume 3 (London and New York, 1929), Chapter XXV (by J. L. Myres). T. J. Dunbabin's *The Western Greeks* (Oxford, 1948) is an exhaustive treatment of the colonization of the west, particularly good on the archaeological side.

There is no adequate account of the ships of this age, although they are discussed in all the handbooks. G. S. Kirk in "Ships on Geometric Vases," *Annual of the British School at Athens* 44 (1949), 93-153, offers a fine collection of material but, because of preconceived notions about ships of earlier and later periods, comes to a number of erroneous conclusions. L. Cohen's "Evidence for the Ram in the Minoan Period," *American Journal of Archaeology* 42 (1938), 486-494, demonstrates that the ram was most likely invented some time between the tenth and eighth centuries B.C. For the hemiolia see L. Casson's "Hemiolia and Triemiolia," *Journal of Hellenic Studies* 78 (1958), 14-18.

Chapter 7

Bibliography

Scholars have debated for centuries about how the oars of a trireme were arranged. In general there have been two schools of thought, one holding for three superimposed banks, the other for one bank of oarsmen grouped in clusters of three as in the galleys called *a zenzile* that the Venetians used in medieval and Renaissance times. The question was settled once and for all in favor of the former by J. S. Morrison in two articles: "The Greek Trireme," *The Mariner's Mirror* 27 (1941), 14-44, and "Notes on Certain Greek Nautical Terms and on Three Passages in I.G. ii² 1632," *The Classical Quarterly* 41 (1947), 122-135. J. A. Davison in "The First Greek Triremes," *The Classical Quarterly* 41 (1947), 18-24, demonstrated that the introduction of the trireme into the fleets, often put as early as 704 B.C., really belongs somewhere beween 550 and 525. Details of rigging and gear can be found in C. Torr's *Ancient Ships* (Cambridge, 1895).

There is an excellent discussion of ancient battle tactics in Chapter V of H. T. Wallinga's *The Boarding-Bridge of the Romans,* Historische Studies uitgegeven vanwege het Instituut voor Geschiedenis der Rijksuniversiteit te Utrecht 6 (Groningen, 1956). The only book devoted to the subject, Vice-Admiral W. L. Rodgers' *Greek and Roman Naval Warfare* (Annapolis, 1937), must be used with caution: the author too often cavalierly relies on his experience and knowledge as a seaman instead of on the accounts of the ancient authorities. A. W. Gomme has some acute observations about the limitations ancient battle fleets faced in "A Forgotten Factor of Greek Naval Strategy," *Essays in Greek History and Literature* (Oxford, 1937), 190-203.

The ancient authority for the battles of Artemisium and Salamis is Herodotus (8. 1-96), but his accounts are in places confused and seemingly contradictory. N. G. L. Hammond has provided a convincing reconstruction of Salamis in "The Battle of Salamis," *Journal of Hellenic Studies* 76 (1956), 32-54. Phormio's victories are described by Thucydides in 2. 83-92, and the complicated land and sea operations about Syracuse fill most of his Books 6 and 7. Accounts of the battles of Arginusae and Aegospotami are in Xenophon's *Hellenica* (1. 6. 24-38 and 2. 1. 16-30).

Chapter 8

References

P. 116, Zenothemis and Hegestratus. Demosthenes, *Orat.* 32, *Against Zenothemis* (text and translation by A. T. Murray in the Loeb Classical Library edition of Demosthenes, Vol. 4 [London 1936], 179-197).

P. 118, the two Lycians. Demosthenes, *Orat.* 35, *Against Lacritus* (text and translation by Murray, *op. cit.*, 279-315; translation in the text is based on Murray's).

P. 122, Heracleides' decree. W. Dittenberger, *Sylloge Inscriptionum Graecarum* (Leipzig, third edition, 1915), Vol. 1, No. 304; cf. G. W. Botsford and E. G. Sihler, *Hellenic Civilization* (New York, 1929; Columbia University Records of Civilization), 586-590.

P. 125, a trierarch's complaints. Demosthenes, *Orat.* 50, *Against Polycles*, sections 14-16 (text and translation by Murray, *op. cit.*, Vol. 6 [London, 1939], 15-17).

Bibliography

G. M. Calhoun's *The Business Life of Ancient Athens* (Chicago, 1926) provides a brief and entertaining survey of the commercial activities of the Peiraeus. For a more detailed treatment see H. Knorringa's *Emporos: Data on Trade and Trader in Greek Literature from Homer to Aristotle* (Amsterdam, 1926). J. Hasebroek's *Trade and Politics in Ancient Greece* (London, 1933, English translation of a work published originally in German in 1928) contains much useful detail, but its picture of the position of trade in the fifth and fourth centuries B.C. must be viewed with a good deal of caution; the distortion is corrected in A. W. Gomme's "Traders and Manufacturers in Greece," *Essays in Greek History and Literature* (Oxford, 1937), 42-66. T. R. Glover's *From Pericles to Philip* (London, fourth edition, 1926) includes an entertaining account of the fortunes of Pasion and his family (Chapter X).

Dionysius' naval innovations are mentioned by Diodorus Siculus (14. 41.

3, 42. 2, 44. 7). For an account of his career see *The Cambridge Ancient History*, Volume 6 (London and New York 1927), Chapter V (by J. B. Bury). On the introduction of quadriremes and quinqueremes into the Athenian navy, see J. S. Morrison in *The Mariner's Mirror* 27 (1941), 41-43, and, for the speed of sailing ships, L. Casson's "Speed Under Sail of Ancient Ships," *Transactions of the American Philological Association* 82 (1951), 136-148.

Chapter 9

References

P. 129, Necho and Sataspes. Herodotus 4. 42-43.
P. 133, Hanno. Translated by M. Cary and E. H. Warmington in *The Ancient Explorers* (New York, 1929), 47-51. This translation has, with minor changes, been reproduced in the text.

Bibliography

Cary and Warmington provide a detailed and interesting account of the major voyages of discovery in the ancient world: Chapter III deals with Pytheas, Hanno, and other expeditions into the Atlantic, and Chapter V with Necho, Sataspes, and other attempts to circumnavigate Africa. More recent treatments of the same material can be found in W. W. Hyde's *Ancient Greek Mariners* (New York, 1947), Chapters VI (Pytheas), VII (Hanno), and XI (Necho, Sataspes), and in J. O. Thomson's *History of Ancient Geography* (Cambridge, 1948), 71-77 (Necho, Sataspes, Hanno) and 143-151 (Pytheas). Thomson's footnotes (whose style is so compressed that they sound at times like the utterances of Dickens' Alfred Jingle) give a good survey of previous writings on the subject and the various points of view they express. A recent article by D. B. Harden, "The Phoenicians on the West Coast of Africa," *Antiquity* 22 (1948), 141-150, argues convincingly that Cerne is to be located at the mouth of the Senegal.

Chapter 10

References

P. 148, letter of Apollodotus. A. S. Hunt and C. C. Edgar, *Select Papyri*, Vol. 2 (Loeb Classical Library, Cambridge, Mass., and London, 1934), No. 410.

P. 153, inscription of Alexidamus. M. Segre, "Dedica votiva dell' equipaggio di una nave Rodia," *Clara Rhodos* 8 (1936), 225-244.

P. 154, inscription of Polycles. A. Maiuri, *Nuova silloge epigrafica di Rodi e Cos* (Florence, 1925), No. 18.

P. 155, inscription of the three brothers. M. Segre, "Due nuovi testi storici," *Rivista di filologia* 60 (1932), 446-461.

Bibliography

A detailed historical narrative of the events in the eastern Mediterranean in the third century B.C. can be found in three fine chapters by W. W. Tarn in *The Cambridge Ancient History*: Volume 6 (1927), Chapter XV; Volume 7 (1928), Chapters III and XXII.

There is no satisfactory work on the great Hellenistic warships. The best is Tarn's *Hellenistic Military and Naval Developments* (Cambridge, 1930), 122-152, although it has a number of serious weaknesses (Tarn refuses to recognize that galleys with superimposed banks ever existed and wrongly states that catapults were never used on shipboard in the Hellenistic Age). The size of the fleets is discussed in detail by Tarn in his *Antigonos Gonatas* (Oxford, 1913), 454-458.

We are badly off for descriptions of battles in which supergalleys took part. Only two have survived: Diodorus Siculus recounts (20. 49-52) the Battle of Salamis between Demetrius and Ptolemy I, and Polybius (16. 2-8) the Battle of Chios in which Rhodes and Pergamum together fought Philip V. Both have been discussed in detail by W. L. Rodgers in *Greek and Roman Naval Warfare* (239-242 and 379-385), but his accounts must be treated with caution (see above, Bibliography to Chapter 7). H. T. Wallinga's *The Boarding-Bridge of the Romans* has (46-48) a short but perceptive description of the Battle of Salamis.

A detailed study of the Rhodian navy and its activities is yet to be written. In "Dedica votiva . . ." cited above, M. Segre, using a newly discovered inscription as his starting point, works out a good many of the details of the crews. For the triemiolia see L. Casson's "Hemiolia and Triemiolia," *Journal of Hellenic Studies* 78 (1958), 14-18.

Chapter 11

References

P. 163, Duilius' inscription. E. H. Warmington, *Remains of Old Latin*, Vol. 4 (Loeb Classical Library, Cambridge, Mass., and London, 1940), 128-131.

Bibliography

A convenient narrative of the wars dealt with in this chapter can be found in *The Cambridge Ancient History*, Volume 7 (1928), Chapter XXI (First Punic War, by T. Frank), and Volume 8 (1930), Chapters II-IV (Second Punic War, by B. L. Hallward), V-VI (war with Philip, by M. Holleaux), and VII (war with Antiochus, by Holleaux). A definitive study of the development of Roman sea power from its beginnings through the period covered in this chapter is provided by two books by J. H. Thiel: *A History of Roman Sea-Power Before the Second Punic War* (Amsterdam, 1954) and *Studies on the History of Roman Sea-Power in Republican Times* (Amsterdam, 1946). The two are somewhat hard to read because they are packed with detail, treat exhaustively every problem large and small, and are rather long-winded and repetitious. There is an excellent brief account of the story of Roman sea power by W. W. Tarn in J. Sandys' *A Companion to Latin Studies* (Cambridge, third edition, 1921), pages 489-501.

The *corvus* has been the subject of much debate and there are long sections devoted to it in both of Thiel's books. But the credit for ending the controversy goes to one of his students, H. T. Wallinga, who in his *The Boarding-Bridge of the Romans* provides what is almost certainly the correct explanation.

Chapter 12

References

P. 173, contract for Red Sea voyage. M. Rostovtzeff (see Bibliography below), 922, 1555.

P. 177, cargo manifest. C. C. Edgar, *Zenon Papyri*, Vol. 1 (Cairo, 1925), No. 59012.

Bibliography

The fullest account of all phases of economic life in the Hellenistic world, including maritime trade, is M. Rostovtzeff's monumental three-volume *The Social and Economic History of the Hellenistic World* (Oxford, 1941). W. W. Tarn in Chapter VII ("Trade and Exploration") of his *Hellenistic Civilization* (London, third edition revised with the aid of G.

T. Griffith, 1952) provides a convenient and well written summary. L. Casson's "The Grain Trade of the Hellenistic World," *Transactions of the American Philological Association* 85 (1954), 168-187, corrects the overemphasis both writers have given to Delos as a figure in the trade in commodities. G. F. Hourani's *Arab Seafaring in the Indian Ocean in Ancient and Early Medieval Times* (Princeton, 1951) contains a useful summary (6-28) of the history of trade with India and is particularly good on the experiences of the Arabs in this region (25-28).

Chapter 13

References

Underwater archaeology is as yet so new a field that there are no scholarly books devoted entirely to it. A number of articles summarize the earlier finds, those chiefly of works of art: A. Merlin, "Submarine Discoveries in the Mediterranean," *Antiquity* 4 (1930), 405-414; S. Casson, "Submarine Research in Greece," *Antiquity* 13 (1939), 80-86; G. Karo, "Art Salvaged from the Sea," *Archaeology* 1 (1948), 179-185. A popular account, good but all too often excessively wordy, of underwater discovery, particularly along the Riviera, is to be found in P. Diolé's *4000 Years Under the Sea* (New York, 1954; an English translation of a work published originally in French in 1952). For a scholarly résumé of all finds along the Riviera up to 1952, see N. Lamboglia and F. Benoit, *Scavi sottomarini in Liguria e in Provenza* (Bordighera, 1953); the section by Lamboglia is in Italian, that by Benoit in French. L. Casson has summarized the sea diggers' activities for the general reader in "Sea-Digging," *Archaeology* 6 (1953), 221-228, and "More Sea-Digging," *Archaeology* 10 (1957), 248-257. In 1957 work began on a very interesting wreck off Spargi in the Strait of Bonifacio between Corsica and Sardinia; see the Italian weekly magazine *L'Europeo*, issues of 20 October 1957 (pp. 27-36) and 29 June 1958 (pp. 14-33). Caligula's barges have been treated exhaustively by G. Ucelli in his *Le Navi di Nemi* (Rome, second edition, 1950).

Chapter 14

References

P. 198, "Strangers, who are you?" *Odyssey* 9. 252-254.

P. 200, inscription from Amorgos. Dittenberger (see *op. cit.*, References Chapter 8), No. 521.
P. 200, inscription from Naxos. Dittenberger, *op. cit.*, No. 520.

Bibliography

The story of the pirates of Cilicia and their defeat is told by Plutarch in Chapter 24 of his Life of Pompey, and the account of Caesar's capture occurs in Chapter 1 of his Life of Caesar. H. A. Ormerod's *Piracy in the Ancient World* (Liverpool, 1924) is a careful, readable account illuminated by numerous parallels from the later ages of Mediterranean piracy.

Chapter 15

References

P. 211, "God willing..." H. C. Youtie and J. G. Winter, *Michigan Papyri*, Vol. 8 (Ann Arbor, 1951), No. 468.
P. 212, Apion's letter. A. S. Hunt and C. C. Edgar, *Select Papyri*, Vol. 1 (Loeb Classical Library, London, 1932), No. 112.

Bibliography

Chester Starr's *The Roman Imperial Navy 31 B.C.-A.D. 324* (Ithaca, 1941) is a thorough study of the organization and personnel of the Roman navy under the emperors, and a review of the history of its operations. There is no single work devoted to the ships of this period. Most of the information available, particularly from the writings of the period, can be found in C. Torr's *Ancient Ships* (Cambridge), a storehouse of material and still the fundamental work on the ships of Greece and Rome, though published in 1895. L. Casson has treated the route and the ships used in the Alexandria-Rome grain trade in "The Isis and Her Voyage," *Transactions of the American Philological Association* 81 (1950), 43-56, and the size of ancient freighters in general in "The Size of Ancient Merchant Ships," *Studi in onore di Aristide Calderini e Roberto Paribeni*, Vol. 1 (Milan, 1956), 231-238. For the lugsail and the sprit-rig in the ancient world, see L. Casson's "The Sails of the Ancient Mariner," *Archaeology* 7 (1954), 214-219, and "Fore-and-Aft Sails in the Ancient World," *The Mariner's Mirror* 42 (1956), 3-5, along with the remarks of R. Le Baron Bowen, Jr., in *The Mariner's Mirror* 43 (1957), 160-164.

Chapter 16

References

P. 223, "I built myself . . ." Petronius, *Satyricon* 76.
P. 227, "The beautiful large . . ." M. Wheeler (see Bibliography below), 132-133.
P. 227, Chinese records. W. Schoff (see Bibliography below), 275-277.
P. 228, "The ladies and their baubles . . ." Tacitus, *Annals* 3. 53.
P. 229, "a little wine . . ." *Periplus* 17 (= Schoff, *op. cit.*, 28-29).
P. 229, "the Sheikh and . . ." *Periplus* 24 (= Schoff, *op. cit.*, 31).
P. 230, "for the rajah . . ." *Periplus* 49 (= Schoff, *op. cit.*, 42).
P. 230, "at the new moon . . ." *Periplus* 46 (= Schoff, *op. cit.*, 41).
P. 231, "because of the enormous . . ." *Periplus* 56 (= Schoff, *op. cit.*, 44-45).
P. 231, "there is a great . . ." *Periplus* 64 (= Schoff, *op. cit.*, 48).
P. 235, "What a size . . ." Lucian, *Navigium (The Ship)* 5.
P. 236, "If you are going . . ." Philo, *Against Flaccus* 5.
P. 237, "Today the ships . . ." Seneca, *Epistles* 77.
P. 237, Irenaeus' letter. Hunt and Edgar, *Select Papyri*, Vol. 1 (Loeb Classical Library, Cambridge, Mass., and London, 1934), No. 113.
P. 238, St. Paul's voyage. Acts 27.

Bibliography

The prime source of information for the trade of the Roman Empire is the comprehensive geography written by Strabo who lived at the time of Augustus; the handiest edition is that in the Loeb Classical Library by H. L. Jones: *The Geography of Strabo*, 8 volumes (London, 1927–1936). M. P. Charlesworth provides a useful survey in his *Trade-Routes and Commerce of the Roman Empire* (Cambridge, second edition, 1926). The part that trade played in the social and economic life of the empire is covered by M. Rostovtzeff in his *The Social and Economic History of the Roman Empire* (Oxford, second edition revised by P. M. Fraser, 1957). The ancient sources of our information are exhaustively treated in the monumental five-volume *An Economic Survey of Ancient Rome*, edited by T. Frank (Baltimore, 1933–1940).

The fundamental work on Rome's trade with India is E. Warmington's *The Commerce Between the Roman Empire and India* (Cambridge, 1928). A brief up-to-date account can be found in Sir Mortimer Wheeler's

Selected Bibliography

Rome Beyond the Imperial Frontiers (London, 1954), Chapters IX-XV. Cary and Warmington (see References, Chapter 9) discuss (73-85) the extent of western exploration in the Indian Ocean and the Far East. The best edition of the text of the *Periplus* is H. Frisk's *Le périple de la Mer Érythrée*, Göteborgs Högskolas Årsskrift 33. 1 (Göteborg, 1927). The best translation, accompanied by an exhaustive and illuminating commentary, is to be found in W. Schoff's *The Periplus of the Erythraean Sea: Travel and Trade in the Indian Ocean by a Merchant of the First Century* (New York and London, 1912).

For the route of the grain ships and their size, see the articles "The Isis and Her Voyage" and "The Size of Ancient Merchant Ships" mentioned in the Bibliography to Chapter 15.

Chapter 17

Bibliography

M. Mercier's *Le feu grégeois, les feux de guerre depuis l'antiquité, la poudre à canon* (Paris, 1952), treats Greek fire exhaustively, convincingly demonstrating the nature of this controversial material and the methods of employing it. Most of the information about the ships of the Byzantine fleets comes from a series of naval handbooks of the tenth century. No useful edition of these was available until A. Dain published his *Naumachica* (Paris, 1943). As a consequence the subject has not yet received extensive treatment. R. H. Dolley's "The Warships of the Later Roman Empire," *Journal of Roman Studies* 38 (1948), 47-53, is an excellent description of what the ships were like, and his "Naval Tactics in the Heyday of the Byzantine Thalassocracy," *Atti dell' VIII Congresso di Studi Bizantini* (Rome, 1953), Volume 1, 324-339, provides a vivid account of what the sea fighting of the time was like. G. F. Hourani (see Bibliography to Chapter 12) includes (53-61) a brief sketch of the Arab navies.

The latest and most complete work on the naval and trade relationships of the age is A. Lewis' *Naval Power and Trade in the Mediterranean A.D. 500–1100* (Princeton, 1951).

Glossary of Greek and Latin Nautical Terms

Words in italics are Greek, those in roman are Latin. Precedence has been given to Greek terms because Roman naval terminology was largely made up of borrowings or adaptations of these (cf. pp. 211, 215).

Number(s) in parentheses after an entry refer(s) to page(s) in the text where further information may be found.

acatus. See *akatos*
adminiculum. See *kamax*
akateion, "boat" mast or sail; small reserve mast and sail used on galleys (97)
akatos (=acatus), boat
akrostolion, ornament at prow or stern (85)
akrōtērion, synonym of *akrostolion*
anakrousis (cf. inhibere), backing water (100)
ancora. See *ankyra*
ancorale. See *ankyreion*
ankoina, forestay (?) (98)
ankyra (=ancora), anchor (98, 197)
ankyra hiera, sheet anchor (literally "holy anchor")
ankyreion (=ancorale), anchor cable (98)
antennae. See *keraiai*
antērides, struts supporting the outrigger (92; see Pl. 8b)
antiprōiros, "prow to prow" (of ramming) (148)
antlētērion (=sentinaculum), bucket for bailing the bilge
antlia, antlos (=sentina), bilge
apertus. See *aphraktos*

Glossary of Greek and Latin Nautical Terms

aphlaston (=aplustre), stern ornament (85; see Pl. 5c)
aphraktos (=apertus), (galley) with open sides (85, 99)
aplustre. See *aphlaston*
apobathra (=pons), gangplank (usually in the form of a ladder) (87, 219; see Pl. 7a)
apogaion, apogeion (=ora), mooring line (98)
architektōn, naval architect
artemōn, bowspritsail (146)
askōma, leather bag closing in an oarport (93; see Pl. 10a)
auchēn, loom of the steering oar
aulētēs, piper who gave the time to the rowers. See also *triēraulēs* (95)

baris, type of boat used on the Nile
bathra, synonym of *apobathra*
biremis, two-banked galley (213-214)

carina. See *tropis*
celoces. See *kelētes*
cercurus. See *kerkouros*
ceruchus. See *kerouchos*
chalinos, backstay (?) (98)
cheir sidēra (=manus ferrea), grapnel (literally "iron hand") (106)
cheirosiphōn, hand-held tube for launching Greek fire (243)
chelysma, false keel
chēniskos, goose-headed device ornamenting the stern of a merchantman (217)
clavus. See *oiax*
codicarius, river boatman (225)
constratum. See *katastrōma*
constratus. See *kataphraktos*
contus. See *kontos*
corvus, boarding bridge (161)

dekērēs, a "ten" (144)
delphines, lead weights hoisted to the yardarms of merchantmen to be dropped on an enemy's deck
diaita, cabin (216)
diekplous, diecplus, a type of naval maneuver (101)
dikrotos, two-banked
dōdekērēs, a "twelve" (144)
dolōn, small reserve mast and sail used on galleys; perhaps the same as *akateion*

dromōn, Byzantine galley (243)
dryochoi, frames for supporting a ship while under construction

eikosērēs, a "twenty" (145)
eikosoros, twenty-oared galley; also a merchantman carrying auxiliary oars (37)
elaiochrēistēs, oiler (154)
embolos (=rostrum), ram (84, 99; see Pls. 3-8, 10)
ennērēs, a "nine" (144)
epholkion, ship's boat towed astern (220)
epibatai (=milites classici), marines (95, 160-162)
epibathra, synonym of *apobathra*
epigyon, synonym of *apogaion*
epikrion, yard (in Homer; the later term was *keraiai*) (38)
epiplous, officer substituting for trierarch as commander of a galley (148, 154)
episēmon, device carved or painted on a ship. See also *parasēmon* and *sēmeion* (217)
epitonos, backstay (in Homer; the later term was perhaps *chalinos*) (38)
epōtides, catheads (105)
eunai, stone anchors (in Homer)

faber navalis. See *naupēgos* (225)
forus, deck

gaulos, type of Phoenician merchantman having a roomy, rounded hull
gerulus, stevedore (226)
gomphos, treenail (39)
gubernaculum. See *pēdalion*
gubernator, helmsman

hapax, catapult-grapnel (207)
hekkaidekērēs, a "sixteen" (144)
hēmiolia, type of pirate craft (86)
hendekērēs, an "eleven" (144)
heptērēs, a "seven" (144)
herma (=saburra), ballast (99)
hexērēs, a "six" (144)
himantes, halyards (?) (98)
hippagōgos, hippēgos, trireme converted to cavalry transport (98, 102)
histion, histia (=velum), sail (38, 87, 98)
histodokē, mast crutch (in Homer) (38)

histopedē, mast wedge (in early writers; the later term was *parastatai*) (38)
histos (=malus), mast (38, 39)
hyperai, braces (38, 39, 98; see Pl. 5c)
hypēresia, rowing complement
hypēresion, cushion for rower's bench
hypozōmata, girding cables (99)

iatros (=medicus), (ship's) doctor (154)
ikria, partial decks at bow and stern (38, 39)
inhibere (cf. *anakrousis*), to back water
insigne. See *sēmeion*

kaloi, kalōs, kalōdia, brails (38, 39, 87, 98; see Pl. 7a)
kamax (=adminiculum), tiller, horizontal bar socketed into the handle of the steering oar. See *oiax* (218)
karchēsion, mast truck
katapeirētēria, lead line (220)
katapeltaphetēs, catapult operator, artilleryman (155)
katapeltēs, catapult (147)
kataphraktos (=tectus, constratus), (galley) protected by decking above and screens along the sides (99)
katastrōma (=constratum), fighting deck of a galley, main deck of a merchantman (84)
keletēs, keletia (=celoces), swift galleys reckoned among the small craft of a fleet
keleustēs, officer in charge of rowing personnel (95)
keraiai (=antennae), yard
kerkouros (=cercurus), swift vessel, of no great size, driven by sail and oar; used as fast merchantman as well as auxiliary in the fleets
kerouchos (=ceruchus), lift, line from mast truck to yardarm (generally in the plural, *kerouchoi*)
klēis, tholepin (in Homer; the later term was *skalmos*) (38, 85)
klimax, klimakis (=scala), landing ladder (87; see Pl. 7a)
kontos (=contus), pole, used for punting or fending off (37)
kōpē (=remus), oar
kōpētēr, leather oar thong. See also *tropos, tropōtēr* (38)
kōpeus (=remex), oarsman
kōpodetēs, oar-thong man (155)
krikoi, rings sewed to the sail as fairleads for the brails (218)
kybernētēs (=magister), executive officer of a galley, captain of a merchantman (94-95, 127)

lamptēr (=lumen), ship's light
lembos, boat, often a ship's boat; from the second century B.C. on, applied to the ships used by Illyrian pirates and later adopted as naval units (167)
lenuncularius, bargeman (225)
Liburna, Liburnian (light Roman galley) (201, 213)
lintrarius, boatman (225)
lithophoroi, "stone carrying," term used of yards fitted to carry weights at the arms which could be dropped on an enemy; cf. *delphines*
longa navis, galley (literally "long ship")
lumen. See *lamptēr*
lusoriae, light Roman galleys used on the frontier rivers

magister, captain of a merchantman; cf. *kybernētēs*
malus. See *histos*
manus ferrea. See *cheir sidēra*
manganon, block; cf. *trochileia*
medicus. See *iatros*
megalai keraiai, main yard (97)
megas histion, mainsail (97)
megas histos, mainmast (97)
mesodmē, mast step (38)
milites classici. See *epibatai*
miltos, ruddle (used in ship's paint) (36, 124)
monokrotos, single-banked
myoparōn, small fast fighting galleys used by pirates or among the small craft of war fleets

nauarchis (=praetoria navis), flagship (162)
nauarchos, admiral (in Greek navies); cf. praefectus classis
nauklēros (=navicularius), shipowner (114)
naumachia, mock sea battle (210)
naupēgos (=faber navalis), shipwright (154)
navarchus, squadron commander (in Roman navy) (211)
navicularius. See *nauklēros*
neōrion, shipyard
neōsoikos, slip, ship shed (93)

oiax (=clavus), helm, tiller; cf. *kamax, plēktron*
oiēion, helm (in Homer) (38)
oktērēs, an "eight" (144)
ora. See *apogaion*

palma (=*pteryx*), oar blade (literally "palm of the hand")
paraseiron (=*supparum*), topsail (174, 218)
parasēmon, device carved or painted on a ship. See also *episēmon* and *sēmeion*
parastatai, mast wedges; cf. *histopedē* (97)
parexeiresia, outrigger (92)
parodos, gangway (99)
pēdalion (=*gubernaculum*), steering oar (38, 85; see Pls. 4-7)
pēdaliouchos, helmsman (154)
peisma, cable (98)
pentekaidekērēs, a "fifteen" (144)
pentēkontarchos, junior officer of a galley (95, 154)
pentēkonteros, penteconter, a fifty-oared galley (37, 59, 81, 85)
pentērēs (=*quinqueremis*), quinquereme (125, 126, 144)
periagōgeus, windlass or capstan; cf. *stropheion* (235)
perineōi, spare oars carried aboard a galley (94)
periplous, periplus, a type of nautical maneuver (101); a "coast pilot" (127)
pes. See *pous*
pharos, lighthouse (180, 225)
phasēlos, a type of boat for passengers or freight, sometimes large enough to be driven by sail alone, sometimes small and driven by sails and oars
phellos, cork, used as floats or buoys
pissa (=pix), pitch (36, 217)
pix. See *pissa*
plēktron, tiller; cf. *oiax*
pons. See *apobathra*
porthmeion, ferry
porthmeus, ferryman (225)
pous, *podes* (=pes, pedes), sheet, sheets (38, 39, 98; see Pls. 5c, 12, 13a)
praefectus classis, admiral (in Roman navy); cf. *nauarchos* (209)
praetoria navis. See *nauarchis* (209)
pristis, light fast warship reckoned among the small craft of a fleet; cf. *lembos*. The word means literally "shark"
proembolion, auxiliary spur set above the main ram (99)
propugnaculum. See *pyrgos*
prōra, prow
prōrētēs, *prōreus*, bow officer of a galley (95, 154)
protonos, forestay; cf. *ankoina* (38)
prymna, *prymnē* (=puppis), stern
prymnēsia, stern cables (98)
pteryx (=palma), oar blade (literally "wing")

Glossary of Greek and Latin Nautical Terms 269

puppis. See *prymna*
pyr automaton, Greek fire (literally "self-igniting fire") (242)
pyr hygron, Greek fire (literally "liquid fire") (242)
pyr thalassion, Greek fire (literally "sea-fire") (242)
pyrgos (=propugnaculum, turris), turret (148)

quadriremis. See *tetrērēs*
quinqueremis. See *pentērēs*

remex. See *kōpeus*
remus. See *kōpē*
restiones, riggers (226)
rostrum. See *embolos*

saburra, ballast (literally "sand"); cf. *herma*
saburrarius, ballast handler (literally "sandman") (226)
scala. See *klimax*
scapharius, boatman (225)
sēmeion (=insigne), device carved or painted on a ship; cf. *episēmon* and *parasēmon*. Also a flag, often used for signaling
sentina. See *antlia*
sentinaculum. See *antlētērion*
siphōn, tube for shooting Greek fire (243)
skalmos, tholepin. See also *kleis* (93)
skaphē, skiff
skēnē, cabin, shelter cabin (213)
stamines (=statumina), ribs
statumina. See *stamines*
steira, cutwater
stropheion, windlass; cf. *periagōgeus*
stuppator, caulker (217, 225)
stylis, ensign consisting of a pole, crossbar and streamer, carried on the stern
supparum. See *paraseiron*

tarsos, oarage
tectus. See *kataphraktos*
tessarakontērēs, Ptolemy IV's great "forty" (145)
tetrērēs (=quadriremis), quadrireme (125, 126, 144, 152)
thalamēgos, boat with a cabin used on the Nile. Ptolemy IV's houseboat was an elephantine version of the type (174)
thalamia, oarport for the thalamite oar (93)
thalamios, thalamite, oarsman in the lowest bank of a galley (93, 145)

thranitēs, thranite, oarsman in the top bank of a galley (93, 145)
transtrum. See *zygon*
treiskaidekērēs, a "thirteen" (144)
triakontērēs, a "thirty" (145)
triakontoros, triacontor, a thirty-oared galley (85, 102)
triarmenos, having three masts or sails (174; see Pl. 11b)
triēmiolia, trireme specially adapted for chasing pirates (152)
triērarchos, trierarch, captain of a galley (95, 148, 211)
triēraulēs, synonym of *aulētēs*
triērēs (=triremis), trireme (92)
trikrotos, three-banked
triremis. See *triērēs*
trochileia, block; cf. *manganon*
tropis (=carina), keel
tropos, tropōtēr, leather thong fastened to an oar and looped about the tholepin; cf *kōpētēr*
turris. See *pyrgos*

urinator, diver (226)

velum. See *histion*

zeuglē, zeuktēria, fitting to hold the steering oar in place (218)
zōstēr, waling piece (see Pl. 12)
zygios, zygite, oarsman in the middle bank of a three-banked ship (93, 145)
zygon, zygos (=transtrum), thwart, rower's bench

Index

Abdera 76
Abdi-Ashirta 30
Achaeans 32
Achilles 34
Actium 208, 213
Adalia, Gulf of 169
Admirals: *see* warships, personnel
Adriatic 24, 125, 166, 168, 198, 201, 209
Aea 58, 59, 61, 63
Aeetes 58, 59, 60
Aegates Islands 165
Aegean 20, 57, 59, 61, 70, 72, 78, 96, 107, 112, 115, 128, 142, 150, 151, 153, 176, 181, 191, 224, 240
Aegina 112
Aegospotami 106
Aeneas 68
Afghanistan 179, 230
Africa 9, 21, 69, 71, 75, 79, 80, 129, 131-136, 159, 163, 164, 165, 166, 187, 216, 224, 226, 229, 232, 233, 234, 239, 241

Africa, circumnavigation of 129-136, 187
Agamemnon 24, 34, 35, 36
Agrippa (admiral) 207, 208
Agrippa (Prince of Judaea) 236
Ajax 37
Akaiwasha 32
Alaric 228
Alasia 56
Albenga 190, 191, 194, 195, 197
Alexander (explorer) 232
Alexander the Great 113, 114, 127, 141, 142, 143, 168, 173
Alexandria 142, 143, 173, 174, 175, 178, 179-180, 181, 183, 184, 186, 187, 189, 210, 211, 225, 226, 234, 235, 236, 237, 238, 239, 245
Alexidamus 153-154
Algeria 181
Algiers 72
Alphabet 70
Alps 166
Altar: *see* ships

Amber: *see* trade
Amenemhet II 21
Amenhotep III 17, 29
Amon 47, 48, 49, 50, 51, 52, 53, 54, 55, 56
Amorgos 200
Amphibious operations 34, 102, 163, 206
Amphorae 190, 191, 192, 193, 194, 219, 234
Amulets: *see* trade
Amurri 30
Anaximander 77
Anchor: *see* ships
Androcles 118
Animals: *see* trade
Annam 228, 232
annona 233
Anthéor 195
Anticythera 189
Antigonus Gonatas 145, 146, 149, 150, 151, 156, 167
Antigonus the One-Eyed 141, 143, 144, 146, 148, 151
Antioch 142, 143, 179, 182
Antiochus III 168, 169, 170, 172
Antipater (*epiplous*) 148
Antisthenes 108
Antony 145, 207, 208
Aphract 99, 154
Apion 212
Apollodorus 118-119
Apollodotus 148
Apollonius 148, 177
Arabia 8, 9, 16, 67, 69, 142, 178, 179, 182, 185, 224, 228, 229, 232
Arabs 128, 178, 179, 181, 184, 186, 241-246
Archaeological remains 3, 4, 8, 20, 21, 23, 24, 35, 57, 67, 76, 79, 80, 180, 184, 189-197, 223, 231
Archestratus 108
Archimedes 161
Arginusae Islands 101
Argo 58, 59, 60, 62, 63, 64
Argonauts 58-65, 76
Armor: *see* ships
Art: *see* trade
Artemisium 90

Artemo 118-119
Artemon: *see* ships
Artillery: *see* ships
Arvad 30
Assyria 86
Astrolabe 189
Atargatis 184
Athens 20, 80, 88, 89-107, 108-127, 128, 142, 148, 151, 153, 170, 174, 175, 176, 181, 182, 183, 184, 189, 190, 198, 199, 216, 224, 226, 235, 236
Atlantic Ocean 71, 72, 81, 82, 128, 140, 187
Augustus 206, 207, 208, 210, 213, 225, 227, 228, 231, 233, 235
Azov, Sea of 64

Babylon 141, 143, 179
Babylonians 5
Backing water 91, 100, 106
Baghdad 179
Bahrein 8
Bakshish 229, 230
Balearic Islands 202
Ballast: *see* ships
Baltic Sea 22, 139
Bankers and banking 9, 109, 114, 116, 117, 118, 120, 173, 180, 181, 183, 187
Barbary pirates 44, 199
Barges 225, 237
Barter 68, 69, 80, 231
Beder 48, 49
Beirut 5, 30, 182, 184, 185
Belerium 138
Bengal, Bay of 232
Benoit, Fernand 192, 193
Berbers 134
Berenice 229
Biscay, Bay of 138
Bissagos Bay 136
Black Sea 59, 61, 63, 64, 65, 73, 76, 77, 78, 81, 88, 111, 115, 118-119, 120, 123, 128, 176, 181, 210, 240, 246
Blockade, naval 30, 102, 113, 153, 159, 165, 170-171, 206
Boat pole: *see* ships
"Boat sail" 97

Index

Boatswain: *see* warships, personnel
Bombay 230
Bonifacio, Strait of 195
Borysthenes River 118
Bosporus 59, 61, 63, 76, 77, 78, 110, 113, 124, 151, 245
Bosporus (in the Crimea) 118
Bow-patches: *see* ships
Britain 137, 138, 139, 182
Brittany 3, 137, 138, 139
Broach 230
Bronze: *see* trade
Brutus 206, 207
Burgundy 223
Burma 232
Bushmen 133
Business methods 8-9, 68-69, 111, 112, 114, 116-120, 174, 181, 226, 228
Byblus 5, 17, 24, 25, 27, 29, 30, 45, 47, 49, 50, 57
Byzantine Empire 241-246
Byzantium 78, 110, 113, 114, 151, 239

Cabins: *see* ships
Cables: *see* ships
Cadiz 71, 88, 128, 138
Caesar 200, 203, 206, 207, 208, 226
Cairo 215
Calicut 245
Caligula 196, 197, 215, 217, 236
Callinicus 241, 242
Camarina 164, 165
Cameroon, Mt. 136
Cameroons 136
Canaan 67
Canals 10, 80, 129, 178, 225, 226, 229
Canary Islands 131
Cannes 195
Cantium 138
Canton 232
Cape: *see under the particular name*
Capri 237
Captain: *see* warships, personnel
Caravan trade 67, 70, 77, 142, 178, 179, 182, 183, 184, 185, 187, 188
Carmel, Mt. 33, 48
Carpenter, ship's: *see* warships, personnel
Carpets: *see* trade

Carrara 226
Cartagena 197
Carthage 68, 72, 82, 83, 112, 133, 134, 135, 136, 138, 157-166, 167, 172, 176, 182, 188, 224, 226
Carthaginians 68, 79, 82, 83, 88, 125, 128, 133-136, 138, 139, 157-166, 173
Cartography 77, 137, 139, 175
Carystus 118
Cassius 206, 207
Cataphract 99, 154
Catapultists: *see* warships, personnel
Catapults: *see* ships
Catapults (land weapons) 125
Caulking 217, 225
Ceos 124
Cephallenia 117
Cerne 134, 135, 136
Ceylon 8, 227
Chalcis 73
Chank: *see* trade
Chariots: *see* trade
Chartering 109, 114, 119
Charts: *see* maps
Cheese: *see* trade
China 224, 227, 228, 230, 231, 232
Chios 112, 167
Chretes 134
Cilicia 201-205
Cinnamon: *see* trade
Circe 63
Circuit of the Earth 77
Cissus 169
Claudius 225, 227, 235, 236
Cleomenes 114
Cleopatra 143
Cnidus 238
Cnossos 20
"Coast pilots" 127, 136, 175, 220, 229
Cochin-China 232
Coinage 80, 112, 113, 231
Colaeus 80, 81, 238
Colchis 59, 63
Colonization
  Carthaginian 72-73, 133-136
  Greek 73-82
  Phoenician 67-72
Colonization, reason for 71, 73
Colony, founding a 73-76

Index

Color of boats: *see* ship
Colossus of Rhodes 175, 181
Columbus 59, 129, 139, 175
Compass 220, 246
Conon 107
Constantine 227, 239, 240, 245
Constantinople 239, 241, 245, 246
Contracts, maritime 118-119, 173
Convoy duty 102, 124, 126, 133, 168
Copper: *see* trade
Coracesium 201, 205
Coral: *see* trade
Corinth 60, 76, 78, 79, 80, 81, 83, 87, 92, 99, 103, 112, 150, 226
Corinth, Gulf of 78, 103, 208
Corinth, Isthmus of 79-80
Cornwall 71, 128, 138, 139
Corsica 82, 83, 191, 209, 241
corvus: *see* ships
Cos 150, 155
Cosmetics: *see* trade
Cottonara 231
Courts, maritime 111, 121
Cousteau, Jacques-Ives 191, 192, 193
Cranganore 230
Cretans: *see* Minoans
Crete 3, 20, 21, 22, 23, 24, 25, 27, 31, 34, 41, 43, 60, 70, 72, 81, 155, 167, 199, 201, 234, 238
Crews: *see* warships, personnel
Crews, training of 160, 207
Crimea 64, 76, 115, 118
Currents
  Agulhas 131
  Dardanelles 71, 77
  Gulf of Guinea 131, 133
  Indian Ocean 131
  Mozambique 131
  North African 71, 131
  Red Sea 131
  West Africa 131, 133
Customs: *see* tariffs
Cyclops 37, 198
Cyprus 5, 16, 17, 22, 24, 25, 30, 31, 45, 56, 70, 72, 115, 149, 176
Cyrene 80
Cyzicus 186, 241

da Gama, Vasco 133, 245

Danube River 210, 214
Dardanelles 33, 59, 76, 77, 90, 106, 112, 124, 170, 171, 208, 245
Dates: *see* trade
Deck hands: *see* warships, personnel
Decks: *see* ships
Deigma 111
Deir-el-Bahari 11
Delos 183, 184, 185, 187, 188, 202, 204
Delphic Oracle 75, 78
Demetrius, Besieger of Cities 143, 144, 145, 146, 147, 149, 151, 153, 199, 208
Demo 116
Demosthenes 116, 117, 118, 120, 123
Demyen 32
Denmark 139
Derna 80
Dido 68, 72
diecplus 101, 162, 170
Diocletian 240
Dionysius I 125, 126, 144, 161, 200
Dispatch boats 102, 210, 237
Diving 189-197
Dnieper River 118
Doctor, ship's: *see* warships, personnel
Dor 48
Double-ax 3, 20, 22
Draa River 134
Dromon: *see* warships
Duilius 162, 163
Dyed textiles: *see* trade

Eastern Roman Empire: *see* Byzantine Empire
Ecnomus 164
Edom 70
Egypt
  Arab 241, 245
  Pharaonic and Persian 1, 2, 3, 4, 5, 9, 10, 12, 16, 17, 18, 21, 23, 24, 25, 27, 29, 30, 31, 32, 33, 42, 43, 45-57, 60, 67, 70, 77, 79, 80, 81, 87, 90, 92, 110, 112, 113, 114, 115, 129, 131, 132, 146, 148
  Ptolemaic 142-150, 151, 152, 153, 156, 166, 168, 174-180, 181, 182, 185-187
  Roman 211, 212, 224, 226, 227, 228, 233, 234, 236, 237, 239
"Eight": *see* warships

Index

"Eighteen": *see* warships
Elbe River 139
"Eleven": *see* warships
Eloth 70
emporion 111
England 71
English Channel 138, 139, 140, 210
Ephesus 169, 170, 172, 179, 182, 226
Eratosthenes 175
Eridu 2
Etesian Winds 115, 182
Ethiopia 45, 129, 178
Etruria: *see* Etruscans
Etruscans 32, 78, 79, 82, 158, 194, 200
Euboea 38, 190
Eubulus 110
Eudamus 169, 170, 171
Eudoxus 186-187
Euneus 58
Euphrates River 5, 179, 214
Euxine 65
Evans, Sir Arthur 20
Executive officer: *see* warships, personnel
Exploration 58-65, 70-82, 128-140, 186-187, 232
Ezion Geber 69-70

Faience: *see* trade
"Fifteen": *see* warships
Figs: *see* trade
Fire: *see* Greek fire
Fire pots 152, 171-172
Fire weapons: *see* ships
First lieutenant: *see* warships, personnel
First Punic War 159-166, 222
Fish: *see* trade
Flagships 149, 155, 162, 208, 210
Flame-thrower 242-243, 244, 246
Flax: *see* trade
Fleets, size of: *see* navies, size of
Fore-and-aft rig 219, 244
"Forty": *see* warships
France 81, 82, 138, 139, 140, 223, 224, 226
Frankincense: *see* trade
Fuller's earth: *see* trade
Furniture: *see* trade

Gadir (*see also* Cadiz) 71
Gaiseric 241
Galley: *see* warship
Ganges River 231
Garum (fish sauce): *see* trade
Gaul 73
Gaza 178, 182
Gems: *see* trade
Genoa 246
Geography, science of 77, 88, 137, 139, 175
Gibraltar, Strait of 61, 63, 71, 81, 82, 88, 128, 129, 131, 132, 133, 134, 136, 138, 140, 172, 175, 205, 208, 224
Ginger: *see* trade
Girding cables: *see* ships
Glass and glassware: *see* trade
Gold and goldware: *see* trade
Golden Fleece 58, 59, 61, 64
Good Hope, Cape of 131
Gorillas 135, 136
Goths 240
Grain: *see* trade
Grand Congloué 192, 193, 194, 195
Grappling 100-101, 106, 148, 161, 162, 207
Greece (*see also under names of Greek cities*) 22, 23, 24, 25, 31, 34, 57, 58, 63, 72, 73, 78, 79, 141, 142, 143, 150, 151, 155, 168, 170, 187, 189, 191, 201, 206, 224, 226
Greek fire 242
Gregale 238
Guardafui, Cape 131
Guinea 132, 136
Guinea, Gulf of 131, 133, 136
Gulf: *see under the particular name*
Gulf Stream 139

Hadad 184
Hadramaut 9, 178, 184
Halicarnassus 148
Hannibal 166, 167, 168, 169, 170, 171
Hannibal (admiral in First Punic War) 163
Hanno 133-136, 138
Hanoi 232
Harpies 59, 62
Hatshepsut 11, 13, 16, 17, 25

Hecataeus 77
Hector 36
Hegestratus 116-118
Heligoland 139
Heliopolis 215
Hellenistic Age 141, 173
Helmsman: *see* warships, personnel
Hemiolia: *see* warships
Hemp: *see* trade
Henu 10
Heraclea 123, 124
Heracleides 122-124
Heracleion 20
Heracles 62
Herihor 47, 48, 49, 53
Hermaeum, Cape 164
Herne Island 134
Herodotus 68, 80, 129, 131, 132
Hesperides 61
Hides: *see* trade
Hippalus 187
Hippocrates 155
Hiram 69-70
Hittites 62
Homer 24, 26, 32, 34, 36, 37, 39, 42, 45, 60, 63, 64, 83, 84, 88, 129, 146, 198, 201
Honey: *see* trade
horrea piperaria 228
Houseboats 174, 196-197, 217
Hull, construction of: *see* ships
Hull, sheathing: *see* ships

Ibiza 71, 81
Iceland 139
Ikhnaton 24, 28, 29, 30, 32
Illyria (*see also* Jugoslavia) 167, 199, 201
Incense: *see* trade
India 8, 67, 69, 70, 77, 128, 142, 175, 178, 179, 182, 185, 186, 187, 224, 227, 228, 229-232, 245
Indian Ocean 3, 5, 8, 128, 131, 140, 227, 228, 229-232, 245
Indians 179, 186, 187, 245
Indus River 228, 230
Insurance 114-115
Iolcus 58, 60, 61, 63
Iran 179, 230

Ireland 137, 138, 140
Iron: *see* trade
Ischia 79, 81
Istanbul 73, 78
Italy 24, 73, 74, 76, 77, 78, 79, 80, 82, 112, 125, 157, 158, 160, 164, 166, 176, 182, 183, 185, 188, 189, 190, 193, 194, 200, 201, 203, 208, 209, 212, 223, 226, 236, 238, 246
Ithaca 43
Ivory: *see* trade

Jars: *see* amphorae
Jason 58-65, 76, 128
Java 232
Jewelry: *see* gems
Jews 184
Josephus 236
Jugoslavia 167, 199, 201, 209, 213
Justinian 245

Kakulima, Mt. 136
Karachi 228
Kenamon 17, 18, 22
Kent 138
Kertsch 110
Khaemwaset 55

Labyrinth 20
Ladders, landing: *see* ships
Lampsacus 106
Land's End 138
Lateen sail 219, 244
Latitude 134, 137, 175
Law, maritime 181, 184
Lead: *see* trade
Lead line: *see* ships
Lebanon 4, 5, 28, 47-57, 60, 67, 69, 176
Lembi: *see* warships
Lesbos 38
Liburnian: *see* warships
Libya 21, 32, 45, 63, 112
Libyphoenicians 133
Lighthouses 175, 180, 225
Lilybaeum 165
Lion, Gulf of 81
Liparite: *see* trade

Index

Loans, maritime 9, 109, 114-115, 116, 118, 120, 173
Longitude 134, 175
Lucian 235
Lugsail 219
Luxuries: *see* trade
Lycia 30, 32, 118
Lycurgus 110

Macedon 21, 124, 142-150, 151, 153, 167-168, 172, 176, 185, 201
Macedonian Wars 167-168, 172
Mahdia 190, 191, 195, 197, 216, 217
Majorca 81
Makkan 8
Malabar 229, 230
Malabathrum: *see* trade
Malacca, Strait of 232
Málaga 72, 82
Malay 231, 232
Malea, Cape 155, 156, 201
Malta 72, 81, 234, 239
Maps 77, 88, 175, 220
Marcus Aurelius 228
Marine railway 80
Marines: *see* warships, personnel
Mark Antony: *see* Antony
Marmora, Sea of 78, 186, 241
Maroneia 125
Marseilles 75, 81, 110, 114, 116, 117, 120, 128, 137, 139, 173, 188, 192, 193, 194, 195, 197, 204
Massilia (*see also Marseilles*) 81
Meat: *see* trade
Mecca 245
Medea 58, 59, 60
Medina 245
Megara 74, 78
Mekmel 49
Meltem 115
Memphis 17
Mende 118, 119
Menelaus 45
Mengebet 47, 50
Mentuhotep III 10
Mercenaries, naval 98
Merchant marine
  Rhodian 151, 172, 180, 181, 183
  Roman 236, 245

Merchantmen
  Early and Classical Greece 87, 126
  Hellenistic Age 174
  Roman Imperial Period 214-222
  Roman Republican Period 193-195
Merchantmen, driven by sail and oar 215
Merlin, Alfred 190
Mesopotamia 2, 3, 5, 8, 142, 179, 227
Messina 158
Messina, Strait of 73, 79, 81, 158, 159, 160, 234
Metals and metalware: *see* trade
Metics 120, 121
Metropolis 76
Miletus 76, 77, 78, 81, 112, 203, 224, 226
Milim 30
Minaeans 184
Minoans 21-24, 28, 31, 35, 41, 61, 64, 70, 78, 216
Minorca 81
Minos 20, 21, 22, 31
Minotaur 20, 21
Misenum 209, 210, 211, 212, 213
Mithridates VI 188, 202
Mizzen: *see* ships
Moneychanging 108, 109, 112
Monsoon 131, 185-186, 187, 228-229, 232
Monte Testaccio 234
Morocco 81, 131, 132, 134, 187
Mount: *see under the particular name*
Murex 67
Mycenae 24, 34, 57, 60
Mycenaean Age 24, 44, 72
Mycenaeans 24-26, 31, 41, 61, 66-67, 70, 78
Mylae 162
Myonnesus, Cape 171
Myos Hormos 228, 229
Myra 238
Myrrh: *see* trade

Nabataeans 178, 184
Naphtha 242-244
Naples 78, 79, 81, 185, 193, 207, 209
Narbonne 226
Nard: *see* trade

Index

Naulochus 208
Nausicrates 118
Naval bases, Roman Imperial 209-210
Naval tactics: *see* warships, tactics
Navies
  composition of 101-102, 146-147, 152, 159, 166, 167, 169, 172, 202, 209, 213, 216, 243
  size of 87, 90, 101, 103, 104-105, 106, 124, 126, 127, 143, 146-147, 149, 152, 153, 156, 159, 162, 163, 164, 165, 166, 168, 169, 171, 172, 201, 202, 206, 207, 208, 209
Navigating officer: *see* warships, personnel
Navigation 38, 77, 127, 137, 139, 175, 185-186, 228, 230, 234, 236, 245
navy
  Arab 241, 244
  Athenian 89-107, 112, 124, 125-126, 143, 162
  Byzantine 241-246
  Carthaginian 87, 157-166
  Corinthian 79, 99, 103, 105
  Egyptian 14-16, 27, 33
  Hellenistic 141-156
  Macedonian 146-150, 151, 156, 167-168, 172
  Phocaean 87
  Phoenician 86, 90, 143
  Ptolemaic 146-150, 151, 156, 175
  Rhodian 150-156, 168, 180, 202
  Roman Imperial 205, 207, 209-214, 240, 241, 243
  Roman Republican 157-172, 202
  Seleucid 168-172, 202
  Spartan 103, 106
  Syracusan 105-106, 160, 161
  Syrian: *see* navy, Seleucid
Naxos 200
Necho 129, 131, 133, 187
Negeb 69
Negroes 18, 132-133, 135
Nemi, Lake 196
Nero 80, 215, 226, 231
Nestor 34, 38
Nesubanebded 47, 49, 52, 54
New Testament: *see* Paul
Nice 82

Nike of Samothrace 150
Nile River 10, 14, 44, 45, 46, 47, 48, 70, 88, 90, 92, 146, 174, 178, 180, 214, 215, 229, 245
"Nine": *see* warships
North Sea 63, 137, 139
"Northerners of the Isles" 31, 32, 42
Norway 139
Nubia 16
Nuts: *see* trade

Oars: *see* ships
Oars, steering: *see* ships
"Oar-thong man": *see* warships, personnel
Obelisks 14, 215, 225
Octavian: *see* Augustus
Odysseus 34, 37, 39, 43, 44, 46, 63, 64, 68, 73, 198
Oecist 74-76
Officers: *see* warships, personnel
Oil: *see* trade
Oil, crude 242
Oiler: *see* warships, personnel
Old Testament 33, 69-70
Olive oil: *see* trade
Oman 8
"One-and-a-half": *see* warships
Ophir 70
Oran 72
Orca 138
Orkney Islands 138
Orpheus 62
Ostia (*see also* Portus) 160, 203, 224, 225-226, 234
Outrigger: *see* ships

Paint, ship's 217
Palermo 72
Palestine 2, 16, 21, 27, 32, 33, 236
Palmas, Cape 131
Pantelleria 72
Papyrus: *see* trade
Papyrus documents 46, 148, 173, 177, 211, 237
Paralus 102
Parthia 230
Pasion 108-110, 114, 120, 121
Passenger service 236, 238, 239

Index

Paul (Apostle) 81, 238-239
Pearls: see trade
Peiraeus 108, 110-113, 114, 115, 116, 117, 120, 122, 124, 125, 127, 174, 235
Peleset 32, 33
Pelias 59, 60
Peloponnese 78
Peloponnesian War 102-107, 108, 113, 124, 125, 170
Penteconter: see warships
Pepi 27
Pepper: see trade
Perfume: see trade
Pergamum 167, 168, 172, 176, 185
Periander 80
Pericles 110
Periplus Maris Erythraei 229
Perseus 172, 201
Persia 74, 76, 82, 89, 90, 91, 92, 97, 103, 112, 133, 141, 142, 245, 246
Persian Gulf 2, 3, 5, 8, 69-70, 179, 229, 230
Petra 178, 184
Petronius 223
Pharos 180
Phaselis 118
Philip, father of Alexander 113
Philip V 156, 167, 168, 172, 199
Philistines 32
Phocaea 81, 82, 83, 97, 137
Phoenicia 4, 5, 9, 16, 17, 18, 21, 24, 25, 28, 30, 31, 32, 45, 69, 70, 72, 77, 90, 143, 144, 169, 178, 185, 204
Phoenicians 57, 66-72, 73, 80, 81, 82, 84, 86, 87, 92, 99, 101, 120, 128, 129, 131, 133, 136, 153, 178, 181, 184, 187, 211, 215, 239
Phormio (admiral) 103-104
Phormio (businessman) 110, 120, 121
Pillars of Hercules 128, 131, 133, 134
Pillows: see trade
Pindar 63
Piracy 10, 29, 30, 31, 32, 33, 42, 43-57, 60, 66, 83, 86, 102, 115, 119, 124, 125, 151, 152, 153, 155, 158, 167, 178, 179, 183, 184, 186, 188, 198-205, 209, 210, 228, 240, 241

Pirates
of Cilicia 201-205, 241

Pirates—Continued
of Crete 167, 199, 201
in Greek literature 198-199
of Illyria 167, 199, 201, 209, 213
in navies 153, 167, 199, 201
punishment of 200, 203-204, 205
of the Red Sea 10, 178, 186, 228
ships: see ships
Tyrrhenian 158, 200, 201
Pisa 246
Pitch: see trade
Plato 73
Pliny the Elder 209, 216, 228, 231
Plutarch 20
Po River 88, 157
Polybius 131
Polycles 154
Polyxenidas 168, 169, 171, 172
Pompeii 209, 223
Pompey 204-205, 206
Pondicherry 231
Pontus 118-119
Port facilities 87, 111-112, 174, 175, 179-180, 216, 224, 225-226, 237, 245
Ports 10, 17, 24-25, 73, 77, 79, 87, 105, 110-112, 113, 174, 177, 178, 179, 181, 184, 188, 224, 225-226, 229, 230, 231
Portus 220, 225, 236, 237
Pottery: see trade
Pozzuoli 185, 188, 224, 234, 236, 237
praefectus annonae 233
Privateering 82-83, 115, 199
Protus 116-118
Prow ornament: see ships
Ptolemy I 141, 143, 144, 145, 146, 147, 148, 149, 175, 176, 180, 208
Ptolemy II 145, 146, 147, 148, 150, 175, 176, 177, 180
Ptolemy III 175, 176
Ptolemy IV 145, 146, 174, 181, 196
Ptolemy VII 186, 187
Punic Wars 159-166, 172, 201
Punt 9, 10, 11, 13, 16, 18
Puteoli (see also Pozzuoli) 185
Pylos 57
Pytheas 128, 136-139

Quadrireme: see warships

Quinquereme: *see* warships

Ram: *see* ships
Ramming 100-101, 104, 148
Ramses III 31, 32, 33, 41, 84
Ramses XI 47
"Raven": *see* ships, *corvus*
Ravenna 209, 210, 211, 213
Red Sea 2, 9, 10, 13, 129, 131, 146, 173, 178, 179, 228, 229, 230, 245
Reefing: *see* shortening sail
Regillus 170, 171
Reinforcing timbers: *see* ships
Rekhmire 18, 20, 23, 24, 31
Rhegium 73
Rhine River 210
Rhodes 22, 24, 70, 72, 79, 114, 115, 150-156, 167, 168, 169-172, 174, 175, 180, 181, 182, 183, 184, 185, 191, 199, 201, 202, 203, 204, 214, 234, 242
  anti-pirate patrols 201, 202
  earthquake at 181
  siege of 153
Rhone River 73, 81
Rib-Addi 29, 30
Rigging: *see* ships
Riviera, French-Italian 190, 191, 194, 226
Rome (city) 156, 157, 167, 196, 203, 204, 210, 216, 220, 223-239, 241
Rome
  grain supply 227, 233-239
  merchant marine 236, 245
  navy: *see* navy, Roman
Rowing 37, 38, 62, 84-85, 93-94, 97, 100-101, 126, 159
Rubicon River 206
Rudder 246
Ruddle: *see* trade
Russia 63, 64, 73, 106, 112, 113, 114, 122, 124, 175, 181, 183, 245

Saba 184
Sabaeans 184
Sabratha 226
Sahara 132
Sahure 14, 21, 27
Sailcloth 175

Sailing season 39, 63, 71, 76, 112, 114, 115, 116, 118, 121, 185-186, 220, 228-229, 234, 235, 236-237, 238, 239
Sails: *see* ships
Sails, left ashore during battle 86, 97, 107, 152; cf. 208, 244
Saint-Tropez 226
Salaminia 102
Salamis 89, 90, 91, 99
Salamis (on Cyprus) 122, 123, 149
Samos 80, 81, 87, 132
Samothrace 150
Sardinia 71, 72, 81, 166, 191, 200, 209, 241
Sataspes 132, 133, 136
Savage, Thomas 136
Scarabs: *see* trade
Scione 118, 119
Scylax the Younger 127, 136
Scythia 73
Sea: *see under the particular name*
Sea battles
  Actium 145, 146, 208
  Aegates Islands 165
  Aegospotami 106, 107
  Amorgos 127
  Andros 150
  Arginusae 101
  Artemisium 90, 92, 101, 103
  Cape Hermaeum 164
  Chios 167
  Cissus 169
  Cos 150
  Ecnomus 164
  Mylae 162-163
  Myonnesus 171
  Naulochus 208
  Patras 103-104
  Salamis (on Cyprus) 149
  Salamis (in Greece) 90-92, 99, 100, 102, 104, 107, 132
  Side 169-170
  Syracuse 105-106
  see also 31, 32, 82, 90-92, 105
Sea battles, mock 210
Sea raiders: *see* piracy
Seals: *see* trade
Second Punic War 166, 204
Seleuceia (in Mesopotamia) 179
Seleuceia (in Syria) 142, 143, 182, 210

Index

Seleucus I 143, 168
Selinus 79
Senate, of Rome 156, 159, 160, 163, 164, 167, 168
Senegal River 134, 135
Senusret 10, 13
Sestus 106
"Seven": *see* warships
Sextus Pompey 207, 208, 211
Sheba 184
Shekelesh 32
Sherboro Sound 136
Ship timber 39, 124, 144, 151, 176, 195, 217
Ship board life 37, 38, 62, 96, 127, 216-217, 236
Shipbuilding 8, 39, 83, 87, 144, 150, 151, 159, 163, 164, 165, 225
Ships: *see also* warships
  multibanked (*see also* warships, types) 144-150
  oarage of 36, 62, 81, 84, 85, 92-94, 125, 144-146, 152-153, 213-214, 215, 243
  pirate 28, 37, 41, 86, 152, 187, 201, 202, 218
  primitive 1-3
  profile of 41, 83-84, 85, 87, 216, 219, 243
  provisioning of 96-97, 102, 106
  Roman grain 235-236, 239, 245
  size of 15, 36, 37, 85, 86, 93-94, 126, 144-145, 174, 176, 193, 194, 195, 196, 215, 216, 235, 236, 243
  speed of 94, 100, 115, 127, 134, 138, 152, 170, 220, 228-229, 234, 236, 245
Ships, chronological and national types
  Arab 186
  Byzantine 243-246
  Egyptian 1, 11, 13, 14, 15, 16, 27, 41, 146
  Greek 26, 36-42, 83-87, 92-95, 125-126
  Hellenistic Age 144-146, 152-153, 174, 213, 215
  Homeric 36-42, 146
  Illyrian 167
  Minoan 25, 41, 146
  Mycenaean 26, 41

Ships, chronological and national types
—*Continued*
  Phoenician 17, 25, 86
  Roman Republic and Imperial period 193-195, 213-222
Ships, equipment and parts of
  altar 219
  anchor 39, 98, 193, 195, 197, 235, 238, 239
  armor 208, 213, 244
  artemon 146, 174, 213, 218, 219, 220, 239
  artillery 147, 242
  ballast 99, 217, 226
  boat pole 37, 104
  bow-patches 37
  cabins 213, 216, 217, 235
  cables 98
  catapults 147, 148, 207, 208, 242
  color 36, 218
  corvus 161, 162, 163, 164, 165, 166
  decks 37, 84, 86, 99, 146, 160, 243
  fire weapons 152, 171-172, 242-243, 244
  girding cables 15, 16, 98-99
  hulls, construction of 1, 14-16, 195, 197, 216, 217
  hulls, sheathing 195, 197, 217
  ladders, landing 17, 87, 219
  lead line 220, 238
  mizzen 146, 174, 218
  oars 1, 15, 38, 85, 93-94, 145, 146, 152-153, 243
  oars, steering 38, 85, 154, 218, 236, 246
  outrigger 92-93, 99, 105, 243
  prow ornament 213, 214, 217, 235
  ram 84, 85, 99, 148, 216, 244
  reinforcing timbers 105, 148
  rigging 2, 15, 16, 38, 86, 87, 97, 98, 146, 152-153, 174, 195, 214, 217, 218-219, 244
  sails 2, 15, 16, 25, 38, 41, 86, 87, 97, 98, 146, 152-153, 174, 218-219, 220, 237, 244
  ship's boat 117, 218, 220
  stern ornament 85, 145, 217, 235
  topsail 174, 218, 235, 237
  turrets 148, 244

Shortening sail 38, 87, 98, 218, 219, 220
Sicily 22, 25, 61, 64, 71, 72, 73, 76, 78, 79, 80, 81, 82, 92, 110, 113, 114, 115, 117, 125, 138, 142, 158, 159, 162, 164, 165, 166, 175, 208, 224, 233, 234, 239
Side 169, 202
Sidon 25, 30, 45, 49, 52, 67, 69, 92, 179, 182
Sierra Leone 136
Signaling 106, 220
Silk: see trade
Silver and silverware: see trade
Simyra 29, 30
Sinai 11
"Six": see warships
"Sixteen": see warships
Skin diving: see underwater archaeology
Slaves (see also trade) 108, 109, 110, 120, 121, 211, 223.
Slaves, as crew members 95, 96, 211
Slavs 211
Smuggling 111, 177
Snefru 4, 5, 21, 67
Solomon 69-70, 158
Somaliland 9, 67, 178
Sophocles 63
Sostratus 180
South China Sea 232
South Vietnam 232
Spain 3, 22, 63, 71, 72, 77, 81, 82, 128, 137, 138, 140, 142, 166, 175, 181, 182, 197, 202, 209, 223, 224, 226, 234, 238
Sparta 74, 91, 102, 103, 104, 113, 125, 173
Spartel, Cape 132
Spice: see trade
Spikenard: see trade
Sponges: see trade
Spritsail 219-222
Squadrons of Roman Imperial Navy 209-210, 211, 213, 228, 240
Stern ornament: see ships
Stone: see trade
Stonehenge 3

Story of the Shipwrecked Mariner 10 11
Strait: *see under the particular name*
Sudan 18
Sumatra 232
Sumerians 5
Susa 90
Syracuse 24, 73, 75, 79, 92, 104, 105-106, 114, 117, 118, 120, 125, 142, 160, 161, 176, 200, 234
Syria 2, 16, 17, 18, 21, 24, 25, 28, 30, 32, 47-57, 80, 112, 120, 142, 143, 168-172, 177, 178, 184, 185, 187, 188, 189, 211, 215, 223, 224, 239, 241, 242, 246
Syrian War 168-172
Syros 41

Tacking 115, 220-222, 234, 238
Tactics: see warships, tactics
Tanetamon 47, 52, 54
Tanetnot 56
Tanis 47, 50, 52
Taranto 74, 158
Tarentum 24, 74
Tariffs 175, 176, 177, 183, 187
Tartessus 71, 81
Tell el-Amarna 24, 29, 31, 45
Telmun 9
"Ten": see warships
Tenedos 38, 245
Teos 74
Teuta 199
Textiles and garments: see trade
Thalamite rowers: see warships, personnel
Thales 77
Thasos 125
Thebes 11, 29, 32, 47, 57
Themistocles 90, 91, 97, 100, 101, 102, 103, 104, 107, 146
Theophrastus 178
Theseus 20, 62
Thieves' Harbor 111, 120
Third Punic War 172
"Thirteenth": see warships
"Thirty": see warships

Index

Thrace 46, 74, 76, 124, 150, 171, 187, 188
Thranite rowers: *see* warships, personnel
Thucydides 20, 21, 31, 46
Thule 138, 139
Thutmose III 16, 18, 20, 27, 28, 29, 31
Tiber River 145, 156, 157, 160, 215, 224, 225, 234, 245
Tiberius 228, 231
Tigris River 5, 179, 214
Timber: *see* trade
Timebeater: *see* warships, personnel
Tin: *see* trade
Tin Isles 71
Tjekers 32, 33, 48, 49, 50, 51, 55, 56, 57, 66
Tolls 81, 111, 151, 181, 182, 183, 229
Topsail: *see* ships
Tortoise shell: *see* trade
Trade
  of Aegina 112
  with Arabia (*see also* trade, Red Sea) 178, 179, 182, 185-187, 228, 229-230, 232
  of Athens 80, 108-124
  Byzantine 245-246
  caravan: *see* caravan
  of Carthage 72, 82, 128, 158, 182
  with China 230-232
  of Corinth 79-80, 112
  of Delos 183-185, 188
  of Egypt, Pharaonic 4-26, 47-57, 128, 133
  of Egypt, Ptolemaic 175-180, 228, 245
  of Egypt, Roman 211, 212, 224, 226, 227, 228, 233, 234, 236, 237, 239
  Etruscan 78-79, 158
  of Greece, early and classical 67, 70, 73-82, 108-124
  of Greece, under the Romans 226
  Hellenistic 142, 173-188, 224
  with India 5-9, 69-70, 178-179, 182, 185-187, 227, 228, 229-231, 232, 245
  Levantine 17, 18, 21, 22, 52, 67-69
  of Marseilles 137-139
  of Mesopotamia 5-9, 69-70
  of Miletus 77-78, 112

Trade—*Continued*
  Minoan 21-23
  Mycenaean 24-26
  Palestinian 69-70
  Persian Gulf 5-9, 69-70, 179
  Phoenician 69-72
  prehistoric 3
  Red Sea 9-14, 70, 173, 178, 179, 185, 228
  of Rhodes 151, 180-184, 185
  of the Roman Empire 223-239
  of the Roman Republic 158, 182-185, 187-188, 193, 194
  of South Italy 78-80, 158, 182-185, 188, 193, 194, 226
Trade, government in 121, 122, 124, 175-177, 179, 187, 233, 235
Trade, objects of
  amber 22, 139
  amulets 79
  animals 13, 16, 112, 216, 229
  art 182, 183, 189, 190, 224, 226
  bronze 22, 71, 78
  carpets 112
  chank 8
  chariots 16, 17
  cheese 112, 176, 177
  cinnamon 179, 231
  copper 5, 8, 16, 17, 22, 25, 71, 176, 224, 231
  coral 231
  cosmetics 13, 179, 224, 230, 231
  dates 112
  dyed textiles 67, 182
  faience 79
  figs 112, 176, 177
  fish 54, 77, 78, 111, 224, 226
  flax 112, 176
  frankincense 9, 178
  fuller's earth 224
  furniture 17, 77, 112
  garum (fish sauce) 226
  gems 8, 143, 178, 224, 230, 231
  ginger 179
  glass and glassware 182, 189, 224, 230, 231
  gold and goldware 13, 16, 22, 54, 61, 64, 69-70, 229

Trade, objects of—*Continued*
  grain 64, 69, 76, 78, 79, 80, 106, 110, 111, 112, 113, 115, 117, 118, 119, 121, 122-124, 125, 126, 152, 166, 175-176, 179, 180, 181, 182, 183, 184, 194, 204, 208, 224, 226, 231, 233-239, 245
  hemp 112
  hides 8, 13, 54, 57, 112, 226
  honey 111, 176, 177, 224
  incense (*see also* myrrh, frankincense) 9, 11, 13, 16, 69, 112, 173, 178, 179, 229, 232
  iron 72, 76, 82, 176
  ivory 8, 13, 22, 69, 112, 178, 224, 226, 229, 231, 232
  jewelry (*see also* gems) 17, 22, 228
  lead 72, 82, 231
  liparite 22
  luxuries 67, 69, 142-143, 174, 177, 178, 182, 183, 184, 224
  malabathrum 231
  meat 112, 177, 233
  metals and metalware 79, 226, 229, 230
  myrrh 9, 10, 11, 13, 178, 230
  nard 179
  nuts 112, 176, 177
  olive oil 8, 17, 18, 69, 78, 79, 110, 111, 113, 126, 176, 177, 182, 185, 191, 193, 194, 224, 226, 233, 234
  papyrus 17, 22, 24, 54, 57, 112, 176, 226
  pearls 8, 178, 224, 231
  pepper 178, 179, 224, 228, 230, 231, 232
  perfume 16, 69, 79, 143, 178, 184, 230
  pillows 112
  pitch 124, 176
  pottery 4, 21, 22, 78, 79, 80, 81, 111, 193, 224, 226
  ruddle 124
  scarabs 79
  seals 8
  silk 69, 178, 224, 228, 230, 231, 232
  silver and silverware 16, 21, 33, 54, 71, 72, 76, 81, 82, 224, 229, 230
  slaves 44, 45, 68-69, 112, 182, 183, 184, 185, 188, 200, 202, 203, 230

Trade, objects of—*Continued*
  spice 21, 69, 112, 143, 179, 184, 187, 228, 230
  spikenard 179, 231
  sponges 177
  stone 8, 22, 79, 190, 224, 226
  textiles and garments 8, 16, 17, 22, 54, 57, 67, 69, 143, 176, 182, 224, 229, 230, 231
  timber 4, 5, 16, 17, 47-57, 67, 69, 124, 176
  tin 22, 71, 72, 81, 82, 128, 138, 139, 140, 176, 182, 231
  tortoise shell 178, 229, 231
  vinegar 177
  wine 18, 48, 57, 78, 81, 110, 111, 112, 113, 118, 126, 176, 177, 180, 181, 182, 183, 185, 191, 193, 194, 219, 223, 224, 226, 227, 230, 231, 233, 234
  woods 8, 13, 16, 224
  wool 8, 77, 143, 224
Trajan 225, 229, 236
Transports 27, 98, 102, 210
Transports for horses 98, 99, 102, 215-216
Triacontor: *see* warships
Triemiolia: *see* warships
Trierarch (*see also* warships, personnel) 109, 125, 148
Trireme: *see* warships
Trireme, uses of 102
Trireme tax 149
Triremes, differences among 99-100, 105
Triremes with reinforced prows 105
Trojan War 33-36, 43
Tropic of Cancer 132, 134
Troy 33, 34, 35, 38, 39, 46, 176
Tugboats 225
Tunis 71, 190
Tunisia 61, 189
Turrets: *see* ships
Tursha 32
"Twelve": *see* warships
"Twenty": *see* warships
"Two-and-a-half": *see* warships
Tyre 30, 45, 49, 67, 69, 70, 71, 72, 82, 92, 179, 182, 185
Tyrrhenian Sea 78, 125, 158, 201

Index

Ugarit 25
Underwater archaeology 189-197, 226
Uni 27
Utica 71, 72

Vandals 241
Venice 246
Ventris, Michael 23
Verdi, Cape 135
Vespasian 228, 234, 236
Vesuvius, Mt. 209
Vikings 37, 38, 44, 45, 61, 243
Vinegar: see trade
Volo 58

Wadi Hammamat 10
Walking the plank 203
Warships: see also ships
  five-banked: see quinquereme
  four-banked: see quadrireme
  life of 98
  names of 212, 214
  personnel
    admirals 97, 153, 154, 170, 209, 211
    boatswain 154
    captain 95, 154, 211
    carpenter 95, 154
    catapultists 147, 155
    crews 93-96, 97, 124-125, 126, 145-146, 153-155, 159, 160, 164, 165, 166, 211
    deck hands 95, 155
    doctor 154, 155
    executive officer 95, 154
    first lieutenant 95, 154
    helmsman 154
    marines 33, 84, 86, 95, 99, 100, 101, 106, 146, 148, 155, 160, 162
    navigating officer 95
    "oar-thong man" 155
    officers 94-95, 153-154, 155, 211, 213
    oiler 154
    thalamite rowers 93, 94, 145
    thranite rowers 93-94, 96, 145, 153
    timebeater 95
    trierarch 95, 154
    zygite rowers 93, 94, 145
  range of 81, 102, 147-148

Warships—*Continued*
  slips 93, 111, 153
  tactics 84, 86, 90-91, 92, 99, 100-101, 103-104, 105-106, 147-148, 149, 152, 153, 161, 162-163, 164, 169-172
  three-banked: see trireme
  two-banked 85-88, 92, 99, 214, 243
  types
    aphract 154
    cataphract 99, 154
    dromon 243-244
    hemiolia 86, 152, 154, 155, 202
    lembi 167
    Liburnian 201, 202, 213, 214, 222
    penteconter 81, 85, 88, 92, 93, 94, 99, 102, 133
    quadrireme 125, 144, 145, 146, 147, 148, 152, 154, 165, 169, 170, 171, 208, 209, 213, 243
    quinquereme 125, 144, 145, 146, 147, 152, 154, 155, 159, 160, 161, 163, 164, 165, 166, 167, 169, 172, 208, 209, 213
    triacontor 85, 102
    triemiolia 152-153, 214
    trireme 86, 92-107, 109, 111, 144, 145, 146, 147, 148, 152, 155, 158, 159, 161, 162, 163, 167, 169, 208, 209, 213, 222, 243
    "one-and-a-half" 86, 152, 154, 155, 202
    "two-and-a-half" 152-153, 214
    "six" 144, 145, 146, 147, 167, 169, 207, 208, 209, 213
    "seven" 144, 145, 146, 147, 149, 162, 163, 167, 169, 170, 208
    "eight" 144, 145, 146, 167, 208
    "nine" 144, 145, 146, 147, 148, 167, 208
    "ten" 144, 145, 146, 167, 208
    "eleven" 144, 147
    "twelve" 147
    "thirteen" 144, 147
    "fifteen" 144, 145
    "sixteen" 144, 145, 146, 149, 150
    "eighteen" 145, 146
    "twenty" 145, 147
    "thirty" 145, 146, 147
    "forty" 145, 146

Wenamon 47-57, 60, 66, 148
Weret 49
Werket-El 52
Weshesh 32
Wheat: see grain
Winds
  Aegean 34, 115
  Bay of Bengal 232
  Black Sea 115
  Dardanelles 76, 77, 107
  Etesian 115, 182
  Gulf of Corinth 104
  Gulf of Guinea 131, 133, 136
  Indian Ocean 131, 185-186, 228-229
  Mediterranean
    central 81, 234, 238
    eastern 43, 56, 115, 169, 234
    western 71, 131
  Monsoon: see Monsoon
  Red Sea 178
  Straits of Salamis 91

Winds—*Continued*
  West African 131, 133
Wine: see trade
Wine, method of shipping 193
Wine jars (*see also* amphorae) 180
Woods: see trade
Wool: see trade
Wrecks, ancient 189-197

Xanthippus 148
Xerxes 89, 90, 91, 102, 112, 132, 133

Yavanas 227
Yemen 178, 184

Zarkar-Baal 49, 50, 51, 52, 53, 54, 55, 56, 57
Zanzibar 229
Zenon 177
Zenothemis 116-118
Zygite rowers: see warships, personnel

dignos y santos por causa del Señor Jesucristo. A los ojos de Dios, somos aptos y dignos; no obstante, cuando nos miramos a nosotros mismos, dejamos de disfrutar esta relación.

"Por esa voluntad somos santificados mediante la ofrenda del cuerpo de Jesucristo hecha una vez para siempre" (He. 10:10). Nuestra santificación se basa en la ofrenda que hizo el Señor Jesucristo de Su propio cuerpo una sola vez y para siempre. "Porque con una sola ofrenda hizo perfectos para siempre a los santificados" (v. 14). Damos gracias a Dios porque nuestra santificación proviene de Cristo y es perfecta para siempre. Algunos temen acercarse al Señor porque son conscientes de su condición. Indudablemente, somos inmundos; nos contaminamos fácilmente; somos impuros e infieles ante Dios. Pero somos santos por Cristo y no por nuestras propias obras. Cristo ofreció Su propio cuerpo una sola vez, lo cual nos pone en la posición de santos ante Dios. Siempre que nos basamos en esta posición y nos acercamos a Dios por medio de Cristo, Dios nos ve santos en Cristo y nos acepta como acepta a Cristo.

3. El fruto de la santificación

"Así como el Santo, quien os llamó, sed también vosotros santos en toda vuestra manera de vivir" (1 P. 1:15). El Señor es santo y puesto que El nos llamó, estamos en la posición de santidad; por eso, también debemos serlo en nuestra vida cotidiana. ¿Cómo podemos ser santos ante Dios sin ser santos ante los hombres? Nuestra vida debe expresar que somos un pueblo santo y separado, santificado para Dios.

"Mas ahora que habéis sido libertados del pecado y hechos esclavos de Dios, tenéis por vuestro fruto la santificación, y como fin, la vida eterna" (Ro. 6:22). Agradecemos a Dios por habernos librado del pecado y apartado para Dios. Ahora somos cautivos de Dios y debemos llevar como fruto la santificación. No debemos presentar nuestros miembros a la iniquidad y la injusticia, sino a la justicia y entregarnos totalmente a Dios como esclavos Suyos, y llevar el fruto de la santificación.

"Así que, amados, puesto que tenemos estas promesas, limpiémonos de toda contaminación de carne y de espíritu, perfeccionando la santidad en el temor de Dios" (2 Co. 7:1). Debemos deshacernos de lo que contamine nuestro cuerpo y espíritu y de todo lo que no sea de Dios, y debemos llevar el fruto de la santificación en el temor de Dios.

"Santifícalos en la verdad; Tu palabra es verdad" (Jn. 17:17). Ser santificado en la verdad equivale a llevar el fruto de la santificación día a día. Dicha verdad es la palabra de Dios. Cuando comparamos nuestra conducta diaria con la verdad de Dios, todo lo que no sea santificado ante Dios es erradicado por la palabra de Dios a fin de que seamos purificados. Esto se relaciona con el avance diario y no se lleva a cabo inmediatamente ya que esto es obra del Espíritu Santo, el cual labora constantemente en nuestra vida según la verdad.

Algunos dicen que la santificación se lleva a cabo de inmediato y que podemos ser santificados instantáneamente; pero esto es imposible. Indudablemente, hay verdaderas experiencias súbitas de victoria sobre los pecados, pero no las podemos llamar santificación. Ser santificado significa ser apartado para Dios; y la victoria instantánea sobre el pecado la llamamos liberación. Una interpretación errónea puede producir un resultado erróneo.

"Porque ellos, por pocos días nos disciplinaban como les parecía, pero El para lo que es provechoso, para que participemos de Su santidad" (He. 12:10). La disciplina es otro medio por el cual podemos producir el fruto de la santificación y cuando nos desviamos, Dios nos regresa a la senda de la santidad por medio de Su disciplina a fin de que seamos partícipes de Su santidad y le pertenezcamos por completo.

Finalmente, vemos que el fruto de la santificación no se relaciona solamente con nuestra conducta, sino con la experiencia de acercarnos a Dios y tener comunión íntima con El. "Seguid ... la santificación, sin la cual nadie verá al Señor" (He. 12:14). Aunque tenemos la posición de ser santos y podemos entrar con confianza al Lugar Santísimo a fin de tener una relación estrecha con Dios, si no nos mantenemos en esa posición, podemos pensar que no podemos tocar a Dios; por lo tanto, debemos procurar la santidad, pues sin ella nadie verá al Señor.

"Y el mismo Dios de paz os santifique por completo; y

vuestro espíritu y vuestra alma y vuestro cuerpo, sean guardados perfectos e irreprensibles para la venida de nuestro Señor Jesucristo" (1 Ts. 5:23-24).

ACERCA DEL AUTOR

Witness Lee nació en 1905 en el seno de una familia cristiana al norte de China. A la edad de diecinueve años fue plenamente cautivado por Cristo y de inmediato dedicó su vida a predicar el evangelio. Poco después de comenzar a servir al Señor, conoció a Watchman Nee, un renombrado predicador, maestro y escritor cristiano. Witness Lee laboró junto con él y bajo su dirección. En 1934 Watchman Nee confió a Witness Lee la responsabilidad de la Librería evangélica de Shanghai, la cual publicaba sus escritos.

En 1949, antes de que el régimen comunista se estableciera en China, Watchman Nee y sus colaboradores enviaron a Witness Lee a Taiwan para que no se perdiera lo que el Señor les había encomendado. Watchman Nee encargó a Witness Lee que continuara la obra de publicación por medio de la Librería evangélica de Taiwan, la cual es reconocida públicamente como la editora de las obras de Watchman Nee fuera de la China. La labor de Witness Lee en Taiwan manifestó la abundante bendición del Señor. Comenzando con un grupo de 350 creyentes, la mayoría de los cuales había huido de la China continental, las iglesias en Taiwan llegaron a 20,000 miembros en cinco años.

En 1962 Witness Lee fue guiado por el Señor a mudarse a los Estados Unidos y se radicó en California. Durante sus 35 años de servicio en dicho país, dio miles de mensajes en reuniones durante la semana y en conferencias los fines de semana. Una gran parte de sus mensajes se ha publicado en más de 400 libros, muchos de los cuales han sido traducidos a más de catorce idiomas. Dio su última conferencia en febrero de 1997 a la edad de 91 años.

Witness Lee deja como legado una amplia presentación de la verdad contenida en la Biblia. Su obra principal, *Estudio-vida de la Biblia,* consta de más de 25,000 páginas de explicaciones sobre todos los libros de la Biblia, desde la perspectiva del disfrute y la experiencia que el creyente tiene de la vida de Dios en Cristo por medio del Espíritu Santo. Witness Lee fue el editor principal de una nueva traducción del Nuevo Testamento al chino, y dirigió la traducción del mismo al inglés. La Versión Recobro también ha sido traducida a otros idiomas, incluyendo el español, y contiene un cuerpo extenso de notas de pie de página, bosquejos y citas paralelas. Los mensajes de Witness Lee se transmiten por la radio en numerosas emisoras cristianas en los Estados Unidos y en otros países. En 1965 Witness Lee fundó Living Stream Ministry, una corporación sin ánimo de lucro radicada en Anaheim California, la cual difunde oficialmente el ministerio de Witness Lee y Watchman Nee.

El ministerio de Witness Lee se centra en la experiencia que el creyente tiene de Cristo como vida y en la unidad práctica de los creyentes como Cuerpo de Cristo. Con este énfasis, él guió a las iglesias que estuvieron bajo su cuidado a crecer en la vida y el servicio cristiano. Fue firme en su convicción de que Dios no se complace en el sectarismo, sino que tiene como meta producir el Cuerpo de Cristo. En respuesta a dicha convicción, los creyentes simplemente empezaron a reunirse como la iglesia en sus localidades. En años recientes, numerosas iglesias han sido establecidas en Rusia y en varios países de Europa.

OTROS LIBROS PUBLICADOS POR
Living Stream Ministry

Títulos por Witness Lee:

La experiencia de vida	978-0-87083-632-9
El conocimiento de la vida	978-0-87083-917-7
El árbol de la vida	978-1-57593-813-4
La economía de Dios	978-0-87083-536-0
La economía divina	978-0-87083-443-1
La economía neotestamentaria de Dios	978-0-87083-252-9
Cristo es contrario a la religión	978-0-7363-1012-3
El Cristo todo-inclusivo	978-0-87083-626-8
La revelación básica contenida en las santas Escrituras	978-1-57593-323-8
La revelación crucial de la vida hallada en las Escrituras	978-1-57593-811-0
El Espíritu con nuestro espíritu	978-0-7363-0259-3
La expresión práctica de la iglesia	978-0-87083-905-4
La especialidad, la generalidad y el sentido práctico de la vida de iglesia	978-0-87083-123-2
La carne y el espíritu	978-0-87083-793-7
Nuestro espíritu humano	978-0-87083-259-8
La autobiografía de una persona que vive en el espíritu	978-0-7263-1126-7
La preciosa sangre de Cristo (folleto)	978-0-7363-0228-9
La certeza, seguridad y gozo de la salvación (folleto)	978-0-7363-0991-2
Los vencedores	978-0-87083-724-1

Títulos por Watchman Nee:

Cómo estudiar la Biblia	978-0-7363-0539-6
Los vencedores que Dios busca	978-0-7363-0651-5
El nuevo pacto	978-0-7363-0064-3
El hombre espiritual	978-0-7363-0699-7
La autoridad y la sumisión	978-0-7363-0987-5
La vida que vence	978-1-57593-909-4
La iglesia gloriosa	978-0-87083-971-9
El ministerio de oración de la iglesia	978-1-57593-908-7
El quebrantamiento del hombre exterior y la liberación del espíritu	978-1-57593-380-1
El misterio de Cristo	978-1-57593-395-5
El Dios de Abraham, de Isaac y de Jacob	978-1-57593-377-1
El cantar de los cantares	978-1-57593-956-8
El evangelio de Dios (2 tomos)	978-1-57593-940-7
La vida cristiana normal de la iglesia	978-0-87083-495-0
El carácter del obrero del Señor	978-0-7363-3278-1
La fe cristiana normal	978-0-87083-779-1

Disponibles en
librerías cristianas o en Living Stream Ministry
2431 W. La Palma Ave. • Anaheim CA 92801
1-800-549-5164 • www.livingstream.com